THE MARX BROTHERS

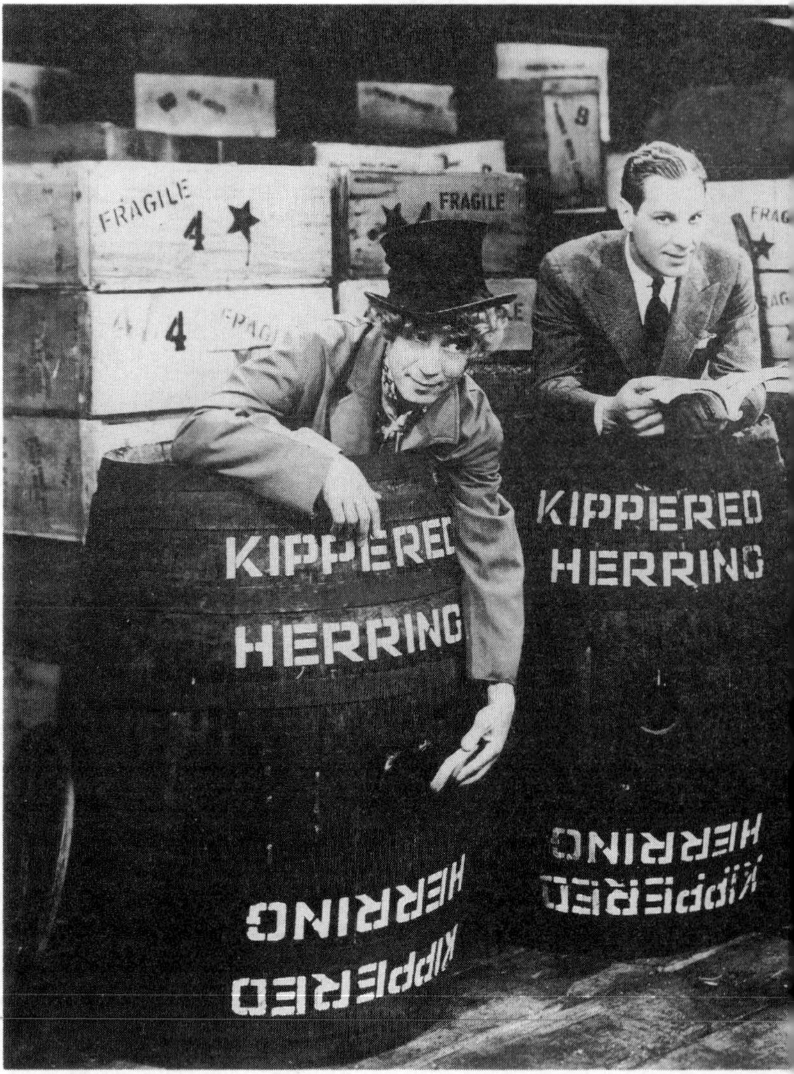
FRAGILE
4
4
FRAGILE
KIPPERED
HERRING
KIPPERED
HERRING

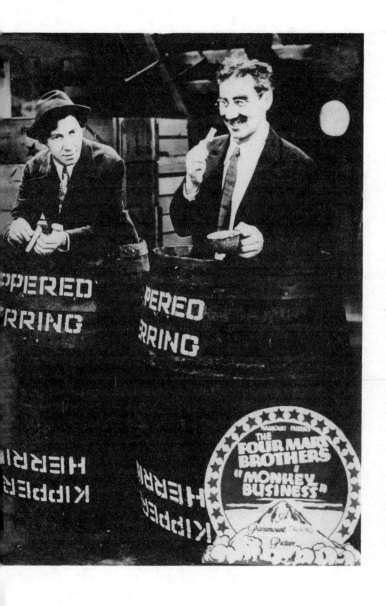

The Marx Brothers

*Monkey Business, Duck Soup
and A Day at the Races*

**WITH AN INTRODUCTION BY
Karl French**

faber and faber
LONDON BOSTON

A Day at the Races first published in 1972 by
The Viking Press, Inc
The Four Marx Brothers in Monkey Business and Duck Soup first
published in 1972 by Lorrimer Publishing Limited
This collection first published in Great Britain in 1993
by Faber and Faber Limited
3 Queen Square London WC1N 3AU

Photoset by Parker Typesetting Service, Leicester
Printed by Mackays of Chatham plc, Chatham, Kent

A CIP record for this book is available from the British
Library

ISBN 0-571-16647-4

4 6 8 10 9 7 5

CONTENTS

INTRODUCTION

'And I went upstairs to the balcony, and I sat down and you know, the movie was a–a–a film that I'd seen many times in my life since I was a kid, an–and I always u–uh, loved it. And, you know, I'm, I'm watching these people up on the screen, and I start getting hooked on the film, you know? And I started to feel how can you even think of killing yourself? I mean, isn't it so stupid? I mean, I–look at the people up there on the screen. You know, they're real funny, and, and what if the worst is true? What if there's no god . . .?'

This is the effect *Duck Soup* has on Woody Allen's suicidally depressed alter ego Mickey Sachs in *Hannah and Her Sisters* (1986). It is, essentially, the same effect the film had on its original audience in 1933. In their films the Marx Brothers provided a relief from the Great Depression as they wreaked havoc on a world filled with hostility, incompetence and corruption.

The four Marx Brothers (Gummo had long since dropped out) were already show-business veterans when they made their film début in *The Cocoanuts* in 1929 – that is excluding Harpo's appearance in a long-forgotten short and the unreleased *Humor Risk*. Their act had evolved over many years, in small theatres in small towns across America from a singing group of varying sizes and names to one in which humour and wild improvisation became increasingly dominant. At the same time their individual personas grew into the forms in which they will always be remembered.

Groucho (1890–1977), was the wise-cracking cynic, in dark, baggy suit, black-rimmed glasses, black grease-paint moustache, permanently smoking a cigar. His talent for improvising one-liners led to a long and successful post 'Brothers' career as host of the game show *You Bet Your Life* on radio and television.

Chico (1886–1961), was the not very bright opportunist

(although he can normally outsmart Groucho) and punster, with a not very good Italian accent. He claimed that Italian was just one of the many ethnic accents he could slip into to escape trouble during his youth in New York. Judging by his Italian accent and the Irish brogue he adopts as the house detective in *A Day at the Races* this was a self-defence weapon of questionable value.

Harpo (1888–1964), was the innocent, woman-chasing, mute clown. Apart from his contribution to the four-part harmony at the beginning of *Monkey Business*, Harpo had remained resolutely dumb on stage and screen since the Brothers appeared in Champaign, Illinois, in 1915. A review of the act stated that although Harpo's stage act was fine and his pantomime amusing, 'Unfortunately the effect is spoiled when he speaks.' Interestingly in the play *The Man Who Came to Dinner* (co-written by his friend George S. Kaufman about his friend Alexander Woolcott), the talkative comic Banjo is based on Harpo.

Zeppo (1901–1979), straight man and occasional romantic lead was, in fact, as embarrassed and uncomfortable in front of the camera as he appeared to be. So, after completing *Duck Soup* and thus fulfilling his contractual obligation at Paramount, he happily left the team to join his brother Gummo in show-business management. While negotiating their new contract MGM suggested that the Brothers should be paid less since there were now fewer of them. Groucho is said to have countered that, 'Without Zeppo we're worth twice as much.'

The three films presented in this collection come from the golden age of the Marx Brothers, which lasted from their second film, *Animal Crackers*, to their second film at MGM, *A Day at the Races*. During this time the genius of the Brothers was encouraged by what would be known in the business as 'highly creative behind-the-scenes talent'. The films of the liberal Brothers were assigned to the right-wing directors Sam Wood (*A Night at the Opera* and *A Day at the Races*) and Leo McCarey (*Duck Soup*) who had also worked with Laurel & Hardy, W. C. Fields and Harold Lloyd and was later to direct *The Awful Truth* with Cary Grant and Irene Dunne.

Herman J. Mankiewicz (a staff producer at Paramount) worked as producer on *Monkey Business*, *Horse Feathers* and did preliminary work on *Duck Soup* before being removed. Mankiewicz, a famous wit, *bon vivant* and loather of Hollywood, was a friend and admirer of the Brothers as well as, briefly, of William Randolph Hearst. He later co-wrote the screenplay of *Citizen Kane* with Orson Welles. He insisted that the focus of the films be on the Brothers and discouraged the possible intrusion of a proper plot, saying, 'If Groucho and Chico stand against a wall for an hour and forty minutes and crack jokes, that's enough for me.'

At MGM, following the almost unaccountably poor box-office performance of *Duck Soup*, producer Irving Thalberg decided that the style of a Marx Brothers film should be drastically revised. The budgets were greater for *A Night at the Opera* and *A Day at the Races*; there are lengthy and lavish musical interludes (including the return of Chico's tricky piano-playing and Harpo's harp-plucking after their absence in *Duck Soup*) and the Brothers commit their mayhem within a consistent narrative plot. The films are longer and were very successful – *A Night at the Opera* and *Duck Soup* still vie with each other as to which is the greater and greatest of all the Marx films. The death of Irving Thalberg at the age of thirty-seven marked the beginning of the Marx Brothers' cinematic decline.

But perhaps the most significant contribution to this golden age was from the screenwriters. *Monkey Business* is a good example of how a Marx Brothers script came into being. S. J. Perelman had his finest screenwriting moments with his first two efforts, *Monkey Business* and *Horse Feathers*, but remained a successful and influential humourist throughout his life. Will Johnstone was a prolific cartoonist and comic writer who had contributed to the Brothers' first Broadway success, *I'll Say She Is*. Together they were commissioned to write the screenplay for what was to be their first Hollywood film. Following a disastrous readthrough of the first draft by a very nervous Perelman, the script was knocked into shape over a period of five months by a team that comprised the original writers, Mankiewicz, the Brothers and their gag writers: J. Carver Pusey (Harpo), Nat Perrin (Chico) and Arthur Sheekman (Groucho). The latter duo along with Tom McNight and George Oppenheimer (one of the writers of *A Day at the Races*) wrote the short-lived but intermittently brilliant Marx

Brothers radio show *Flywheel, Shyster and Flywheel*. It ran for twenty-six episodes in 1932 and 1933 borrowing from previous films but also lending specific gags to later ones.

A similar process of creative collaboration continued up to *Duck Soup* with the original script written by the established songwriting team of Bert Kalmar and Harry Ruby. At MGM this process was enhanced at Thalberg's insistence. Key sequences of *A Night at the Opera* and *A Day at the Races* were taken on the road as theatrical plays for eight weeks each, performed up to five times a day in movie houses and adjusted according to audience response. The results are memorable and justify the elaborate preparations.

By experiencing these films in script form you will miss out on Harpo's contribution, especially the extraordinary mirror scene from *Duck Soup* in which Groucho aims to prove that Harpo is Harpo and not his (Groucho's) mirror image; the musical interludes – no great loss on the whole; and, finally, Zeppo's acting – no loss at all. What you have is the chance to relive, in your own time, some of the most brilliantly inane puns, one-liners and comic exchanges in the history of cinema. For example, and to whet your appetite . . .

In *Monkey Business*, after a typically painful Chico pun, Groucho inquires, 'Do you suppose I could buy back my introduction to you?' Later the neglected gangster's moll complains, 'I've been married for four years. Four years of neglect, four years of battling, four years of hardship . . .' Groucho replies, 'That makes twelve years. You must have been married in rompers . . .'

In *Duck Soup*, Groucho as Rufus T. Firefly aggressively woos Margaret Dumont as Mrs Teasdale: 'You can leave in a taxi. If you can't leave in a taxi you can leave in a huff. If that's too soon, you can leave in a minute and a huff.' Then on hearing of her husband's death he continues, 'Will you marry me? Did he leave you any money? Answer the second question first.'

In *A Day at the Races*, Whitmore, suspecting Groucho (Dr Hackenbush, originally conceived as Dr Quackenbush) of being a quack, questions the medication (a horse pill) he has prescribed to Margaret Dumont (Mrs Upjohn): 'Isn't that awfully large for a pill?' Groucho replies, 'No. It was too small for a basketball and I didn't know what to do with it.' Later, when Chico shouts that Flo, the woman with whom Groucho is dining, is out to get him she cries, 'Why, I've never been so insulted in my life.' Groucho replies 'Well, it's early yet.'

KARL FRENCH
London
December 1992

PUBLISHER'S NOTE

As no original scripts were available for *Monkey Business* and *Duck Soup*, the versions presented here were built up from a dialogue continuity provided by Universal City Studios Inc., amplified with material gained from a shot-by-shot viewing of the two films.

During filming of *A Day at the Races*, the action moved away considerably from the original script. The version presented here combines the script with the dialogue and action in the film itself.

Monkey Business

CAST

THE STOWAWAYS	Groucho
	Harpo
	Chico
	Zeppo
LUCILLE	Thelma Todd
JOE HELTON	Rockliffe Fellowes
GIBSON	Tom Kennedy
MARY HELTON	Ruth Hall
ALKY BRIGGS	Harry Woods
THE CAPTAIN	Ben Taggart
OFFICER	Otto Fries
MANICURIST	Evelyn Pierce
MADAME SWEMPSKI	Maxine Castle

Directed by	Norman McLeod
Screenplay by	S. J. Perelman and
	Will Johnstone
Additional dialogue by	Arthur Sheekman and
	Nat Perrin
Director of photography	Arthur L. Todd
Running time	77 minutes
Released by	Paramount, 19 September 1931

On the surface of a slowly revolving wooden barrel, the opening credits appear.
Then four more barrels in turn come rolling down a ship's gangplank and fill the screen, showing the credits for GROUCHO, HARPO, CHICO *and* ZEPPO MARX. *The last barrel turns to show the names of the rest of the cast.*
Fade out and in to a shot of an ocean liner ploughing through the waves, then dissolve to the deck of the liner, where the CAPTAIN *is standing at the rail with a pair of binoculars. Some passengers are chatting in the background. First Officer* GIBSON *runs up with a note in his hand.*

CAPTAIN: What is it?
GIBSON: (*Saluting*) Sorry to have to report there are four stowaways in the forward hatch.
CAPTAIN: Stowaways? How do you know there are four of 'em?
GIBSON: Why, they were singing 'Sweet Adeline'.
CAPTAIN: Well, get them out of there, you hear?
GIBSON: But we can't find 'em. And besides, they've been writing insulting notes.
    (*He hands the note to the* CAPTAIN.)
CAPTAIN: (*Reading the note*) So I'm an old goat, am I?
    (GIBSON, *looking over his shoulder, nods.*)
    Listen to me – find them if you have to clear out that whole hatch.
GIBSON: (*Saluting*) Yes, sir.
    (*He runs off while the* CAPTAIN, *furious, looks out to sea through his binoculars. A* GIRL *passenger comes up to him.*)
GIRL: (*Brightly*) Oh, Captain, when do we get in?
CAPTAIN: (*Snapping at her*) Wednesday!
    (*She winces.*)
    Oh, I . . . I beg your pardon. Wednesday.
GIRL: I thank you. (*She starts to go off.*)

Down in the forward hatch, camera tracks in on four large barrels labelled KIPPERED HERRING. *Voices issue from inside, singing in close harmony.*

ZEPPO: (*Off*) 'In all my dreams . . .'
ALL: (*Off*) 'In all my dreams . . .'
ZEPPO: (*Off*) 'Your fair face beams . . .'
ALL: (*Off*) Your fair face beams . . .
        You're the idol of my heart
        Sweet Adeline.'
GROUCHO: (*Off*) 'My Ad–e–line.'
        (GROUCHO, HARPO, CHICO *and* ZEPPO *lift the lids, rise from the barrels and take a bow.*
        HARPO, *in close-up, brushes his hair with a boot brush.*)
        (*Off*) Ah, this is the only way to travel, boys . . . the only way.
        (*Now we see the four of them, with* GROUCHO *cleaning his teeth,* CHICO *buffing his nails, while* ZEPPO *reads a book.*)
        I was gonna bring along the wife and kiddies but the grocer couldn't spare another barrel.
        (HARPO *drops into his barrel, and we cut to* CHICO *and* GROUCHO.)
CHICO: I was goin' ta bring my grandfather, but there's no room for his beard.
GROUCHO: (*Waving his toothbrush*) Why don't you send for the old swine and let his beard come later?
CHICO: I sent for his beard.
GROUCHO: You did?
CHICO: Yeah, it's coming by hairmail.
ZEPPO: (*Off*) Sssh!
        (*Back to the group.*)
        Say, fellas, I think I hear someone.
GROUCHO: Well, if it's the Captain, I'm gonna have a few words with him.
        (*Cut to him and* CHICO.)
        My hot water's been cold for three days and I haven't got room enough in here to swing a cat. In fact I haven't even got a cat.

(*Resume on all three.*)

CHICO: My grandfather can swing a cat.

GROUCHO: Yeah?

CHICO: Hey, that'd make a good job for him.

GROUCHO: Yes.

GIBSON: (*Off*) Come on, men.

ZEPPO: Hey, someone's coming.

> (*They drop hastily into the barrels as we cut to* GIBSON *entering in the background with some sailors.*)

GIBSON: Come on, gang, snap it up. Listen, fellows . . .

> (*We see them come round and stand in front of the barrels.*)
> We've gotta find those stowaways, and when we do we'll put 'em in irons.

A SAILOR: (*Saluting*) Aye, aye, sir.

> (*The others go off.*)

GIBSON: (*Pointing*) Take a look in behind those cases. You fellows look behind those boxes. (*He exits.*)

> (*The remaining* SAILOR, *in close-up, bends down and listens at* HARPO's *barrel.*
> GIBSON *stands with his back turned beyond the barrels, as* GROUCHO *pops out of his.*)

GROUCHO: Never mind the barrels. (*He drops into his barrel.*)

> (*Back by* HARPO's *barrel, the* SAILOR *springs to attention.*)

SAILOR: (*Saluting*) Aye, aye, sir!

> (GIBSON *turns in bewilderment.*)

GIBSON: What's that?

SAILOR: I just said 'Aye, aye, sir.'

GIBSON: Never mind that. Find those men.

SAILOR: Aye, aye, sir. (*He goes off.*)

> (GIBSON *turns his back again, peering to and fro. The* MARX BROTHERS *rise from their barrels, then pop back again, slamming the lids.* GIBSON *whips round, then goes off. Seen from behind,* GIBSON *hurries to another part of the hold.* HARPO *rises from his barrel, in close-up, chewing.* GIBSON *hears a noise and goes off in the wrong direction.* HARPO *scratches his chin with his hooter. It makes a noise and he drops hurriedly into the barrel.* GIBSON, *walking away, hears the noise and turns.*)

13

Resume on the barrels as he hurries back and stands with his back to them, hands on hips. A SAILOR *enters.*)

SAILOR: They're not here, sir.

(*A closer shot of the two of them.*)

GIBSON: Oh, yes they are. Hoist all this stuff up on deck. Get these barrels out of the way.

SAILOR: Very well, sir. (*He exits.*)

(*Back to the scene, as* GIBSON *pulls out a whistle and signals to the derrick operator up on deck.*)

GIBSON: Lower away up there.

(*The sailors roll the barrels into position as the hoist appears from above.*

GIBSON, *in medium close-up, points at the barrels.*)

Hurry up with that sling.

(*Back to* GIBSON *and the sailors as they start to put a rope sling round the barrels.*

Another OFFICER *comes up to some sailors who are standing about watching.*)

OFFICER: Well, you'll never find 'em standing around this way!

SAILOR: Yes, sir.

OFFICER: (*Pointing*) Now you look in back o' those bales. You look in those boxes.

SAILOR: Yes, sir.

(*Resume on the barrels.*)

GIBSON: All right, boys.

(*Seen from above, he shouts up to the derrick operator.*)

Make it snappy up there.

(*Back to the barrels as they are hoisted out of shot, revealing* GROUCHO, CHICO, HARPO *and* ZEPPO *squatting on the floor with their belongings.* GIBSON *has his back to them and starts to walk away.*

In a closer shot, he starts to climb a companion way, then turns and sees . . .

The four MARX BROTHERS *squatting on the floor.*

GIBSON *can't believe his eyes . . .*

And seen from his point of view the MARX BROTHERS *turn as he shouts:*)

(*Off*) Hey!

(*They run for it, leaving their belongings as* GIBSON *gives chase in the background.*)

There they are!

(*Seen from behind, they run past some bales.*)

CHICO: Hurry! Hurry!

(GIBSON *and the sailors give chase.*

CHICO, GROUCHO, ZEPPO *and* HARPO *start up a flight of stairs . . .*

While the sailors run past the bales in pursuit.

Resume on the stairs as HARPO, *last up, looks back and sounds his hooter. Then* GIBSON *and the sailors reach the bottom and start up.*

We see the MARX BROTHERS *again arriving at the top of the stairs. Some passengers watch in bewilderment as they chase off . . .*

While down below the sailors run up the stairs after them.

Long shot of the crowded promenade deck. There is a general hum of voices as the MARX BROTHERS *pelt towards us,* HARPO *bowling a lifebelt along the floor. He drops it over a passenger's head as they run off.*

Meanwhile GIBSON *and the sailors reach the top of the stairs and look from side to side . . .*

They charge along the promenade deck in a body, scattering the passengers.

GROUCHO, CHICO, HARPO *and* ZEPPO *run down the staircase into the main saloon. Camera follows as they race once round the fountain at the bottom, then across to the piano, where they grab up some instruments and break into a swinging jazz number, brash and out of tune. There is loud applause as they finish with a flourish, then we cut to long shot as they race out of the saloon again, the sailors thundering after them.*

Back on the promenade deck, they take refuge behind some passengers sitting in deck-chairs.

Camera moves with GIBSON *and the sailors as they come running up and halt in front of the deck-chairs.* GIBSON *issues orders.*)

GIBSON: (*Pointing*) You fellows go aft. You fellows take a look in behind those lifeboats.

(*The sailors run off.* GIBSON *paces to and fro, oblivious, as*

ZEPPO *sneaks away behind him, while* GROUCHO *stands in a corner with a rug over his head. Then he turns and looks suspiciously at the occupant of one of the deck-chairs.*
It is CHICO *in a woman's hat; seen in close-up, he coyly picks his teeth.*
Resume on the scene as GIBSON *leans towards him, turns away, then does a double take.* CHICO *runs for it and* GIBSON *gives chase.*
A woman sitting in another deck-chair rises, revealing a grinning HARPO *beneath her. She screams.*
Back to the scene as she runs off. HARPO *rises and does likewise, while another passenger emerges from the depths of the deck-chair, looking crushed.* GROUCHO *runs past amid the general confusion.*)

We now see the CAPTAIN *about to go into his quarters; he is stopped by a group of girls.*
GIRL: (*Eagerly*) Oh, Captain, tell us about the stowaways.
CAPTAIN: (*Bragging*) Oh, I'll have them in the brig before long.
GIRL: Oh, that's terribly romantic. I'd love to meet a stowaway. (*She laughs.*)
(*Suddenly* GROUCHO *slides down a companion way and lands beside the group. He starts back up the stairs, but the* CAPTAIN *stops him.*)
CAPTAIN: Hey, you!
(GROUCHO *holds out his gloved hands.*)
GROUCHO: Are these your gloves? I found 'em in your trunk. (*To the girls*) You girls go to your rooms. I'll be down shortly. (*The girls exit meekly.*)
CAPTAIN: Who are you?
GROUCHO: (*Ignoring the question*) Are you the floorwalker on this ship?
CAPTAIN: (*Indignantly*) Floor – !
GROUCHO: If you are . . .
(*A closer shot of the two of them.*)
. . . I want to register a complaint.
CAPTAIN: Why, what's the matter?
GROUCHO: Matter enough. Do you know who sneaked into my

stateroom at three o'clock this morning?

CAPTAIN: Who did that?

GROUCHO: Nobody, and that's my complaint. I'm young. I want gaiety, laughter, ha-cha-cha.

(*He breaks into a dance step, seen in a wider angle.*)

I want to dance. I want to dance till the cows come home.

CAPTAIN: Just what do you mean by this?

(*Resume on the previous shot.*)

GROUCHO: Another thing. I don't care for the way you're running this boat. Why don't you get in the back seat for a while and let your wife drive. (*He walks away, puffing at his cigar.*)

CAPTAIN: I want you to know I've been Captain of this ship for twenty-two years.

GROUCHO: (*Coming back*) Twenty-two years, eh? If you were a man, you'd go into business for yourself. I know a fella who started only last year with just a canoe. Now he's got more women than you could shake a stick at, if that's your idea of a good time.

(*Back to the wider angle.*)

CAPTAIN: One more word out of you and I'll throw you in irons.

(GROUCHO *sits in a deck-chair and puts his feet up.*)

GROUCHO: You can't do it with irons. It's a mashie shot.

(*Seen in medium close-up, he gets up and comes back towards the* CAPTAIN.)

It's a mashie shot if the wind is against you, and if the wind isn't, I am . . . And how about those barrels down below?

CAPTAIN: Barrels?

GROUCHO: (*Indignantly*) Yeah. I wouldn't put a pig in one of those barrels.

CAPTAIN: (*Getting angry*) Now, see here, you . . .

GROUCHO: No, not even if you got down on your knees. (*He holds out the gloves.*) And here's your gloves (*Snatching them away again.*) You would take them, wouldn't you?

(*He turns towards the door of the chart room behind him. Close-up of the* CAPTAIN.)

CAPTAIN: (*Hands on hips*) Why you . . .

(*Resume on* GROUCHO *in the door of the chart room.*)

GROUCHO: And keep away from my office.

(*Back to the scene as he goes in and shuts the door.*)

CAPTAIN: Now, see here, you . . .

(*The* CAPTAIN *starts forward angrily and pulls open the door. Simultaneously,* CHICO *slides down the companion way behind him, dodges under his arm and goes in.*

Reverse shot inside the CAPTAIN'S *quarters.* CHICO *comes in, slams the door and hides behind a chair, while* GROUCHO *puts on an officer's coat and cap. The door opens and the* CAPTAIN *comes in; he looks round suspiciously and crosses to another door,* GROUCHO *loping after him with his cap on sideways. The* CAPTAIN *goes into the next room and shuts the door.*

GROUCHO, *in medium shot, locks the door and turns to* CHICO *behind him.*)

GROUCHO: How dare you invade the sanctity of the Captain's quarters?

CHICO: (*Laughing*) I thought he was the Captain. Hey, I'm hungry. I'm a-lookin' for somet'ing to eat. (*He opens a cupboard.*)

GROUCHO: I'll take care of that.

(*Seen in close-up, he picks up a phone.*)

(*Into the phone*) Hello. Send up the Captain's lunch.

CHICO: (*Over his shoulder*) Hey, two.

GROUCHO: Send up his dinner too. Who am I? (*He takes off his cap, looks at the braid and puts it on again.*) I'm the Captain. You want to choose up sides?

(*Another shot as he puts back the phone and picks up the engine-room intercom.*)

Oh engineer, will you tell 'em to stop the boat from rocking? I'm gonna have lunch.

(*He taps his cigar ash into the speaking tube, then turns to* CHICO, *who is still rummaging around just behind him. They both face camera.*)

Well, what's the matter with you?

CHICO: What's the matter with me? I'm hungry. I didn't eat in three days.

GROUCHO: Three days? We've only been on the boat two days.

CHICO: (*Counting on his fingers*) Well, I didn't eat yesterday, I didn't eat today, and I'm not goin' to eat tomorrow. That makes three days.

GROUCHO: Well, state your business. I've got to shiver my
    timbers. (*He hums a tune.*)
    (*Seen in a longer shot, he dances a hornpipe, humming.*)
CHICO: I got no business. I come up to see the Captain's bridge.
GROUCHO: The Captain's bridge? I'm sorry, he always keeps it in
    a glass of water while he's eating. (*He takes* CHICO'*s hand and
    leads him towards the locked door.*) Would you like to see
    where he sleeps?
CHICO: (*Not interested*) Aw, I saw that. That'sa the bunk.
GROUCHO: You're just wasting your breath, and that's no great
    loss, either. A fine sailor you are.
    (*We follow them to the chart table in the centre of the room.*
    CHICO *sits on a corner of the table,* GROUCHO *on a chair.*)
CHICO: Hmm, you bet I'm a fine sailor. You know my whole
    family was a-sailors? My father was-a partners with
    Columbus.
GROUCHO: Well, what do you think of that, eh? Your father and
    Columbus were partners?
CHICO: You bet.
GROUCHO: Columbus has been dead for four hundred years.
CHICO: Well, they told me it was my father.
GROUCHO: Well now, just hop up there, little Johnny, and I'll
    show you a few things you don't know about history. Now
    look . . .
    (CHICO *sits up on the table as* GROUCHO *gets up and reaches for
    a globe.*
    They are seen in a closer shot.)
    (*Drawing a circle on the globe*) Now, there's Columbus.
CHICO: (*Pointing at it*) That's-a Columbus Circle.
GROUCHO: Would you mind getting up off that fly-paper and
    giving the flies a chance?
    (CHICO *lifts his backside off the table, sees he is sitting on a
    newspaper and grins.*)
CHICO: Aw, you're crazy. Flies can't read papers.
GROUCHO: (*Pointing to the globe again*) Now, Columbus sailed
    from Spain to India looking for a short cut.
CHICO: Oh, you mean strawberry short cut.
    (GROUCHO *takes off his cap and rubs his head.*)

GROUCHO: I don't know. When I woke up, there was the nurse taking care of me.

CHICO: What's the matter? Couldn't the nurse take care of herself?

GROUCHO: You bet she could, but I found it out too late. Well, enough of this. Let's get back to Columbus. (*He puts on his cap again.*)

CHICO: I'd rather get back to the nurse.

GROUCHO: (*Drawing on the globe*) So would I. But Columbus was sailing along on his vessel . . .

CHICO: On his what?

GROUCHO: Not on his what – on his vessel. Don't you know what vessel is?

CHICO: Sure. I can vessel.

(*He whistles the tune of 'Sugar in the morning . . .' GROUCHO throws down his pencil in disgust. CHICO gets off the table and goes out of shot.*)

GROUCHO: Do you suppose I could buy back my introduction to you?

(*A medium shot includes CHICO again as he sits in a chair on the other side of the table. GROUCHO resumes his discourse.*)

Now, one night Columbus' sailors started a mutiny . . .

CHICO: Naw, no mutinies at night. They're in the afternoon. You know, mutinies Wednesdays and Saturdays.

GROUCHO: (*Throwing down his cap*) There's my argument. Restrict immigration.

(*Silhouetted against the glass partition behind them, GIBSON comes down the companion way and pauses outside the door. GROUCHO and CHICO exit under the table.*

GIBSON opens the door, looking over his shoulder . . .

He comes into the chart room . . .

He turns, in close-up, and finds the room apparently empty. Under the table, GROUCHO and CHICO watch over their shoulders as GIBSON's legs exit in the background, then they turn towards camera, grinning.

Resume on the scene. CHICO and GROUCHO rise from under the table as a waiter comes in through the door, carrying a tray. They follow him across to the door of the CAPTAIN's cabin, mimicking him with upturned palms.)

Inside the CAPTAIN's *cabin, the waiter enters and sets the tray down on the table.* GROUCHO *and* CHICO *hover in the doorway, then stride into the room, as the* CAPTAIN *dismisses the waiter and sits down at the table.*)

CAPTAIN: (*To the waiter*) All right.

(GROUCHO *sits down at table with the* CAPTAIN, *while* CHICO *stands opposite. The* CAPTAIN *is amazed.*)

Well, of all the colossal impudence!

(GROUCHO *removes the napkin from the lunch tray.*)

GROUCHO: Why don't you stand up? Can't you see he has no chair?

(CHICO *pulls up a chair and sits down, while* GROUCHO *tucks the napkin into his collar.*)

CAPTAIN: (*Speechless*) Why . . . ugh . . . you . . .!

(CHICO, *in medium close-up, grabs his table napkin.*)

CHICO: You better keep quiet. We're a coupla big stockholders in this company.

(*Resume on the three men at table.*)

CAPTAIN: Stockholders, huh? Well, you look like a couple of stowaways to me.

GROUCHO: (*Standing up*) Well, don't forget, my fine fellow, that the stockholder of yesteryear is the stowaway of today.

CAPTAIN: Well, you look exactly like 'em.

CHICO: Yeah? What do they look like?

(*Close-up of the* CAPTAIN. *He looks meaningfully at* GROUCHO.)

CAPTAIN: One of them goes around with a black moustache.

(*Camera on* GROUCHO.)

GROUCHO: So do I. If I had my choice I'd go around with a little blonde. (*He waggles his eyebrows.*)

(*Back to the* CAPTAIN.)

CAPTAIN: (*With emphasis*) I said, one goes around with a black moustache!

(*Resume on* GROUCHO.)

GROUCHO: Well, you couldn't expect a moustache to go around by itself.

(*Pan to include the* CAPTAIN. GROUCHO *lays a hand on his arm.*)

(*Coyly*) Don't you think a moustache ever gets lonely, Captain?

(*Resume on the scene as the* CAPTAIN *shrugs him off.*)

CHICO: Hey, sure it gets-a lonely. Hey, when my grandfather's beard gets here, I'd like it to meet your moustache.

(GROUCHO *is seen in medium close-up*).

GROUCHO: Well, I'll think it over. I'll talk it over with my moustache. (*He leans forward.*) Tell me, has your grandfather's beard got any money?

CHICO: Money? Why, he fell hair to a fortune.

(*Back to the scene as the* CAPTAIN *rises indignantly.*)

CAPTAIN: Now listen, stockholders or no stockholders, you clear out of here.

(*The others rise also.*)

GROUCHO: All right.

(*Sound of knocking, off.*)

CHICO: Hey! Maybe there's somebody in that room.

GROUCHO: (*Pointing*) There's somebody in that closet there . . .

(*The* CAPTAIN *hurries across the cabin, followed by* CHICO *and* GROUCHO.)

. . . And I think it's you, Captain.

(*They push him into the closet and lock the door.*

[*In the National Film Archive print, the scene between* MARY *and* ZEPPO, *which comes a little later, is inserted at this point.*]

Out on deck, GIBSON *comes down the companion way by the chart room door and looks from side to side.*

Meanwhile, inside the CAPTAIN'*s cabin,* GROUCHO *and* CHICO *settle down to their meal.*)

Well, now we can eat in peace.

CHICO: All right. Here's a piece for you.

GROUCHO: Atta boy.

(*There is a knock at the door and* GIBSON *hurries in in the background.* GROUCHO *springs to his feet, turning his back on him, and puts on his captain's cap.*)

GIBSON: (*Saluting*) Beg pardon, Captain . . .

(*Medium close-up of* GROUCHO.)

GROUCHO: (*Eyebrows working*) How dare you enter the Captain's quarters while I'm eating!

(*Resume on the scene.*)

GIBSON: (*Saluting*) Sorry, sir.

(*He goes towards the door, while* GROUCHO *sits down, laughing, and shakes hands with* CHICO *across the table. At that moment there is thunderous knocking from the imprisoned* CAPTAIN *off-screen.*

Seen by the door, GIBSON *turns and comes forward again, peering through his spectacles.*

Resume on the scene.)

Now I got you!

(*He chases them round the table,* GROUCHO *and* CHICO *grabbing up the food as they go.*)

CHICO: Don't forget the butter.

(*They run for the door.*)

The scene changes to a corridor by the cloakrooms. HARPO *is leaning against a sign which reads* MEN *on the wall. A man comes up, looks at the sign and goes into the cloakroom, then reappears, catapulted through the door. He gets up, peers from the sign to* HARPO, *then hurries off in bewilderment.* HARPO *moves to reveal the entire sign, which now reads* WOMEN. *At that moment a chambermaid passes down the corridor.* HARPO *grins and starts off after her as the chambermaid takes to her heels.*

Seen from behind, HARPO *chases her down the corridor.*

On the promenade deck, ZEPPO *skids past and through a doorway with* GIBSON *in hot pursuit. He reappears through another glass door and crouches down, hiding from* GIBSON, *as a girl – MARY – walks through.* ZEPPO *springs up and strolls along beside her, taking her by the arm. Camera tracks ahead of them.*

ZEPPO: (*Expansively*) You know, there's some mighty pretty country round here. I've . . .

MARY: I beg your pardon?

(*She disengages herself and walks on.* ZEPPO *strides ahead of her, whistling. He drops his handkerchief, picks it up, and steps up to* MARY *again.*)

ZEPPO: Pardon me, is this yours?

MARY: Why no.

23

(*She walks on.* ZEPPO *hesitates, then tries again.*)

ZEPPO: Are you sure?

MARY: (*Sweetly*) I'm positive.

(*A smile comes over her face as she walks on. She drops her own handkerchief and waits. Then, as* ZEPPO *hurries up again, she picks it up and holds it out to him.*)

Is this yours?

ZEPPO: (*Pocketing the handkerchief*) Yes, it is.

(*He takes her by the arms and they stroll on.*

Well, as I was saying, there's some mighty beautiful country round here.

MARY: (*Enthusiastically*) The trees are lovely.

ZEPPO: Oh, you bet they are. I love 'em.

(*They go off in the foreground.*)

The scene changes to another corridor. HARPO *runs up to a door. Inside is the nursery, where the children are watching a Punch and Judy show. We hear squeaking voices and laughter, as* HARPO *runs in through the door and hides beside the Punch and Judy booth.*

In a closer shot, he looks up and notices the puppets. Grinning from ear to ear, he goes to sit with the children and settles down to enjoy the show.

In the corridor outside, GIBSON *runs up to the nursery door.*

We see him come in through the door, then cut to HARPO, *who takes refuge inside the Punch and Judy booth.*

Camera moves with GIBSON *as he hurries across the room, almost knocking over a child.*

GIBSON: (*To the child*) Get out of my way.

(*He stands in front of the booth, peering to and fro, while* HARPO's *head appears between Punch and Judy.*

In a closer shot, GIBSON *walks to and fro in front of the booth; then he peers myopically at the puppets and taps Punch on the nose to see if he's real. Punch and Judy hit* HARPO *on the head with their sticks, and the children shout with glee.*)

PUNCH: Whoopee! Whoopee!

(HARPO *slaps* GIBSON's *face from behind, then dodges down out of sight.* GIBSON *whips round and peers down into the booth.*

Shot of the scene as he goes round the side.
Round the back, HARPO's *backside protrudes between the curtains as* GIBSON *appears.*
HARPO's *face is seen between Punch and Judy, rocking to and fro.*
Resume on GIBSON, *who has an idea.*
Seen in close-up, he removes his tie-pin . . .
And jabs it into HARPO's *backside.*
HARPO, *between Punch and Judy, screams with pain.*
GIBSON *grabs a cricket bat and hurries round the front, while* HARPO's *face emerges at the back.*
His backside is now protruding between the front curtains; GIBSON *swipes it with the cricket bat.*
And HARPO, *eyes bulging, blows a squeaker.*
Resume on the scene from the front. Punch and Judy watch as GIBSON *drops the bat and goes inside the booth.*
Seen in close-up the puppets disappear, while GIBSON *pops up, throttling* HARPO.
The children in the audience shout and scream with glee, laughing and applauding the show.
At that moment the door opens and the CAPTAIN *enters, led by a little girl and smiling benignly.*
Close-up of GIBSON *in the booth, throttling* HARPO.
The CAPTAIN *sees them, his smile fades, and he calls out sternly:*)

CAPTAIN: Gibson!
(GIBSON *releases* HARPO *and looks around.*
Resume on the CAPTAIN.)
Come out of there!
(*We now see him standing in front of the booth, with* GIBSON *and* HARPO *inside.*)
GIBSON: Yes, sir.
(*He disappears from view, then emerges from the booth.*)
I want to report I found a . . .
CAPTAIN: Gibson, you've been drinking again and you know what my orders were.
(*Behind them* HARPO *disappears and* PUNCH *bobs up in his place.*)

GIBSON: But those stowaways – I just caught one of them in
 there.

CAPTAIN: Stowaway, huh?

GIBSON: (*Turning*) Yes. There he is.

 (*Cut to medium shot as he grabs* PUNCH *by the neck.*)

PUNCH: (*Squeaking*) Ouch! Look out, you're choking me. Look
 out!

 (*The* CAPTAIN *taps* PUNCH's *nose; it makes a hollow sound.*)

CAPTAIN: (*To* GIBSON) I thought so. Go to your quarters.

 (*Behind them,* HARPO *replaces* PUNCH *again, and blows his
 squeaker at the* CAPTAIN *as he turns away.*

 In a closer shot, HARPO *whips round, revealing a false face on
 the back of his head. The audience shouts with glee, while the*
 CAPTAIN *reappears.*)

GIBSON: That's him now.

CAPTAIN: (*Tapping the mask*) That's a dummy. Come with me.

 (*He exits as* HARPO *turns and blows the squeaker at* GIBSON.
 Laughter. GIBSON *taps* HARPO's *face.*

 Back to the scene as HARPO *whips round, showing the mask
 again. The* CAPTAIN, *who has started for the door, comes back
 towards the booth.*)

 (*Sternly*) First Officer!

GIBSON: I'm telling you that's him!

CAPTAIN: This has gone far enough. Get up to your quarters.

 (GIBSON *goes past him, then* HARPO *turns and kicks the*
 CAPTAIN *through the front of the booth.*)

 Oh!

 (GIBSON *whips round and salutes.*)

GIBSON: Yes, sir.

 (*Laughter off.*)

CAPTAIN: (*To the children*) Quiet!

 (*He pokes* HARPO's *cheek, then says to* GIBSON:)

 I think you're right.

 (HARPO *kicks him again, and this time the* CAPTAIN *grabs his
 leg and pulls.*)

 I know you're right!

PUNCH: (*Reappearing next to* HARPO) Look out there. What're
 you doing? What're you doing?

(In the audience, the children shout and clap with glee.
Back to the scene as the CAPTAIN *and* GIBSON *both start*
heaving at HARPO's *leg. The children laugh and Punch squeaks,*
while HARPO *whistles encouragement. Suddenly, he disappears*
from the booth, emerges behind GIBSON *and starts heaving with*
the other two. The false leg finally gives way and they collapse in
a heap on the floor.
HARPO *goes into the booth again . . .*
He reappears on the other side, where the Crocodile is now
visible, its jaws flapping. He picks up his hat and hooter from a
chair.
We see the CAPTAIN *and* GIBSON *on the floor, embracing the*
false leg . . .
Then resume on HARPO. *He sticks the bulb of the hooter between*
the Crocodile's jaws; it sounds the hooter.
At the side of the room, he gets on to a kiddy-car and rides it down
a track towards the door; the camera follows and the children
scream with glee.
Seen from behind, he trundles off down the corridor, the mask
still fixed to the back of his head. Two passengers skip out of the
way as he signals a left turn and rounds the corner, sounding his
hooter.)

In the barber's shop, CHICO *is sitting in a chair, being given a*
manicure by a blond MANICURIST. *The* BARKER *comes up.*

BARKER: Er – would you like to have anything before lunch?
CHICO: Yes, breakfast.
BARKER: Why, nobody eats in here.
   (CHICO *gets out a sandwich.*)
CHICO: I do. (*He takes a bite and makes a face.*) Mustard's no good
   without roast beef.
   (*He throws the sandwich away and the* BARBER *exits.*)
MANICURIST: Do you want your nails trimmed long?
CHICO: Oh, about an hour and a half. I got nothin' to do. (*He*
   grins.) Hey, you're a nice-a lookin' gal, all right. You got it.
MANICURIST: (*Smiling*) Thank you.
CHICO: And you can keep it.

(There are noises off as we cut to a medium shot of the doorway.
HARPO *trundles up on his kiddy-car, hits the door sill and falls to
the floor. He hides his head under the carpet as* GIBSON *thunders
past outside.*
In a closer shot, HARPO *looks out from under the rug, sees* CHICO
and grins.
Resume on the scene as CHICO *approaches with the*
MANICURIST. HARPO *gets up, holds up his mask and pulls a
face. The* MANICURIST *screams and runs off.*
A closer shot of CHICO *and* HARPO.)
Yeah, that's a nice girl, hey?
(In the corridor outside, the SECOND OFFICER *approaches. He
has a luxuriant moustache.*
Back to HARPO *and* CHICO.)
Somebody's comin'!
(They exit.
In the corridor, the OFFICER *reaches the door of the barber's shop
and beckons to some* SAILORS.)
OFFICER: Come on, boys.
(The SAILORS *appear and follow him in.*
Inside, HARPO *and* CHICO *are standing by the chair in barber's
aprons as the* OFFICER *and* SAILORS *enter.* HARPO *whistles.)*
CHICO: You're next, Cap.
OFFICER: Say, I'm looking for a couple of mugs.
*(HARPO *holds out a couple of shaving mugs.)*
No, no! *(To the* SAILORS) Say, you boys look on B deck.
SAILORS: Aye, aye, sir. *(They go off.)*
(Medium shot of the three of them.)
CHICO: Well, how about a shave, huh?
OFFICER: Sure. Gimme a once-over.
CHICO: *(To* HARPO) Once over, partner.
(They crouch on either side of the OFFICER *and* HARPO *whistles,
indicating a somersault.)*
OFFICER: *(Tapping his face)* No, a shave.
CHICO: On the face. All right.
(The OFFICER *gets into the chair.)*
OFFICER: Say, wake me up when you get through.
CHICO: You bet.

28

(*A closer shot, with the* OFFICER *seated in the chair.*)
(*Taking his cap*) We take care of you, all right.
(*The* OFFICER *yawns hugely and shuts his eyes.* HARPO *ties him to the chair with an apron, while* CHICO *grabs a cut-throat razor and looks down his throat.*)
We take-a the tonsils last. I think we work the moustache first . . . Give 'im a little snoop.
(HARPO *brandishes the scissors.*
In a medium close-up, camera follows HARPO *as he moves to and fro. He cuts a piece off one side of the* OFFICER's *moustache, then stands back to admire the effect.*)
(*Off at first*) This side's too long. Give 'im a little snoop this side.
(HARPO *snips a piece off the other side.*)
Now this side's too short.
(HARPO *looks indignant and makes as if to cut the same side again.*)
It's too short. The other side is too long. Snoop 'im up.
HARPO *cuts far too much off the other side.*
Shot of CHICO *as he stands back to inspect* HARPO's *handiwork.*)
That's better, but the side's too short now is too long, the side's too long is too short . . . I think we gotta give 'im one more snoop.
(*Resume on the three of them as* HARPO *takes too much off the other side again, then cut to a shot of the scene.*)
I think we better measure.
(*They both grab tape measures, measure a yard or so out from the* OFFICER's *moustache and compare lengths.* CHICO *points at* HARPO's *measure.*)
It's about a foot too much.
(HARPO *grabs a hammer and the* OFFICER's *foot.*)
(*Restraining him*) Hey, no! The measure's a foot too much!
(HARPO *cuts a foot off the tape measure.*
Shot of CHICO.)
Now, looks much better.
(*Close-up of* HARPO *and the* OFFICER.)

It can stand one more snoop in the middle, I think . . .
(HARPO *looks bewildered.*)
. . . In the middle, one snoop.
(HARPO *snips the moustache straight across; it is now no more than a toothbrush.*)
'At's-a fine. (*He laughs.*) 'At's-a very good.
(HARPO *looks pleased, and we cut to* CHICO, *pointing.*)
I think – I think it's a little bit rough right here . . .
(*Pan to include the* OFFICER.)
I fix that.
(*We now see* HARPO *stropping a razor on the shower tube by the basin.*)
(*Off*) You know, I'm never goin' on this boat again. The food's no good.
(HARPO *slices up a block of wood, testing the razor.*)
(*Off*) Of course, I no eat yet, but even if I don't eat I like the food good.
(HARPO *whistles, satisfied, and strops the razor once more on the marble counter.*
Back to the scene. CHICO *has now lathered the* OFFICER's *moustache.*)
One more snoop.
(HARPO *wields the razor and* CHICO *wipes away the lather.*)
Hah! 'At's-a beautiful, hey! 'At's-a what you call a work of art.
(*He peers more closely.* HARPO *has shaved off the whole moustache.*)
Hey, you know, I think you give 'im one snoop too much.

We move to the state room occupied by ALKY BRIGGS *and his wife* LUCILLE. BRIGGS *sits pulling on his spats while* LUCILLE *paces angrily to and fro.*
Seen in medium shot, she comes and stands over him.

LUCILLE: And I want you to know, I'm fed up with your alibis.
BRIGGS: Aw, take it easy. You're getting all excited.
(*He gets up and takes his hat from the table.*)
LUCILLE: (*Hands on hips*) Now where do you think you're going?

BRIGGS: Never mind. I'm running this racket. Just stay here and
keep out of sight like I told you.
(*He walks to the door; she runs in front and stops him.*)
LUCILLE: Oh no, you don't.
(*The two of them are seen in medium close-up,* LUCILLE *with her
back to the door.*)
Now listen to me, Mr Alky Briggs. You can't keep me
cooped up like this. I've played second fiddle on this ship
long enough.
(BRIGGS *pulls her away from the door.*)
BRIGGS: Now you listen. I'm not after any dames. I'm after Joe
Helton, I tell you, and he can't get away from me on this
boat . . .
(LUCILLE *folds her arms.*)
He's gonna put his OK on my gang or he's gonna get this.
(*He taps his pocket.*)

Out on the promenade deck, GIBSON *spots* GROUCHO *in a deck-chair
and gives chase.* GROUCHO *shoves the chair in* GIBSON's *way,
tripping him up, and runs off.*
In the corridor outside BRIGGS's *state room,* GROUCHO *runs towards
camera but skids to a halt, falling over, as he sees . . . an officer with a
couple of passengers at the other end.*
GROUCHO *starts back in the opposite direction but skids to a halt
again as* GIBSON *appears, blocking his exit. At that moment a tailor
approaches carrying a couple of dresses on hangers, and knocks at a
cabin door.* GROUCHO *grabs one of the dresses and, using it as a
shield, makes for the door of* BRIGGS's *state room, while* GIBSON *spots
him and follows.*
GIBSON: Hey, who are you?
(*We see* GROUCHO *at the door.*)
GROUCHO: I'm the tailor.
(*Shot of* GIBSON *approaching.*)
GIBSON: Oh! That reminds me, where are my pants?
(*Resume on* GROUCHO.)
GROUCHO: You've got 'em on.
(*Back to* GIBSON: *he looks down at his pants.*
Seen from inside, GROUCHO *barges into the state room and comes*

31

face to face with BRIGGS *and* LUCILLE.)

Er . . . pardon me while I step into the closet.

(*Camera pans as he crosses to the closet and steps inside.*)

LUCILLE: (*Off*) And get a load of this . . .

(*Resume on her and* BRIGGS.)

If you come in again at three o'clock in the morning, I'm going . . .

BRIGGS: Aw, stop bothering me. Tell it to the tailor. (*He opens the door.*)

LUCILLE: Alky!

(*Cut to a longer shot as he goes out.*)

Alky!

(*She takes a few paces back and hurls something at the door, then we cut to a long shot as she crosses to the closet by the bed. We see her approaching the closet door, where she calls out:*)

Say, what are you doing in there?

(*Cut to the door of the closet as* GROUCHO *opens it and sticks his head out.*)

GROUCHO: (*In a whisper*) Nothing. Come on in.

(*He beckons, rolling his eyes, and goes back into the closet. Resume on* LUCILLE.)

LUCILLE: You can't stay in that closet.

(GROUCHO *steps out again beside her.*)

GROUCHO: Oh, I can't, can I? That's what they said to Thomas Edison, mighty inventor . . . Thomas Lindberg, mighty flier, and Thomas Shefsky, mighty like a rose. (*He chucks her cheek.*) Just remember, my little cabbage, that if there weren't any closets, there wouldn't be any hooks, and if there weren't any hooks, there wouldn't be any fish, and that would suit me fine.

(*Shot of the scene as he goes back into the closet.*)

LUCILLE: (*Leaning against the door*) Don't try to hide. I know you're in that closet.

(GROUCHO *steps out of another door behind her.*)

GROUCHO: Did you see me go in the closet?

LUCILLE: (*Turning*) No.

GROUCHO: Am I in the closet now?

LUCILLE: Well, no.

GROUCHO: (*Theatrically*) Then how do you know I was in the
closet? Your honour, I rest my case.
(*He throws himself down on the bed.*
LUCILLE, *in medium close-up, glances towards the door.*)
LUCILLE: (*Invitingly*) Come here, brown eyes.
(GROUCHO *snuggles against the pillow.*)
GROUCHO: Oh, no. You're not going to get me off this bed.
(LUCILLE *stands over him.*)
LUCILLE: I didn't know you were a lawyer. You're awfully shy
for a lawyer.
(*Back to* GROUCHO.)
GROUCHO: You bet I'm shy. I'm a shyster lawyer.
(*Shot of the scene.*)
LUCILLE: Well then, what do you think of an egg that would give
me . . .
GROUCHO: (*Sitting up*) I know, I know. You're a woman who's
been getting nothing but dirty breaks.
(*Close-up of* GROUCHO, *with* LUCILLE'*s bosom over him.*)
Well, we can clean and tighten your brakes, but you'll have
to stay in the garage all night. (*He lies down.*)
(*Shot of* LUCILLE.)
LUCILLE: I want excitement. I want to ha-cha-cha-cha. (*She
breaks into a dance step.*)
(*Back to the scene as* GROUCHO *picks up a guitar and strums it
while she dances. Then he throws it down and lies back again.*)
You don't realize it . . .
(*We see her from the end of the bed, standing over him.*)
. . . but from the time he got the marriage licence, I've led a
dog's life. (*She goes off.*)
GROUCHO: Are you sure he didn't get a dog's licence?
(*Cut to show them from the side of the bed.*)
LUCILLE: Oh, Alky can't make a fool of me.
(*We see them from the foot of the bed again.*)
(*Excitedly*) I want to go places. I want to do things. I want
freedom, I want liberty, I want justice . . . (*She goes off.*)
GROUCHO: (*Trumpeting*) Ta-ra-ta-da-da . . .
(*He sits up as* LUCILLE *reappears.*)
Madam, you're making history. In fact, you're making me,

and I wish you'd keep my hands to yourself.
(*Resume on the side of the bed as* GROUCHO *lies down again.*)

LUCILLE: (*Excitedly*) Oh, you know what I want. I want life, I want laughter, I want gaiety. I want to ha-cha-cha-cha . . .
(*She does a dance step – he strums the guitar.*
Shot of GROUCHO *from the end of the bed.*)

GROUCHO: Madam, before I get through with you, you will have a clear case for divorce, and so will my wife.
(*Camera pans as he gets up and approaches* LUCILLE.)
Now, the first thing to do is to arrange for a settlement. You take the children, your husband takes the house. Junior burns down the house, you take the insurance, and I take you. (*He puts his arms round her.*)

LUCILLE: But I haven't any children.

GROUCHO: That's just the trouble with this country. You haven't any children, and as for me . . . (*Dramatically*) I'm going back in the closet, where men are empty overcoats. (*He opens the door and steps in.*)
(*Cut to a longer shot.*)

LUCILLE: Oh, brown eyes!
(*She follows him into the closet and closes the door.* GROUCHO *emerges from the other door and leans against the wall.* LUCILLE *comes out after him and throws herself into his arms.*)

GROUCHO: (*Tossing away his cigar*) Wheee!
(*Loud tango music; camera pans as they dance across the room, round the table, up on to the bed and off again. They dance back to back, then* LUCILLE *disappears while* GROUCHO *cavorts solo by the door. It opens, and* BRIGGS *comes in.*
Oblivious, GROUCHO *backs up to* BRIGGS *takes his hands and dances with him.*
Seen in close-up, he holds up his mouth to be kissed. Then he opens his eyes and winces. The music stops, and we cut back to the two of them.
Sir, this is an outrage, breaking into a man's home. I'm not in the habit of making threats, but there'll be a letter about this in *The Times* tomorrow morning. (*He flaps his coat-tails in indignation.*)

BRIGGS: (*Threateningly*) Yeah? But you won't read it, 'cause I'm gonna lay you out pretty.

GROUCHO: Oh, you're gonna lay me out pretty, eh? That's the thanks I get for freeing an innocent girl who, although she is hiding in the closet at this moment, has promised to become the mother of her children. And with that, sir, I bid you a fond farewell. Good day, sir.

(*Pan as he moves towards the closet with the utmost dignity. Shot of the state room.*)

Good day! (*He exits into the closet.*)

BRIGGS: (*Going up to the door*) Come out of there. I want to talk to you.

(*They are seen in medium close-up as* GROUCHO *opens the door.*)

GROUCHO: I'm sorry, but we're using the old-fashioned ice man, and we find him very satisfactory for keeping the house warm. (*He shuts the door.*)

(*Back to the scene as* BRIGGS *opens the door of the closet again.* GROUCHO *comes out, crouched behind a dress, and makes for the door of the state room.*

As he gets there, BRIGGS *catches him up and grabs the dress.*)

Just as I thought, you're yellow – grabbing at a woman's skirts!

BRIGGS: (*Throwing down the dress*) I'm wise! I'm wise!

(*A closer shot of the two of them.*)

GROUCHO: You're wise, eh? Well, what's the capital of Nebraska? What's the capital of the Chase National Bank? Give up?

BRIGGS: (*Growling*) You . . .

GROUCHO: Now, I'll try you on an easy one. How many Frenchmen can't be wrong?

BRIGGS: I know, but . . .

GROUCHO: You were warm and so was she. But don't be discouraged . . . (*He pats his arm*) . . . With a little study you'll go a long ways, and I wish you'd start now.

(*Shot of the scene as* GROUCHO *turns to go.* BRIGGS *holds out a gun in his jacket pocket.*)

BRIGGS: Do you see this gat?

(GROUCHO *peers into the pocket.*)

GROUCHO: Cute, isn't it? Santa Claus bring it for Christmas?

(*Preening*) I got a fire engine.

BRIGGS: Listen, mug, do you know who I am?

GROUCHO: Now don't tell me. (*He leans his head against the door, pondering.*) Are you animal or vegetable?

(BRIGGS *growls with fury.*)

Animal.

BRIGGS: Get this. I'm Alky Briggs.

GROUCHO: (*Taken aback*) And I . . . I'm the fella who talks too much. Fancy meeting you here after all these drinks. (*He slaps him on the back.*)

(*Seen in close-up at the closet door,* LUCILLE *puts a finger to her lips.*

We see GROUCHO *and* BRIGGS *again as* GROUCHO *blows* LUCILLE *a kiss.*

LUCILLE *exits into the closet.*

And we resume on the scene as GROUCHO *edges towards the door.*)

BRIGGS: (*Holding him back*) Wait a minute.

GROUCHO: Sorry, I can't stay. The Captain's waiting to chase me round the deck. (*He turns to go.*)

BRIGGS: (*Brandishing the gun*) You can stay, all right, until I finish with you.

(*On his last words, we cut to* LUCILLE *as she runs out of the closet.*

She comes up and throws herself on BRIGGS.)

LUCILLE: Alky, darling, please . . .

BRIGGS: Don't 'darling' me. Get in that next room and stay there.

(*She hesitates.*)

Get in that next room!

(*She goes off and* GROUCHO *starts after her, but* BRIGGS *stops him.*)

GROUCHO: Oh, I'm not good enough for her, am I?

(*We see* LUCILLE *go into the next room and slam the door. Then resume on the two men.*)

BRIGGS: Is there anything you've got to say before I drill ya?

GROUCHO: Yes, I'd like to ask you one question.

BRIGGS: Go ahead.

GROUCHO: (*Coyly*) Do you think that girls think less of a boy if he lets himself be kissed?

(BRIGGS *backs away and sits down as* GROUCHO *advances on him.*)

I mean, don't you think that although girls go out with boys like me – they always marry the other kind?

(*He works his eyebrows.* BRIGGS *stares at him.*)

(*Opening his jacket*) Well, all right, if you're gonna kill me, hurry up. I have to take my tonic at two.

(*Close-up of* BRIGGS.)

BRIGGS: (*Amused*) Say, I can use a guy with your nerve.

(*Resume on the two of them.*)

(*Getting up*) I think we could get along well together.

GROUCHO: (*Coyly*) Well, of course, the first year we might have our little squabbles, but then that's inevitable, don't you think?

(*In the corridor outside,* ZEPPO *dodges away from an officer and opens the state room door.*

We see him again as he comes into the state room, shuts the door and listens for sounds of pursuit, watched by GROUCHO *and* BRIGGS.)

BRIGGS: (*Threatening*) And what do you want here?

(ZEPPO *whips round at the sound of his voice and* GROUCHO *motions him away.*)

ZEPPO: (*Embarrassed*) Why, I was . . . (*Indicating* GROUCHO) I was just looking for him.

BRIGGS: (*To* GROUCHO) Do you know this guy?

(*The three of them are seen in medium shot.*)

GROUCHO: Why, I've known him for years. He used to live in the next barrel to me.

BRIGGS: Oh, I see. The stowaways . . .

(GROUCHO *makes a face.*)

Say, I can help you bozos.

GROUCHO: Mr Bozos to you.

BRIGGS: All right. Mr Bozo. And you can help me. I'm short-handed, and I want to get a guy on this boat.

GROUCHO: Well, it's too late to get him on now. You should have said something before we sailed.

37

(BRIGGS *pulls out a bit of paper.*)

BRIGGS: Listen. This is a map of B deck. There's Joe Helton's
state room . . .

(*A closer shot of the three of them.*)

. . . and he's a tough egg. And you're coming with me while I
have it out with Joe.

(*He puts away the paper and goes off.* ZEPPO *crosses to*
GROUCHO.)

ZEPPO: Say, do you know who Joe Helton is?

GROUCHO: I think I'll get off this boat until this blows over.

(*They make for the door but* BRIGGS *reappears with a couple of
guns.*)

BRIGGS: If you know what's good for you, you'll stick with me.
(*He shoves the guns into their hands.*) Now, you keep the
windows covered while I go in. Now move!

(*Unwillingly,* GROUCHO *opens the door.*

Seen from outside, GROUCHO *and* ZEPPO *come out of the state
room, looking uncertainly at their guns.* BRIGGS *appears in the
doorway behind them.*

*In the corridor, a sailor is washing down a handrail with a tub of
water on the floor beside him.* GROUCHO *and* ZEPPO *drop their
guns in the tub and run off, while* BRIGGS *comes out of the door.*)

Meanwhile, in the main saloon, HARPO *comes up to some children
playing round the fountain at the bottom of the staircase. The children
shout and laugh at him, and he shoos them away. Then he looks down
into the water, sounds his hooter and takes off his hat.*

In a closer shot, HARPO *kneels down by the fountain, holding out his
hat. He whistles and sounds his hooter and a frog jumps out of the
water into the hat. He gets up.*

Cut to close-up as HARPO *puts on his hat. The frog croaks inside it and
the crown moves up and down.* HARPO *grins and rolls his eyes.*

We move to the promenade deck as CHICO *comes running towards us,
looking over his shoulder. He cannons into a man, knocking him over,
picks him up and dusts him down with a laugh, then rushes off in the
foreground. Immediately afterwards,* GIBSON *appears in pursuit and
knocks the same man flying again, then rushes off after* CHICO.

Resume on the main saloon, where two MEN *are sitting absorbed in a*

MONKEY BUSINESS

game of chess. HARPO *wanders up, whistling, and sits down between them.*
A closer shot as one of the men leans forward to make a move; his
OPPONENT *and* HARPO *start forward too. However, he thinks better of it and leans back again; so do the other two. The same thing happens again, then* CHICO *enters and leans over them. The* FIRST MAN *starts to make a move again, but* HARPO *restrains him, shaking his head. The other man looks up.*)

OPPONENT: (*Indignantly*) What is the idea of this?
CHICO: That's all right. I make a move for you.
   (*He takes a white piece with a black and* HARPO *removes it from the board.*)
FIRST MAN: (*Furious*) Why, this is an outrage.
OPPONENT: I'll call the Captain.
CHICO: The Captain don't play chess.
FIRST MAN: (*Getting up*) Purser! Purser!
OPPONENT: (*Getting up*) Steward! Steward! Come here.
CHICO: (*To* HARPO) Too much noise here for us. We better go
   some place where it's quiet.
   (*Camera pans as he and* HARPO *pick up the chessboard and start off, leaving general confusion behind them.*
   The scene changes to JOE HELTON's *state room.* HELTON *is sitting finishing his breakfast, wearing a dressing-gown and reading a newspaper. There is a knock at the door.*)
HELTON: Come in.
   (*A steward enters with a tray.*)
STEWARD: Your cigars, sir.
   (*Seen in a medium shot,* HELTON *takes the cigars from the tray.*)
HELTON: Thank you.
   (*The steward picks up the breakfast tray from the table and starts to go out.* HELTON *gets up.*)
   Wait a minute.
   (*He pulls out a bundle of notes and throws one down on the tray. Resume on the scene.*)
STEWARD: Oh, thank you, sir. (*He starts out.*)
   (HELTON *is now seen in medium close-up as he sits down and picks up the newspaper.*

39

Close-up of the paper with the headline: 'MILLIONAIRE
RACKETEER RETURNS TO AMERICA', *then dissolve to
an insert of* HELTON's *photograph beside it.*
HELTON *looks at the paper and nods with satisfaction.*
In the corridor outside, MARY, *the girl whom we saw with*
ZEPPO, *approaches the door of the state room, back to camera.*
Inside the state room, camera pans with MARY *as she comes in
through the door and goes across to her father, who has now got
up.*)

MARY: (*Pointing at his dressing-gown*) Aw, Dad, now look at you.
You aren't even dressed yet.

(*A closer shot of the two of them, as* HELTON *pats her on the
arm.*)

HELTON: You can do all the dressing for the family, Mary. Old
Joe Helton is taking things easy for the rest of his life. (*He sits
down.*) We're big shots now, baby.

(*Out in the corridor,* BRIGGS *goes up to the door in back view.
He looks furtively round, then knocks.*
*On the sound of the knock, we cut back to the interior of the state
room.*)

Come in.

(BRIGGS *comes in and* HELTON *gets up, holding* MARY *by the
hand.*)

BRIGGS: (*Breezily*) Hello, Joe.

HELTON: (*Unenthusiastic*) Hello, Briggs.

(*A closer shot of the three of them.*)

What do you want?

(BRIGGS *eyes* MARY *appreciatively.*)

BRIGGS: Oh, I just wanted to have a friendly talk. You know, I'm
sort-a worried about business.

HELTON: (*To* MARY) Step into the other room, baby.

MARY: Oh, but Dad . . .

HELTON: (*Firmly*) Run along, honey.

(MARY *exits and* BRIGGS *turns to watch her go.*)

BRIGGS: Your kid?

(*We see* MARY *going through the door into the next room; she
looks suspiciously back.*
Then we resume on the two men.)

She's cute, isn't she?

HELTON: I don't think we've got anything to talk about. Get out!

BRIGGS: Not before I get your OK on my gang.

HELTON: I'm not doing you any favours.

BRIGGS: Oh yes, you are . . .

(*He puts his hand in his breast pocket.* HELTON *reaches for his gun, but* BRIGGS *only pulls out a bit of paper.*)

You're gonna sign this. (*He hands it to* HELTON.)

(*In the corridor,* HARPO *and* CHICO *approach the door of the state room, carrying the chessboard between them. A dog barks off-screen and* HARPO *turns angrily to silence it.* CHICO *motions him into the room.*

Resume on the scene inside the state room. Engaged in their argument, HELTON *and* BRIGGS *do not notice as* HARPO *and* CHICO *come in through the door and settle down to their chess game on the bed.*)

I'm taking over your territory or there's gonna be trouble.

HELTON: I'm taking no sides. You'll have to fight it out with Butch and the gang.

BRIGGS: (*Loudly*) I'm stepping into your shoes as boss.

(HARPO *turns and shushes* BRIGGS, *who has his back to him.*)

HELTON: I'm not backing up any small-time chiseller.

(*We see* HARPO *and* CHICO *engrossed in their game, as the argument gets fiercer off-screen.*)

BRIGGS: (*Off*) Aw, don't put on the Ritz with me.

HELTON: (*Off*) Say, don't get cocky with me, Briggs.

(HARPO *turns indignantly and mouths 'shut up' at the two men.*)

BRIGGS: (*Off*) I'm talking turkey. You can't make all the dough and then run out on your pals.

(*Resume on the scene.*)

HELTON: I'm not taking orders from a mug like you. Scram!

(*He tears up the paper and throws it on the ground.*)

BRIGGS: So that's your answer, huh? Well, here's mine . . .

(*He brings up his gun in his jacket pocket, but at the same time* HARPO *gets up and hits him over the head with his hooter. A closer shot, by the bed.* HARPO *points the hooter at* BRIGGS *as he turns.* BRIGGS *thinks it's a gun and puts up his hands.* HARPO *slaps hands with him and* BRIGGS *knocks him over on the bed.*)

41

Resume on HELTON *as* BRIGGS *comes up to him.*)

(*Furious*) So you got your gang with you, hey? Well, I'll get you later. (*He goes off.*)

(*By the bed,* CHICO *and* HARPO *return to their game while* BRIGGS *slams out of the door in the background.* HELTON *appears and stands over them.*)

HELTON: Who are you guys?

(*They signal to him to keep quiet.*)

What are you doing in my room?

CHICO: 'Ats-a my partner, but he no speak. He's-a dem an a-duff. (HELTON *picks up the hooter from the bed and* HARPO *squeezes the bulb. Sound of the hooter.*)

HELTON: (*Laughing*) You guys don't know it, but you just scared a pretty tough egg out of this room.

CHICO: Sure, we're a couple tough guys.

(HELTON *leans forward, in medium close-up.*)

HELTON: Do you wanna make some money?

(*Resume on the three of them.* CHICO *and* HARPO *are on their feet and standing beside him almost before he has got out the words. They rub their hands with glee.*)

CHICO: Money? (*He chuckles.*) Money, hey? Feela this mos'le. (HELTON *does so.*) Feela his mos'le.

(HARPO *gives him his leg.* HELTON *laughs and squeezes it;* HARPO *winces.*)

All right, all right. How much you pay?

(*A closer shot of the three of them.*)

HELTON: Well, just how tough are you?

CHICO: Well, you pay little bit, we little bit tough. You pay very much, very much tough. You pay too much, we too much tough. How much you pay?

HELTON: I pay plenty.

CHICO: Well, then we're plenty tough. And we show you, too. (*He pushes* HELTON *off and beckons to* HARPO.)

Hey, partner, show 'im how tough we are.

(HARPO *rolls up his sleeve and hits* CHICO *on the jaw.*)

(*Turning to* HELTON) See? 'At's-a nothing, 'ats-a free.

(HELTON *is seen from a low angle, watching sceptically.*)

(*Off*) Now, we give you da real stuff this time.

(*Resume on the other two.*)

(*To* HARPO) Hey, come on, put some pep into it. The one-two uppercut. You know, on the button.

(HARPO *takes aim at his navel.*)

No, no – no downstairs button, upstairs button.

(HARPO *cracks him on the jaw . . .*

CHICO *flies through the air . . .*

And lands on his back on the floor.

HELTON *stands watching. He looks from* CHICO *to* HARPO *and grins.*

Resume on HARPO: *he grins back at* HELTON, *teeth bared.*

CHICO *gets up in front of him.*)

(*Pushing him around*) 'At's-a fine, hey? 'At's good, all right. I tell him you're tough and you punch like a lily. What's-a matter with you? You wanna lose-a this job? Give 'im the stuff this time.

(*Camera pans with* CHICO *as he goes across to* HELTON.)

Excusa me, boss, he canna do much better, but he no work good today. You see, he's-a no getta paid. But when he getta paid, you watch him.

(*We follow him back to* HARPO *again.*)

Come on. This time we give 'im the works. Come on, hurry up. On the button this time. (*He pushes him, egging him on.*) Come on. I tell you, on the button. Come on, hurry. Come on. Give him da punch.

(HARPO *clenches his fists and starts to pant, rolling his eyes and baring his teeth.*)

(*Urgently*) Come on, come on, come on. All right, all right.

(*Close-up of* HARPO, *panting and glaring.*)

(*Off*) Come on. Punch! Punch!

(HARPO *swings at* CHICO.

In a general shot of the scene, he cracks him on the jaw again.

CHICO *flies through the air, lands on the bed . . .*

And somersaults on to the floor, seen from a high angle.

Resume on HARPO, *still panting and glaring. Suddenly the frog croaks inside his hat and the crown moves up and down.*

HARPO *looks up and grins.*

Laid out on the floor beside the bed, CHICO *starts to come to . . .*

43

While HARPO *starts glaring again and runs forward.*
Back to the scene. HELTON *comes across and helps* CHICO *to his feet, while* HARPO *grabs the hooter from the bed and takes a swing at him.*)
(*Restraining* HARPO) Hey, 'at's-a nuf. Wait. (*To* HELTON) Well, what you think of us?

HELTON: You're great.

CHICO: Sssh! Not so loud. You want him to getta swell head?

HELTON: You guys are plenty tough all right.
(*He turns and opens a closet beside the bed.*
At that moment GROUCHO, *in close-up, pokes his head through the window and calls out:*)

GROUCHO: I'm spying on you!
(*Shot of* HARPO *and* CHICO. CHICO *shushes* GROUCHO, *off;* HARPO *shushes* CHICO.
Back to the scene as HELTON *comes up to the two of them again.*)

HELTON: You're just the fellows I need. You're hired.
(*He exits into the closet, taking off his dressing-gown.* CHICO *holds out his hand to shake with* HARPO; HARPO *gives him the bulb of the hooter; the hooter sounds and* CHICO *runs into the closet.*
CHICO *comes up to* HELTON *inside the closet. As they talk,* HELTON *takes off his dressing-gown and reaches for a jacket.*)

CHICO: Hey, we're great, huh?

HELTON: You're great.

CHICO: Sure, my partner's great.

HELTON: He's great.

CHICO: My grandfather's great. He a great-grandfather.
(*On the deck outside,* BRIGGS, GROUCHO *and* ZEPPO *emerge from behind a companionway and look off.*)

BRIGGS: Now when Helton comes out of his room, plug him.

ZEPPO: Yeah? What'll we plug him with?

BRIGGS: Didn't I give you two gats?

GROUCHO: Well, we had to drowns the gats, but we saved you a little black gitten.
(BRIGGS *pulls out two more guns.*)

BRIGGS: Here, take these, and hang on to 'em now.

(*He gives them the guns and they look at them nervously.
Inside the state-room,* HELTON *gives a gun each to* HARPO *and* CHICO.)

HELTON: Don't leave me for a minute. And keep your eyes on that guy that just went out of here. (*He goes off to the closet again.*)

CHICO: (*To* HARPO) Now, you understand? Anybody comes near da boss, let 'im have it.

(*He slaps his hand with the gun butt.* HELTON *reappears, putting on a cloth cap.* CHICO *steps up to him.*)

You're all right now, boss. Anybody comes near you . . .

(HARPO *hits him on the head with the gun butt.*)

Hey, what's-a matter with you? Look out. (*To* HELTON) That's all right, he was just practising.

(*He mutters at* HARPO *who gives him his leg;* CHICO *thrusts him aside.*)

HELTON: Now I can take a walk out on deck and feel safe. Come on, let's go.

(*In a closer shot, the three of them pass by the bed and go towards the door,* HARPO *brandishing his hooter.*

As they are about to leave, HARPO *dodges back to the chessboard, makes a final move and returns to the door, putting a piece in his pocket.*

Out on the deck, BRIGGS, GROUCHO *and* ZEPPO *are seen by the companionway, looking off.*)

BRIGGS: There he comes now. Get him. (*He goes off.*)

GROUCHO: Don't worry, we'll get him. I've got my finger on the trigger.

(*He unconsciously points his gun at* ZEPPO'S *stomach and* ZEPPO *dodges back nervously.*

HELTON *now appears in a doorway, flanked by* HARPO *and* CHICO *with their guns. He looks round warily and exits to the left, while the other two peer behind them. Simultaneously* GIBSON *appears, going towards the right, and* HARPO *and* CHICO *follow him off, unaware, searching to and fro for potential enemies.* HARPO *holds his gun butt-forwards.*

In a long shot of the promenade deck, GIBSON *strides towards us with* HARPO *and* CHICO *prowling behind, guns at the ready.*)

45

There is a buzz of voices as the passengers leap up in alarm.
Camera tracks ahead of HARPO *and* CHICO *as they walk along.*)
CHICO: Hey, don't forget, anybody comes near the boss, let 'im
    have it.
    (*Resume on all three of them as* GIBSON *arrives at the bottom of a*
    stairway and looks up it, then goes off in the opposite direction.
    HARPO *tries to follow a couple of passing girls, but* CHICO *hauls*
    him back and they follow a passenger in a white cap as he mounts
    the stairs.
    At the top of the stairs, two passengers hurry off in alarm as the
    man comes into view, followed by CHICO *and* HARPO. *We move*
    with them past a row of deck-chairs; a woman jumps up with a
    scream.
    We now see the trio coming along the boat deck towards us.
    HARPO *and* CHICO *turn round, grinning at the frightened*
    passengers. In so doing, they lose the man in the white hat and
    start following a passenger with a beard, who gets up from a
    deck-chair just in front of them.
    The MAN *moves away from camera, then stops and turns.*
    HARPO *and* CHICO *stand amazed as they see his face, then*
    CHICO *bursts out laughing.*
    A closer shot of the three of them.)
    (*Pointing*) Hey, it's da boss. He's gotta disguise. Take off the
    whiskers, we know ya.
    (HARPO *puts his knee against the* MAN's *chest and tugs at the*
    beard.)
MAN: (*Indignant*) Ouch! What do you mean? (*Waving*) Officer!
    Officer!
    (*Resume on the previous shot as* HARPO *and* CHICO *exit in*
    opposite directions.)
    Officer!

    (GIBSON *passes at a run.*
    On another part of the boat deck, BRIGGS *appears in the*
    foreground and signals to GROUCHO *and* ZEPPO. *They hurry up*
    and stand on either side of him.)
BRIGGS: Well, why didn't you get him? Not afraid, are you?
ZEPPO: Well, we were . . .
GROUCHO: Afraid? Me? A man who's licked his weight in wild

caterpillars? Afraid! . . . You bet I'm afraid.

(LUCILLE *comes up behind them, furious.*)

LUCILLE: So . . .!

GROUCHO: Hello. How are things in the closet? You know, I still smell of mothballs.

LUCILLE: (*Standing nose to nose with him*) Oh, I don't want to talk to you.

(*She stamps her foot and turns away.* GROUCHO *grabs her from behind and sweeps her into a tango, humming. They circle round the deck.*

In a reverse shot they return to the other two. GROUCHO *does a final pirouette.*)

(*To* BRIGGS) So, here you are, loafing around with these tramps!

BRIGGS: I tell you, I came down to see Joe Helton.

ZEPPO: (*To* GROUCHO) Don't you think we'd better go?

GROUCHO: What, and leave this woman alone with her husband? Suppose her sweetheart came in?

LUCILLE: (*Poking* BRIGGS *in the chest*) Let me tell you, Alky Briggs, don't think you can keep me cooped up in that state room below, because you're crazy.

(ZEPPO *leans back against the wall, while* GROUCHO *stands between* BRIGGS *and* LUCILLE, *listening.*)

BRIGGS: You're going to stay down there like I told you and keep out of my business, do you understand? Keep out of my business.

(*Medium close-up of* BRIGGS, GROUCHO *and* LUCILLE.)

GROUCHO: Your turn.

LUCILLE: Oh, you were going to show me a good time. A good time! Well, I might as well have stayed at home and played solitaire.

GROUCHO: (*To* BRIGGS) Your turn.

BRIGGS: Pipe down, will ya? I have more important things than you to worry about.

GROUCHO: (*To* LUCILLE) Your turn.

LUCILLE: (*Advancing on* BRIGGS) You say that again to me and I'll scratch your eyes out.

GROUCHO: Here, big boy, you take this gun. You're going to

need it more than I will.
(*He hands* BRIGGS *his gun and steps between them.*
Shot of the scene as GROUCHO *and* ZEPPO *exit on the left.*)
LUCILLE: Oh, you . . . !
(*She exits to the right, followed by* BRIGGS.)

In the main salon, HARPO *chases the chambermaid down the stairs and round the fountain at the bottom. He passes a female on the stairs. On the boat deck,* HELTON *is sitting back in a deck-chair, reading a magazine.* GROUCHO *strides up and slaps him on the foot.*

GROUCHO: (*Standing over him*) You're just the man I want to see. If I could show you how to save 20 per cent, would you be interested? Of course you would . . . In the first place, your overhead is too high and your brow is too low. Interested already, aren't you?
HELTON: I . . .
(*A close shot of both.*)
GROUCHO: (*Raising a hand*) Now, just wait till I get through.
HELTON: I haven't got time.
GROUCHO: Now, there are two fellas trying to attack you, aren't there? And there are two fellas trying to defend you.
HELTON: Why . . .
GROUCHO: Now that's 50 per cent waste. Now why can't you be attacked by your own bodyguards? Your life will be saved, and that's . . . that's 100 per cent waste.
(HELTON *stares at him, bewildered.*)
Now what have you got? You've still got me and I'll attack you for nothing.
HELTON: Say, what are you getting at?
GROUCHO: I anticipated that question. How does an army travel? On its stomach. How do you travel? On a ship. (*Waving his cigar*) Of course, you're saving your stomach. Now, that same common sense will . . .
HELTON: I don't think you realize . . .
GROUCHO: Oh I realize it's a penny here and a penny there, but look at me. I've worked myself up from nothing to a state of extreme poverty. Now what do you say?

48

HELTON: I'll tell you what I say, I say . . .
(The two of them are seen in medium close-up.)
GROUCHO: All right. Then it's all settled. I'm to be your new
bodyguard. In case I'm gonna attack you, I'll have to be
there to defend you, too.
(HELTON springs to his feet.)
Now, let me know when you want to be attacked, and I'll be
there ten minutes later to defend you.
HELTON: I've already got two bodyguards, but I'll think it over.
*(We cut to the corridor outside the barber's shop, where HARPO is
strolling to and fro, whistling. He suddenly slips on the polished
floor, losing his hat, and the frog escapes.*
Seen from above, it leaps away across the floor.
*Inside the barber's shop, a customer is just putting on his jacket as
HARPO enters in search of the frog, whistling. The man tips the
BARBER.)*
BARBER: Thank you.
MAN: *(Croaking)* You're welcome.
BARBER: Why, what's the matter with you?
MAN: *(Croaking)* I've got a frog in my throat.
*(A closer shot of the two of them as HARPO, who is searching
round in the background, turns to listen.)*
BARBER: What?
MAN: *(Croaking)* A frog – a frog in my throat.
BARBER: *(Loudly)* Oh, you've got a frog in your throat.
MAN: *(Croaking)* Yes.
*(HARPO grabs the man and wrenches open his jaw, looking down
his throat.*
*Resume on the scene as he turns the man upside-down, shaking
him.)*
BARBER: Hey! You can't do that to my customers. Cut it out.
Say, what's the matter with you? Are you crazy or
something?
*(At that moment the frog croaks off-screen and we cut back to the
previous shot as HARPO looks round wildly, clapping his hand
over the man's mouth.*
*Back to the scene. Camera pans as HARPO thrusts the man aside,
grabs his hat and hooter, and runs to the door, whistling.*

49

We see the frog on the floor of the corridor outside. HARPO
*appears in the foreground and kneels down, whistling and
beckoning. The frog jumps into the hat and* HARPO *gets up,
scolding it. It croaks in reply and he puts on his hat, looking
relieved. Fade out.)*

*On the sound of the ship's siren, we fade in to the New York shoreline
in the distance.*
*General shot of the deck. The passengers are sitting or standing around
with their luggage.* GIBSON *steps forward and calls out:*

GIBSON: Have your landing cards and passports ready, please.
   (*On another part of the deck, a tall, opulently dressed middle-
   aged* WOMAN *comes and stands by some luggage; a couple of
   reporters step up to her.*)
FIRST REPORTER: How do you do, Madame Swempski?
MADAME SWEMPSKI: Oh, hello boys.
   (*A closer shot of the three of them.*)
FIRST REPORTER: Any statement for the press this time?
MADAME SWEMPSKI: (*Affably*) No, I'm afraid not. Nothing of
   interest on this last tour.
FIRST REPORTER: Is it true that the opera is on the decline in
   Central Europe, Madame?
MADAME SWEMPSKI: Absurd. I predict they're going to have the
   greatest year they've ever had in grand opera.
   (*They write in their notebooks, as* GROUCHO *comes up and
   stands on the luggage behind them, looking over their shoulders*.)
SECOND REPORTER: Pardon me, is it true that you're going to get
   married again while on this tour?
MADAME SWEMPSKI: (*Coyly*) Why, gentlemen. (*She laughs.*) I . . .
   I don't know what to say . . .
   (GROUCHO *steps down between her and the reporters.*)
GROUCHO: (*Waving his cigar*) Gentlemen, I'd say just this. The
   bicycle will never replace the horse. On the other hand the
   horse will never replace the bicycle . . .
   (MADAME SWEMPSKI *looks indignant.*)
   . . . which is quite a horse on the bicycle if I ever saw one,
   and I don't think I ever saw one. (*He snaps his fingers at the*

reporters.) I dare you to print that, you muck-rakers! Have a cigar, babe?

(*He takes a cigar from his breast pocket and offers it to* MADAME SWEMPSKI.)

FIRST REPORTER: (*To a photographer, off-screen*) OK for the picture, Joe.

(*Shot of the scene as* GROUCHO *sits down on the luggage and pulls up his trouser leg.*)

GROUCHO: Pictures? Here's a little sex stuff for your front page.

(*We see the photographer standing by his camera, which is on a tripod with a black cloth over it.*)

PHOTOGRAPHER: Now hold it steady, please.

(*He presses the bulb; it makes a noise like a hooter.*

Cut to a closer shot as he whips off the cover in amazement, revealing HARPO *standing underneath.* HARPO *exits, scattering the tripod legs.*

We return to the other four.)

GROUCHO: (*Getting up*) And you can say it was a real love match. We married for money . . .

(*He puts his arm round* MADAME SWEMPSKI, *in medium close-up.*)

Eh, my shrinking violet? (*Prodding her*) Say, it wouldn't hurt you to shrink thirty or forty pounds.

MADAME SWEMPSKI: Oh, you impudent cad! I'll report you to your paper.

(*Back to the four of them.*)

GROUCHO: I'll thank you to let me do the reporting. (*He grabs the first reporter's notebook.*) Is it true you're getting a divorce as soon as your husband recovers his eyesight? Is it true that you wash your hair in clam broth? Is it true you used to dance in a flea circus?

MADAME SWEMPSKI: (*Indignantly*) This is outrageous! If you don't stop, I'll call the Captain.

GROUCHO: Oh, so that's it. Infatuated with a pretty uniform! (*Gesturing to the reporters*) We don't count, after we've given you the best years of our lives. You have to have an officer. (*He hands back the notebook.*)

MADAME SWEMPSKI: I don't like this innuendo.

GROUCHO: That's what I always say. Love flies out the door when money comes innuendo. Well, goodbye. (*He picks up a suitcase and shakes her hand.*) It's nice to have seen you, but I've got nobody to blame but myself. Ta-ta.

(*Shot of the scene as* GROUCHO *goes off, camera panning with him.*)

REPORTER: (*Off*) Now, could you tell me . . .

MADAM SWEMPSKI: (*In a tired voice, off*) Oh, please . . .

(*Music as we move to a shot of* ZEPPO *and* MARY, *sitting side by side.*)

MARY: You're awfully glum.

ZEPPO: (*Taking her hand*) I was just thinking, after the boat lands I may never see you again.

MARY: Does it matter to you whether you ever see me again?

ZEPPO: I can't think of anything in the world that matters more. Mary, I'll never leave you.

(*Sound of running feet, off.* ZEPPO *leaps up, and we cut to a longer shot as he exits, pursued by* GIBSON.

Shot of the passengers standing amid their luggage, waiting to get off the boat. A STEWARD *is squatting on the floor, handing out luggage tags as* GROUCHO, HARPO *and* CHICO *come up. They each grab a bag and hurry past.*)

STEWARD: (*To each of them in turn*) Tag. Tag. Tag.

(HARPO *doesn't take his.*)

. . . Tag.

(HARPO *tags the steward and runs off.*

We are now looking on to the boat from the top of the gangway, with an OFFICER *standing on each side.* HARPO, CHICO *and* GROUCHO *hurry forward with their bags, but the* OFFICERS *hold them back.*)

OFFICER: Wait a minute. Wait a minute.

GROUCHO: Well, I'm just trying to sneak off the boat, that's all.

CHICO: I'm lookin' for the man who owns this grip.

(ZEPPO *comes up behind them.*)

OFFICER: Where's your passport?

(*They back off and go into a huddle.*)

GROUCHO: Wait a minute. Wait a minute. Let me handle this.

(*He goes up to the officer on the right, and we cut to a shot of the two of them.*)

Ahem! I don't like to speak about it, officer, but I happen to be a good friend of the man who supplies the meat for this boat.

OFFICER: (*Unimpressed*) Well?

GROUCHO: Well, do you like lamb chops?

OFFICER: Yes. What of it?

GROUCHO: Well, this man doesn't handle any lamb chops, but the roast beef is very good today.

(*Resume on the scene from the top of the gangway.*)

OFFICER: Say, now listen, you fellas can't get off the boat without showing passports.

(*There is more shouting and arguing as they are pushed away from the gangway.* HARPO *swings from the* SECOND OFFICER's *arm.*)

Go on, get back.

(*We move to a shot of the swing doors near the top of the gangway; camera pans with the* MARX BROTHERS *as they come through and* ZEPPO *goes off.*)

GROUCHO: Stuffed shirt! You know, when he said that to me, you could have knocked me over with a feather.

(HARPO *takes a feather from his pocket and hits* GROUCHO *over the head;* GROUCHO *falls in* CHICO's *arms.*)

CHICO: He gives you service.

(*Seen in close-up,* HARPO *takes an iron bar from inside the feather and drops it.*

It lands with a crash on the floor.

Then we resume on the three of them.)

GROUCHO: Well, it looks like we're up against it. (*To* HARPO) It's up to you to get us a passport.

(*A* MAN *goes past towards the swing doors.* HARPO *follows and puts a hand in the* MAN's *pocket. The* MAN *stops and grabs him by the wrist.*)

MAN: I got you, didn't I! Well, you'll have to get up pretty early in the morning to steal from me.

GROUCHO: He did get up early this morning, but you weren't here. Could he see you some time tomorrow?

MAN: Aww!

(*He lets go of* HARPO *and exits through the swing doors.*)

GROUCHO: Well, come on, let's try another one, huh?

(*Another* MAN *passes.* CHICO *follows and puts a hand in his pocket. The* MAN *turns and grabs him by the wrist.*)

MAN: What's the idea, putting your hand in my pocket?

CHICO: Just a little mistake. I had a suit once looked just like that, and for a moment I thought those were my pants.

MAN: How could they be your pants when I've got them on?

CHICO: Well, this suit had two pair of pants.

MAN: (*Releasing him*) You'd better keep your hands to yourself.

(*Shot of the group as the* MAN *exits through the swing doors and* ZEPPO *enters from the right.*)

ZEPPO: Do you know who's on this boat?

GROUCHO: No.

ZEPPO: Maurice Chevalier, the movie actor. I just ran into him.

GROUCHO: Did you hurt him?

CHICO: How did you know it was Chevalier?

(ZEPPO *pulls out a passport.*)

ZEPPO: I got his passport. Right here.

(*A closer shot of the four of them as they pass it round.*)

GROUCHO: Now he can't get off the boat.

(HARPO *grabs the passport, looks at the photograph and grimaces, thrusting out his lower lip.*)

CHICO: Hey, he looks like Chevalier.

GROUCHO: Yes, that's true.

CHICO: (*Grimacing*) And I can look like Chevalier.

GROUCHO: (*Grimacing*) And I certainly look like Chevalier.

(*Camera pans towards* ZEPPO.)

ZEPPO: But that's not enough. You've gotta sing one of Chevalier's songs to get off this boat.

(*He sings, with his hand on his heart:*)

'If a nightingale

Could sing like you,

They'd sing much better

Than you do . . .'

GROUCHO: That's dandy. If you sing like that, they'll throw us all off the boat.

(*Resume on the scene.*)

CHICO: Well, let's try it.

GROUCHO: All right. Come on, come on. Let's go.
  (*They all hurry off.*)

The scene moves to the passport control in the main saloon.
The passengers are queuing at a long table with several passport
officers at its head, one of them standing and calling out instructions.

OFFICER: Have your passports ready. (*To a passenger*) Right
  straight up, you'll find the baggage on the deck. (*Inspecting*
  another's passport) OK . . . Have your passports ready. Keep
  in line, everybody. Nine forty-five. Keep in line, everybody.
  Have your passports ready.
  (*A closer shot of the passengers queuing at the table as the four*
  MARX BROTHERS *come up in the background, all wearing straw*
  boaters, except for HARPO. *Camera pans with them as they crawl*
  under the table and along on the opposite side to the queue.
  HARPO *tries to ride on* GROUCHO's *back.*
  We now see the end of the table as the MARX BROTHERS *crawl*
  back under it and come up at the head of the queue.)
  Ten ninety-two . . .
  (*Another shot of the head of the table, with the passport officers*
  seated in back view as the MARX BROTHERS *surface on the other*
  side. HARPO *grabs a rubber stamp and starts stamping everything*
  in sight. General shouts and confusion.)
PASSPORT OFFICERS: Hey! Hey! Hey!
  (*The standing* OFFICER *addresses them.*)
OFFICER: Hey, if you want to get off the boat, get in the back.
GROUCHO: (*Swapping hats with him*) Oh, I didn't get on in the
  back. I got on in the front.
OFFICER: (*Swapping the hats back*) Never mind where you got on.
  (GROUCHO, HARPO *and* CHICO *leave, shoved by the*
  OFFICER.)
ZEPPO: You're perfectly right, officer. I told those fellows to stay
  in line.
OFFICER: Yeah? Well, let me see your passport.
ZEPPO: Yeah, right here.
  (*They are seen in medium close-up as* ZEPPO *hands over the*
  passport.)

55

That's my name.

OFFICER: (*Sceptically*) Maurice Chevalier, eh?

ZEPPO: Yeah.

OFFICER: Say, this picture doesn't look like you.

ZEPPO: Sure I'm Maurice Chevalier. I'll sing for you.

> (*Music. We cut to a medium shot as* ZEPPO *does his Chevalier routine, dancing and waving his boater.*)

>> 'If a nightingale
>> Could sing like you,
>> They'd sing much better
>> Than they do . . .'

> (*He tries to dance past the* OFFICER, *but the latter grabs him.*)

OFFICER: Here. Never mind this! Get back in line where you belong! (*He shoves him to the back of the queue.*)

> (*Resume on the other end of the table as* CHICO *now runs up with the passport, followed by* GROUCHO. *Camera moves with them as they push their way to the head of the table, where* CHICO *engages the standing* OFFICER *while* GROUCHO *turns to the indignant* MADAME SWEMPSKI *just behind him.*)

> (*To* CHICO) Let me have your passport. Say, this picture doesn't look like you.

CHICO: I know it don't look like me from the front, but you go in the back of the boat – it just like me.

OFFICER: You're not Maurice Chevalier.

CHICO: Are you Maurice Chevalier?

OFFICER: No.

CHICO: Well, there you are. Wait, I prove it.

> (*Music; he sings, waving his boater.*)

>> 'If a nightingale
>> Could sing like you,
>> He sing much better
>> Than you do,
>> And . . .'

> (*The* OFFICER *grabs him and shoves him to the back.*)

OFFICER: Hey! Out! Out!

CHICO: Hey! No pusha me!

OFFICER: Get out of here! Get back in line where you belong!

> (CHICO *leaves, handing the passport to* GROUCHO, *who steps up*

to the OFFICER.)

Passport!

(GROUCHO *hands it over, tilting his boater to hide his face.*)

Say, this picture doesn't look like you.

GROUCHO: Well, it doesn't look like you either.

OFFICER: This man has no moustache.

GROUCHO: Well, the barber shop wasn't open this morning.

OFFICER: Why, look at that face.

GROUCHO: (*Pointing to* MADAME SWEMPSKI) Well, look at that face.

MADAME SWEMPSKI: Ohhh!

GROUCHO: (*Pointing back at the* OFFICER) All right, look at that face.

OFFICER: Hey, are you going to identify yourself, or else . . .

(*Music;* GROUCHO *sings, waving his boater.*)

GROUCHO: 'If a nightingale

Could sing like you,

They'd sing much sweeter

Than they do,

You brought a new kind of love

To me . . .'

(*The* OFFICER *grabs him and shoves him to the back.*)

OFFICER: Outside! Back in line where you belong.

(GROUCHO *leaves.*

Resume on the other end of the table. Camera pans with HARPO *as he climbs on to it and strolls along the top with his hooter, nodding to the indignant passengers.*

We see him again as he arrives at the head of the table and stands over the passport officers amid their papers. General confusion.)

PASSPORT OFFICERS: (*Shouting*) Get off that table! What do you think . . . Get him off that table anyway!

(HARPO *works a date stamp with his foot; the standing* OFFICER *yells at him.*)

OFFICER: Come off there!

(HARPO *jumps down and starts throwing papers in the air. The* OFFICER *grabs him round the waist.*)

Lunatic!

(HARPO *carries on throwing papers, jiggles the pens in the pen*

57

holder and drums his hands on the table in maniac glee.
A closer shot of him and the OFFICER.)
(*Beside himself*) Passport!
(HARPO *produces a piece of pasteboard.*)
I said passport . . .
(*Resume on the scene.*)
(*Throwing it down*) . . . not pasteboard!
(HARPO *offers his leg.*)
Come on with that passport.
(HARPO *produces a washboard. The* OFFICER *throws it down.*)
Not washboard. (*Beating his fist on the table*) Passport!
(HARPO *finally produces the passport, stamps it and hands it to the* OFFICER.
Close-up of the passport with Chevalier's photograph.)
(*Practically speechless, off*) Chevalier . . . eh?
(*Resume on the two of them.* HARPO *restrains the* OFFICER *and starts miming to a record of the Chevalier song.*)
CHEVALIER'S VOICE: 'If a nightingale
    Could sing like you,
    They'd sing much sweeter
    Than they do,
    For you brought a new kind of love
    To me.
    If the sandman brought me dreams of you
    I'd like to . . .'
(*The record runs down and* HARPO *turns to reveal a gramophone strapped to his back, which he winds furiously. The record picks up again.*)
    '. . . To sleep my whole life through,
    For you brought a new kind of love
    To me . . .'
(*Shot of the scene as the* OFFICER *grabs* HARPO, *losing his cap.* HARPO *goes wild, stamping everything in sight – the papers, the table, the* OFFICER's *bald head – while everyone tries to restrain him.*)
PASSPORT OFFICERS: (*Shouting*) Get him out of here! Put him back! Put him back where he belongs!
(*The* OFFICER *finally ejects him.*)

On the deck, GIBSON is standing by the swing doors leading out to the gangplank, a stream of passengers moving slowly towards him. A fat man in a straw boater hurries into view.

GIBSON: Take it easy, folks. The gangplank is to the left, please. Don't crowd.

(*In a closer shot the camera pans with the* FAT MAN *as he pushes his way to the head of the queue.*)

Don't crowd.

(*The* FAT MAN *reaches* GIBSON, *almost knocking over* MADAME SWEMPSKI.)

Take your time. Ladies first.

FAT MAN: Let me off the boat. I'm a sick man. I feel faint.

GIBSON: I don't care. Take your time.

FAT MAN: (*Frantically, mopping his face*) I tell you I feel faint. I'm going . . . I'm going to faint.

(*He collapses into* GIBSON'*s arms.*)

MADAME SWEMPSKI: Oh! Oh, someone get a doctor!

(*Back to the scene as she hurries along the corridor towards us, then cut to a closer shot, camera panning as she hurries along.*)

Where's a doctor? A doctor! I want a doctor!

(*She encounters* HARPO *and* CHICO *who grab her and lay her in a deck-chair.*)

CHICO: She's-a sick. All right, all right, we take care of you . . .

(*She drums her feet, speechless.*)

Look, she's gotta chill. Cover her up. Cover her up.

(HARPO *sits on top of her.*)

MADAME SWEMPSKI: (*In a muffled voice*) Oh! Oh! Oh!

CHICO: Oh, no, no, no. Get up, get up! Take her pulse!

(*A closer shot of the three of them.* HARPO *grabs her purse and pockets it.*)

Take her pulse. No, purse – put it back . . .

(HARPO *does so . . .*)

Pulse.

(MADAME SWEMPSKI *struggles wildly, but* CHICO *holds her down.*)

(*To* HARPO) I think you best take the temperature. That's good. All right, we take care of you, lady.'

(HARPO *pulls out a pipe, shakes it and thrusts it into her mouth*.)
All right, all right, all right, all right.
(*Resume on the scene as she finally springs up and throws down the pipe*.)

MADAME SWEMPSKI: Oh, you fools! I'm not the patient!
(CHICO *hands her her fur coat*.)

CHICO: Well, we're not the doctor . . . Come on.
(*He leads* HARPO *off*.)
(*On another part of the deck, a middle-aged passenger is sitting asleep, wearing dark glasses. Other passengers pass to and fro in front of him, then a* MAN *in a white cap hurries into view*.)

MAN: Doctor! Doctor! Is there a doctor on the boat? Doctor!
(*He goes off;* GROUCHO *appears from the right; a* SECOND MAN *enters*.)

SECOND MAN: Doctor! Doctor! (*To* GROUCHO) Are you a doctor?

GROUCHO: Sure, I'm a doctor. Where's the horse?

SECOND MAN: (*Pointing*) Why, a man's fainted over here.

GROUCHO: A man's fainted? I'll soon fix that . . .
(*The* MAN *goes off;* GROUCHO *grabs the dark glasses from the sleeping passenger and lopes after him*.)
Just my hard luck it couldn't be a woman!
(*Camera pans with* GROUCHO *as he runs along the corridor, grabbing a black bag from a pile of luggage as he passes. He reaches a group of passengers gathered round the fainted man.* GIBSON *is bent over him, while another man fans him with his hat.* GROUCHO *grabs one of the standing passengers by the wrist and take his pulse*.)
Hmmm. Just as I thought – smoking too much.

GIBSON: (*On his knees*) Here he is here, doctor.

GROUCHO: Don't tell me, I'll find him myself.
(*In a closer shot,* GROUCHO *kneels down beside the man and pulls out a stethoscope. He puts it in the man's ears and listens at the wrong end, then gets up again*.)
I can't do anything for that man. He's fainted. What he needs is an ocean voyage. (*He pulls out a pad and writes a prescription*.) In the meantime, get him off the boat and have his baggage examined.
(*He hands the prescription to* GIBSON *off-screen*.)

A MAN: (*Off*) Gangway!
GROUCHO: (*Beckoning to the passengers*) Will you all get close so he
    won't recover? Here, right this way.
    (*Shot of the scene as everyone closes in around the man.*)
    Step right around here.
    (*He steps over the man's body and makes off.*
    On the other side of the swing doors, some sailors carry a covered
    stretcher out towards the gangway.
    GIBSON *is seen in back view at the top of the gangway.*)
GIBSON: Step lively down there.
    (*The sailors carry the stretcher down the gangplank and* GIBSON
    follows them part of the way down.
    A high-angle shot shows the scene at the bottom of the gangway,
    as the sailors lay down the stretcher on the quay.)
SAILOR: Hey, back that ambulance in here.
    (*The sailors go off.* GROUCHO, HARPO, CHICO *and* ZEPPO
    throw the cover aside and rise from the stretcher. General
    laughter.
    GROUCHO *waves up to* GIBSON.
    We see GIBSON *from below on the gangway.*)
GIBSON: Hey!
    (*Resume on the quayside; the* MARX BROTHERS *stand in a row*
    grinning up at him.)
    (*Off*) Hey!

The scene dissolves to an insert of a newspaper headline which reads:
'BIG JOE HELTON HOME FROM ABROAD PLANS
ELABORATE PARTY TO INTRODUCE DAUGHTER.'
Dissolve again to a poorly furnished room, where BRIGGS *is standing*
over two of his gang – BUTCH *and* SHORTY *– who are seated at a*
table. SHORTY *is holding a saxophone; another man,* SPIKE, *is seen*
reflected in a mirror.

BRIGGS: Helton's throwing his party tonight, and this time we
    blow the works. Now you guys are going in as musicians,
    and stay that way until I give you the office.
SPIKE: Say, what about those four guys in the house, the ones
    that you said were on the boat?

BRIGGS: Aw, don't worry about them. They eat out of my hand.
(SPIKE *comes up to them, holding a bottle of milk.*)
The thing for you to worry about is that girl. Keep an eye on her. Get me? (*He lights a cigarette.*)

SPIKE: That ought to be easy to take.
(*He picks up a sandwich from the table and drinks from the milk bottle.*)

BRIGGS: OK. Sit tight and I'll give you a call.
(*He moves off. Fade out.*)

Fade in to the exterior of JOE HELTON's *palatial residence. It is night; light floods from the windows and gay music is heard. A large limousine drives up to the front steps and several people in party clothes get out.*
Dissolve to the interior of the house; in the drawing room a band is playing and couples are dancing, seen from above.
A closer shot of the dancers; most of them are in fancy dress.
Outside, another car full of guests draws up, with CHICO *and* HARPO *riding on the offside running board. The guests get out, while* HARPO *and* CHICO *clamber into the car, leave again from the near side and follow them up the steps. The car drives off. As* HARPO *and* CHICO *reach the top of the steps, the door is slammed in their faces.*
A closer shot shows HARPO *and* CHICO *peering in through the glass door. It opens and two thugs in evening dress come out.*

MAN: (*Threatening*) Say, have you guys got an invitation?

CHICO: We give you invitation of Chevalier.
(*He sings, while* HARPO *whistles in accompaniment.*)
    'When the nightingale
    Sing like you,
    He sing much . . .'

MAN: Hey! Cut it out! And stay away from this door, see?
(*He goes in and slams the door.*
We return to the drawing room, where ZEPPO *appears in back view, peering around among the guests.*
He is seen again standing by an open doorway leading out into the hall. MARY *comes down the staircase in the background and he calls up to her.*)

ZEPPO: Mary!

(*Camera tracks forward into the hall as he meets her at the bottom of the stairs and takes her by the hand.*)

You certainly had me worried. I thought you'd forgotten your own party.

(*Track out again as they advance to the door of the drawing room.*)

MARY: You haven't been doing all the worrying. I was afraid you wouldn't come.

(BUTCH, SHORTY *and* SPIKE *are seen playing in the band.* SHORTY *nudges* BUTCH.

The couple dance away from the drawing room door . . .

And the three thugs follow them with their eyes.

We see the couple in medium close-up, dancing.)

(*Looking round*) My, but there's a lot of strange-looking people here.

(*On the other side of the room, camera moves with* GROUCHO *as he lopes past the band and in among the dancing couples. He climbs on to a couch at the end of the room and calls for silence.*)

GROUCHO: Ladies and gentlemen!

(*The music stops.*)

Quiet, everybody, quiet!

(*A closer shot of him.*)

A lady's diamond earring has been lost. It looks exactly like this. (*He holds up an earring.*) In fact, this is it.

(*Resume on the scene as he vaults over a balustrade behind the couch, then cut to reverse shot as he lands beside a tall woman sitting on another couch on the other side.*)

WOMAN: (*Haughtily*) I beg your pardon!

GROUCHO: How about you and I passing out on the veranda, or would you rather pass out here?

(*He grabs her by the hand and pulls her to her feet.*)

WOMAN: (*Looking down her nose*) Sir, you have the advantage of me!

(*She is a good head taller than he is.*)

GROUCHO: (*Rolling his eyes*) Not yet I haven't, but wait till I get you outside.

(*He grabs her; she pushes him away.*)

WOMAN: You're pretty fresh, aren't you?

(GROUCHO *starts to take off his jacket.*

Shot of the scene as a MAN *in Indian costume comes up and grabs* GROUCHO *by the shoulder.*)

MAN: Hey, that's my wife and I don't like the way you're acting around here.

GROUCHO: Well, if you don't like our country, why don't you go back where you came from.

(*The man brandishes his tomahawk.*)

MAN: Say, I ought to sink that right in your scalp.

(*He takes a swing at* GROUCHO, *but is restrained by his* WIFE. GROUCHO *dodges past her and taps a* FAT MAN *standing nearby on the back.*)

GROUCHO: Run for your life. The Indians are coming!

FAT MAN: (*Turning in alarm*) What?

GROUCHO: Put your scalp in your pocket. (*He takes off the* MAN's *toupée and hands it to him.*) Here. The Indians.

FAT MAN: Oh!

(GROUCHO *exits with a warwhoop. The* HUSBAND *starts after him and bumps into the* FAT MAN.)

MAN: (*Waving his tomahawk*) I'll get him!

(*Out in the hall,* HELTON *is welcoming a couple of guests as* GROUCHO *comes out doing an Indian dance and whooping. The guests go into the drawing room.* HELTON *slaps* GROUCHO *on the back.*)

HELTON: Have a good time, kid.

(*A closer shot of the two of them.*)

This is gonna be a real party.

GROUCHO: You call this a party? The beer is warm, the women are cold and I'm hot under the collar . . . In fact, a more poisonous little barbecue I've never attended.

HELTON: Say, you're a funny kind of a duck, but I like you. You stuck by me, and I'll stick by you.

(GROUCHO *claps him on the shoulder, clasps his hand and addresses him in a Texan drawl.*)

GROUCHO: Sheriff, I ain't much on flowery sentiments, but there's somethin' I jes' got to tell yuh . . . Shucks, man, I'd be nuthin' but a pizenous varmint and not fitten to touch the

64

hem of yo' pants if I didn't tell you you've treated me squar, mighty squar, and I ain't fergettin' it.

(*With bowed legs, he walks into the drawing room, past a couple standing in the doorway, the* MAN *wearing a cowboy outfit. Then he comes back towards* HELTON, *grabbing the* MAN's *ten-gallon hat as he passes.*)

Sheriff, I ain't fergettin'.

(*He goes off in the foreground with legs bowed, wearing the hat. Sound of a horse neighing.*)

Whoa theah, Bessie, whoa theah.

(*Hoofbeats.* HELTON *and his guests burst out laughing. We move to the interior of the drawing room as a large floral decoration is carried in.* HELTON *enters and stands in front of it. Applause.*)

HELTON: My friends, this is indeed a surprise . . .

(*He beckons, and* MARY *appears, followed by* ZEPPO.)

. . . You couldn't have pleased me better.

(*A closer shot of* HELTON *and* MARY.)

And now I want you to meet the sweetest little thing in the whole wide world.

(*Music and applause as* HELTON *holds out his hand to* MARY. *Suddenly* HARPO *springs between them from the centre of the wreath and strikes a pose, holding his hooter, a rose clasped between his teeth.* MARY *backs off, while* HELTON *looks amazed. Shot of the scene as the two thugs in evening dress rush forward and carry* HARPO *off.*

We see them again from the drawing room door as they hustle him out, his feet waving in the air, gleefully sounding his hooter. Camera pans as they exit.

In a corner of the drawing room, GROUCHO *stops the* BUTLER *as he passes carrying a champagne bottle and some glasses on a tray.*)

BUTLER: Oh! Oh, no, sir. This is special for Mr Helton, sir.

GROUCHO: (*Pulling out a note*) You see this?

(*The* BUTLER *grins and looks round furtively, while* GROUCHO *pours himself a glass of champagne and drinks.*)

(*Holding up the note again*) Come back in a half-hour and I'll give you another look at it. (*He exits.*)

65

The scene changes to the terrace outside the house. BRIGGS *is prowling to and fro beneath it as* GROUCHO *comes out of the french windows and reclines on top of the balustrade.*
A closer shot as BRIGGS *comes up to him. He sits up.*

BRIGGS: Listen, keep your eye on Helton. We're gonna grab his daughter and take her to the old barn.

GROUCHO: Old barn? A fine tinhorn sport you are. With all the good shows in town, taking a girl to an old barn! (*Nose in air*) Huh!

BRIGGS: Once we get hold of that girl, he'll take orders from me, and believe me, I'll show him who's . . .

GROUCHO: Enough of this small talk! Where's your wife Lucille?

BRIGGS: (*Angrily*) Would you . . . (*He turns.*) Shhh. Someone's coming. I'll be back.

GROUCHO: (*Seizing him by the wrist*) All right, be back next Thursday and bring a specimen of your handwriting, and above all, don't worry!

BRIGGS: Aww! (*He exits with an angry gesture.*)
(*We now see* LUCILLE *in the garden, looking from side to side.* GROUCHO, *in medium close-up, climbs back on to the balustrade and starts acting like a tomcat.*)

GROUCHO: Miaow!
(LUCILLE, *in the garden, turns at the sound.*)
(*Off*) Miaow!
(*Resume on him on all fours, prowling to and fro on the balustrade.*)
Mia–a–a–ow.
(*Camera pans with* LUCILLE *as she hurries across the garden and up on to the terrace.*)
(*Off*) Mia–a–a–ow. Miaow!
(*She passes behind him, going towards the house.*
A closer shot of GROUCHO *on the balustrade. He wiggles his behind and miaows again.*)
Mia–a–a–ow!
(*He jumps down as* LUCILLE *comes up to him.*)

LUCILLE: What brought you here?

GROUCHO: (*Dramatically*) Ah, 'tis midsummer madness, the

music is in my temples, the hot blood of youth! Come,
Kapellmeister, let the violas throb. My regiment leaves at
dawn!
(Bugle and drums off. LUCILLE *throws off her wrap and*
GROUCHO *takes her in his arms.*
Music over a shot of the scene as they waltz round and round the
terrace, fall over a couch, then get up again.
They dance back to back, then waltz towards the couch again —
and fall straight over the end.
Cut to medium close-up as they land. A bugle sounds off.)
Aw, I guess my regiment can go without me!
(Seen in a medium shot, they sit up on the couch. GROUCHO *grabs*
LUCILLE *and tries to kiss her.)*

LUCILLE: *(Pushing him away)* Oh, no, no no, don't. My husband
might be inside, and if he finds me out here he'll wallop me.
(A closer shot of the two of them. She smooths her hair.)

GROUCHO: Always thinking of your husband. Couldn't I wallop
you just as well?

LUCILLE: Oh, I heard Alky talking about this party.

GROUCHO: *(Putting an arm round her)* Oh, I've dreamed of a night
like this, I tell you. Now you tell me about some of your
dreams.

LUCILLE: Dreams! Ha! I can't even sleep any more wondering who
he's chasing around with.

GROUCHO: *(Expansively)* Oh, why can't we break away from all
this, just you and I, and lodge with my fleas in the hills . . .
(She looks at him doubtfully.)
. . . I mean flee to my lodge in the hills.
(Camera tilts as she rises.)

LUCILLE: Oh, no, I couldn't think of it.

GROUCHO: *(Also rising)* Don't be afraid. You can join this lodge for
a few pennies, and you won't even have to take a physical
examination, unless you insist on one.
(Resume on the previous shot. She sits down and he sits under her.
Then we cut back to the closer shot again.)

LUCILLE: *(Chin on hand)* What a swell home life I've got. *(She turns*
and leans over him.) Why, I think I'd almost marry you to spite
that double-crossing crook.

(*Resume on the medium shot as they rise and* GROUCHO *stands with his hands on her shoulders.*)

GROUCHO: Mrs Briggs, I've known and respected your husband Alky for many years . . . and what's good enough for him is good enough for me.

(*He suddenly throws himself down on the couch, dragging* LUCILLE *with him.*)

LUCILLE: Ughh!

(*We now see a couple in evening dress emerge from the french windows on to the terrace; camera pans as they walk towards the balustrade, revealing* GROUCHO *and* LUCILLE *hiding on the couch.*

The couple are seen from beyond the balustrade as they come up to it; in the background, GROUCHO *and* LUCILLE *lean forward to listen.*)

MAN: (*Looking round nervously*) Oh, Emily!

(*He grabs her in his arms.* GROUCHO *climbs on to the couch to get a better view.*)

WOMAN: Oh, Henry, carefully. Somebody may see us.

MAN: (*Hungrily*) Oh, I've been careful too long.

GROUCHO: Well, now that you've brought that up, just how long have you been careful?

(*They whip round.*)

WOMAN: Oh, they saw us!

MAN: Now, be calm, Emily. I'll talk to them. (*To* GROUCHO) You won't say anything about this will you?

GROUCHO: (*Drawing himself up*) Sir, are you trying to offer me a bribe? . . . How much?

WOMAN: Oh, but you don't understand. You see, I'm not happy with my husband. (*Scornfully*) He should have married some little housewife!

(GROUCHO, *in close-up, wags a finger.*)

GROUCHO: Madam, I resent that. Some of my best friends are housewives.

(*He works his eyebrows at* LUCILLE.)

(LUCILLE, *in close-up, smooths her hair.*)

LUCILLE: Ahem!

(*We see* GROUCHO *standing over the couple again.*)

MAN: Now see here, if you're going to talk like that . . .

GROUCHO: Listen here, you're living in a fool's paradise. You intend to spend ten dollars and buy this woman a ring? Look at this. (*He holds up a ring.*) It's solid brass and a buck and a half takes it away. What do you say? . . . I know it'll fit her. I got it from the nose of a savage.

MAN: (*Indignant*) Wh–!

GROUCHO: Well?

WOMAN: (*Indignant*) Oh!

(*Shot of the group.*)

GROUCHO: A buck and a half. You can have it for a dollar.

(*The couple exit indignantly and* GROUCHO *shouts after them:*)

Fifty cents and not a nickel under!

(*He pats* LUCILLE *on the head and steps down from the couch.*)

Now then, my friends, what am I offered for this fine French piece of bric-a-brac?

(*A closer shot of the two of them as he sits down beside her.*)

LUCILLE: Oh, I know what it is to be unhappy.

GROUCHO: How do you think I feel? Here I am stuck with this ring.

LUCILLE: (*Disgustedly*) I've been married for four years. Four years of neglect, four years of battling, four years of heartbreak . . .

(*The two of them are seen in medium close-up.*)

GROUCHO: That makes twelve years. You must have been married in rompers . . . Mighty pretty country round there. You think you'll ever go back? (*He tries to draw her down on the couch.*) Come here, babe, I like you.

LUCILLE: (*Pulling away*) Oh, I shouldn't. What about my husband?

GROUCHO: That's all right. Maybe we can get a girl for him.

(LUCILLE *looks off and gives a little scream.*)

LUCILLE: Ohh!

(*Shot of the scene as she grabs her wrap and runs off in the foreground, while* BRIGGS *runs up in the background.* GROUCHO *tries to hide under a cushion, but* BRIGGS *comes and grabs it.*)

69

BRIGGS: (*Standing over him*) Who was that? My wife?

GROUCHO: Married to her twelve years and you have to ask me?

BRIGGS: What are you doing out here? I thought I told you to spy on Helton.

GROUCHO: I did spy on him.

BRIGGS: What was he doing?

GROUCHO: He was spying on me.

BRIGGS: Did he see you?

GROUCHO: No. I was too foxy for him. All he could do was spy on me.

BRIGGS: Well, get back in there. We're all set to cop his girl.

GROUCHO: OK, chief.

> (BRIGGS *runs off in the background again, and we cut to a closer shot of* GROUCHO *as he pulls out a cigar and leans back. His hand lights the cigar with a lighter.*
> *He throws away the lighter and settles himself on the couch, smoking.*
> *Out in the garden, a* GIRL *appears, running across the lawns. Camera pans as* HARPO *chases her on a bicycle. The* GIRL *screams.*)

We return to the interior of the drawing room; the band is seen at one end of the room as CHICO *enters through the french windows in the background.*
In a closer shot, camera pans as he comes up and taps the pianist on the arm.

CHICO: Hey! They gotta some good stuff outside. You wanna drink?

> (*The pianist nods and exits.*
> *Shot of* CHICO *as he sits down at the piano.*)

CHICO: Ready, boys? (*He raps the piano.*) Let's go.

> (*He starts to play the* divertissement *from Delibes's* Sylvia. *Camera shows his hands on the keyboard as he plays with his forefinger.*
> *Then we resume on him as he hurries to the end of the piece.*)
> (*To the other musicians*) Ha-ha. I beat you that time.
> (*He starts playing again, ending up with 'Ain't she sweet?'*

There is applause as he finishes and he turns in surprise.
Reverse shot of the guests, who have gathered round,
applauding.
CHICO, *at the piano, bows, then leaves.*
We move to the doorway leading into the drawing room.
HELTON *comes through accompanied by a very tall* WOMAN *in*
a frilled dress with an enormous bustle.)

HELTON: Mary's swell. Say, let me get you a glass of punch.
WOMAN: I'd love it.

(Camera pans as they cross to the punch bowl; the bustle follows
a few feet behind.
In a closer shot, HELTON *and the* WOMAN *raise their cups and*
drink. HARPO's *head emerges from the bustle, looks to and fro,*
then disappears again.)

Just what I needed, Joe. *(She takes* HELTON's *arm.)*
HELTON: Ah!

(Resume on the previous shot as the band starts playing and
HELTON *and the* WOMAN *exit, leaving the bustle behind.*
HARPO *looks out again and grins.*
We see couples dancing in the drawing room. HARPO *comes up*
in the bustle and attaches himself to a dancing WOMAN. *She*
turns and cries out.)

WOMAN: Ohhh!

(Shot of HELTON *standing at the side of the room as* CHICO
comes up and taps him on the shoulder.)

HELTON: *(Affably)* Well, well, how're they coming, kid?
CHICO: Fine.
HELTON: Getting everything you want?

(A closer shot of both.)

CHICO: Sure, but how about a job for my grandfather?
HELTON: Your grandfather? What does he do?
CHICO: He puts cheese in-a mousetraps.
HELTON: Why, we haven't got any mice here.
CHICO: Oh, 'at's-a all right. He brings his own mice with him.

*(*HELTON *laughs and slaps him on the shoulder.*
HARPO *is meanwhile sitting on the couch by the balustrade at*
the end of the room, enveloped in the bustle. A GIRL *in fancy*
dress passes; HARPO *throws aside the bustle and chases her*

round and round, leaping over the balustrade. They finally run off. The band continues to play.

We follow MARY *and* ZEPPO *as the music ends and they come to a halt by the doorway into the hall. There is a buzz of voices.*)

ZEPPO: You know, Mary, everyone seems to be having nearly as much fun as I am.

(*The* BUTLER *comes up to them from the hall.*)

BUTLER: I beg your pardon, but there's someone to see you, Miss Helton.

MARY: (*To* ZEPPO) Pardon me a minute, and I'll hurry right back.

ZEPPO: Surely.

(MARY *goes into the hall.*

We see SHORTY, BUTCH *and* SPIKE *rise from the band and start out with determined expressions.*

In the hall, HARPO *chases a* GIRL *in a short skirt down the stairs. The* GIRL *runs past another in a fairy godmother costume who is standing at the bottom.*

In a closer shot, HARPO *stops by the* SECOND GIRL *and whistles. She turns towards him.*

Resume on the scene as he jumps on the panière of her skirt and it collapses; he beats down the other side, messes her headdress and exits gleefully.

In the drawing room, GROUCHO *stands wearing a jockey cap, surrounded by a crowd of admiring girls. One of them strokes his chest.*)

GROUCHO: No, you're wrong, girls. You're wrong. In the first place, Gary Cooper is much taller than I am.

GIRL: Ohhh!

(HELTON *comes up and hands* GROUCHO *a piece of paper.*)

HELTON: I wish you'd announce this singer. I can't make out the name.

(*He exits and* GROUCHO *steps forward, tearing up the piece of paper.*)

GROUCHO: Ladies and gentlemen.

(*A closer shot of him.*)

I wish to announce that a buffet supper will be served in the next room in five minutes. In order to get you in that room quickly, Mrs Schmalhausen will sing a soprano solo in this room. (*He gestures off.*)

(*We see a tall, well-developed* LADY *standing beside the piano. She sings, accompanied by a female harpist.*)

WOMAN: (*Singing*) 'Que bella cosa 'na iurnata'e sole
    N'aria serena doppo 'na tempesta.'

(HARPO *appears behind the harp and grins through it at the harpist, who exits with a scream.*

A closer shot shows HARPO *grinning through the harp strings, gibbering like an ape.*)

(*Singing, off*) 'Pe' ll'aria fresca . . .'

(*Resume on the scene as* HARPO *takes the harpist's place and starts to accompany the* SINGER.)

(*Singing*) '. . . pare gia 'na festa'

(HARPO'*s hand gets stuck in the harp; he disengages it.*)

(*Singing*) 'Che bella cosa 'na iurnata'e . . .'

(*Shot of* HARPO; *he unscrews the false hand, scratches his chin with it and throws it away. Then he rolls up his sleeve and continues playing.*)

(*Singing, off*) '. . . sole.
    Ma n'atu sole cchiu bello chine'
    O sole mio stan' frontea te'

(HARPO *plucks too hard and hits himself on the chin.*)

(*Singing, off*) 'O sole, o sole mio, sta'n frontea te
    Sta'n . . .'

(*Back to the scene.*)

(*Singing*) '. . . frontea te.'

(HARPO *rises to take a bow.*

Resume on the previous shot. He sits down hurriedly as the WOMAN *continues to sing, and drops the harp on his foot. He rubs his foot, scratches the sole of his shoe, then continues playing.*)

(*Singing, off*) 'Ma n'atu sole cchiu bello ohine''

(HARPO *thumbs his nose at the* WOMAN *as he plays.*)

(*Singing, off*) 'O sole mio, sta'n frontea te.'

(*He clicks his nose as he plucks at the strings.*)

(*Singing, off*) 'O sole, o sole mio, sta'n frontea te
    Sta'n frontea . . .'

(*The* SINGER *starts a high-pitched trill.* HARPO *looks alarmed and tugs wildly at one of the base strings of the harp.*
We see the SINGER, *trilling.*
HARPO *stuffs his fingers in his ears, looks round for his hat and puts it on.*
In a shot of the scene, HARPO *finally flings his coat over his head as he plays the final bars.*)
(*Trilling*) '. . .te.'
(*She finally makes it to the end of the song. Loud applause; she bows and exits, and* HARPO *waves his arms in relief.*
We see CHICO *among the applauding guests. He steps forward and goes off.*
He comes up to the grinning HARPO, *by the musicians.*)

CHICO: Hey, 'at's-a no good. You want to get thrown out again? Play something nice. I tell you what to play. Play . . .

(*He sings the tune of 'Sugar in the morning . . .'* HARPO *gets it, whistles along, then grabs a seat and starts to play the tune on the harp.*)

'At's-a it. Ah, 'at's beautiful. 'At's-a magnifico. Umm, boy, I like that. (*He leaves.*)

(*A closer shot of* HARPO *playing. The orchestra accompanies him to the end of the piece. Applause off.*
HARPO, *in close-up, grins; the frog croaks inside his hat, moving the crown up and down.*
By the doorway into the hall, the guests stand applauding while one of them beckons wildly to HELTON *off-screen. It is the man* GROUCHO *accosted on the terrace earlier.* HELTON *hurries in and the man speaks in his ear.*)

HELTON: (*Wildly*) Oh! Oh! Mary! They've kidnapped her!

(ZEPPO *runs in.*)

ZEPPO: Who's been kidnapped?

HELTON: Mary! My daughter! Do something!

ZEPPO: Well, who could have done it?

HELTON: It's that Alky Briggs.

(*A closer shot as* HELTON *goes up to the* MAN *who called him over.*)

You saw them drag her into the car. Where did they take her? Where did they take her?

74

MAN: Well, you see, first they blindfolded me, and then they
turned me around this way . . .
(GROUCHO *enters.*)
GROUCHO: Of course, of course. They took her to the barn. Say,
fellows, let's all pack up a nice little lunch and go down to the
old barn, eh?
(*The two thugs in evening dress enter from the hall.*)
HELTON: Red, you go down by the North Road.
(*One of the thugs runs off.*) Jack, you head down by Front
Street. I'll go and pick up a couple of the boys. Come on!
Come on!
GROUCHO: And I'll stay here and pick up a couple of dames.
(*Shot of the scene as the guests all pour out into the hall and*
CHICO *appears in the foreground.*)
(*Taking off his jacket*) This is no time for women. On to the
barn!
(HARPO *comes up, hops on the back of the tall* WOMAN *in the*
frilled dress and rides out.)
CHICO: (*Turning in the doorway*) Gee, I wish I had a horse!
(*They all exit, to the sound of* HARPO's *hooter.*)

The scene changes to the exterior of the old barn, in darkness.
A car drives up and BRIGGS *and his henchmen hustle* MARY *into the*
barn.

BRIGGS: Hurry up. Come on.
(*The car drives off.*
Inside the barn, they enter through the door, MARY *struggling*
between BUTCH *and* SPIKE.)
MARY: Let me go! Let me go! Let me go!
BRIGGS: No use yelling, kid. Nobody'll hear you here.
(*Pan as they cross the floor amid piles of hay and cartwheels.*)
MARY: You wait until my father hears about this.
BRIGGS: (*Pausing*) Well, he's gonna hear about it, because I'm
gonna tell him myself.
(MARY *struggles wildly.*)
Listen, take it easy. You're not goin' any place. Don't get all
excited. Come on.

MARY: You take your hands off me, I tell you.

BUTCH: Go on!

(They arrive at the bottom of some stairs leading up to the loft.)

BRIGGS: Listen, kid, nobody's gonna hurt you. You'll be out of
here in an hour if your old man comes through . . . Butch, you
take care of the girl while I telephone Joe. Come on, you guys.
*(BUTCH hauls her screaming up the stairs, while camera pans with
BRIGGS, SPIKE and SHORTY as they go to the door and exit.
We follow BUTCH from a low angle as he carries MARY along the
gallery at the top of the stairs.)*

MARY: Don't! Stop! Stop!

*(In a room in the loft, BUTCH carries MARY in through the door
and deposits her on a chair. She screams and struggles.)*

MARY: You take your hands off me!

BUTCH: *(Roughly)* Now, make yourself at home, but shut up!

*(Pan as he goes to the door.
Outside the barn a taxi drives up and stops.
We see the DRIVER in the foreground as GROUCHO and CHICO get
out on the other side.)*

DRIVER: Dollar-ten.

GROUCHO: *(Holding out a note)* Here's a dollar. Keep the change.

DRIVER: But I said a dollar-ten.

GROUCHO: *(Grabbing back the note)* All right. Give me the dollar.
I'll keep the change.

(They walk away.)

CHICO: *(To GROUCHO)* That's half a dollar I owe you.

*(In a longer shot, the taxi drives off and they go up to the barn door
in the background.
At the door, CHICO AND GROUCHO enter from foreground and
turn to face camera; GROUCHO is carrying a picnic basket.)*
You call this a barn? This looks like a stable.

(A closer shot of the two of them.)

GROUCHO: Well, if you look at it, it's a barn. If you smell it, it's a
stable.

CHICO: Well, let's just look at it.

*(Seen from below, BUTCH leans out of the loft window above
them. He bellows threateningly:)*

BUTCH: Get out of here!

(GROUCHO *and* CHICO *start and look upwards.*)

GROUCHO: Say, have you got a girl up in that hay loft?

BUTCH: (*Off*) No.

GROUCHO: Then you're a bigger fool than I thought you were.

    (*We see* BUTCH *holding up a sack.*)

BUTCH: Beat it, I tell you!

    (*Back to the other two.*)

GROUCHO: What'd you say?

    (*Resume on* BUTCH *at the window.*)

BUTCH: I said beat it. (*He throws down the sack.*)

    (*The sack whistles down and lands with a crash by* GROUCHO *and* CHICO.

    A closer shot of the two of them.)

GROUCHO: (*Dead pan*) Pardon me. What did you say?

BUTCH: (*Off*) I said beat it.

GROUCHO: He said beat it. Gee, I wish I'd have said that. Everybody's repeating it around the club.

    (*A closer shot of* BUTCH *at the window.*)

BUTCH: I'm coming down to get you. (*He goes inside.*)

    (*Resume on* CHICO *and* GROUCHO.)

GROUCHO: Don't bother. We'll come right up. (*He picks up the picnic basket; to* CHICO) Come on, I'm going in to get him.

    (*We move to the interior of the old barn.* CHICO *and* GROUCHO *enter in the background and walk towards us. Hens cluck; a cow moos loudly off-screen.*

    In a closer shot, camera pans as they walk across and sit down on a pile of hay.)

Well, here we are in the old barn, all set for a nice picnic lunch. (*He opens the picnic basket.*) Oh gosh, the picnic is off. We haven't got any red ants.

CHICO: (*Chewing a bit of hay*) I know an Indian who's got a couple of red aunts . . .

    (GROUCHO *pulls out a napkin and lays it on the ground.*)

Hey, don't you think we'd better go look for the girl?

GROUCHO: Let's wait till we get through eating. There's hardly enough lunch for two.

CHICO: I don't see why she couldn't get kidnapped near a restaurant.

GROUCHO: (*Pulling out some plates*) Some dark night I think I'll come here and lay for you if the hens don't get sore. (*He hands* CHICO *a tin cup.*) Here, go over to that filling station and get some milk – Grade A.

(*Shot of the scene. There is a cow in the background, and as* CHICO *turns, a calf runs up to it and starts to suckle. The cow moos. Resume on the two men as* GROUCHO *pulls food out of the basket.*) Well, come on, come on, where's the milk?

CHICO: There's a customer ahead of me.

(*Camera follows* BUTCH *from a low angle as he walks along the gallery of the loft, then we cut to a shot of the scene as he looks down.*)

BUTCH: Hey!

(GROUCHO *and* CHICO *rise.*

A closer shot of BUTCH, *from below.*)

What're you doin' here?

(*We see* CHICO *and* GROUCHO, *looking up.*)

GROUCHO: What are we doing? What about you, kidnapping a girl! Nice old-fashioned piece of melodrama, kidnapping a girl! (*He wags a finger.*) You've been reading too many dime novels.

CHICO: Go on, you get 'im. I'll wait for you outside.

(*In a shot of the scene,* CHICO *stands aside as* GROUCHO *starts for the stairs.*

Then we resume on BUTCH.)

BUTCH: (*Savagely*) Keep out of this loft!

(*Back to the other two,* GROUCHO *on the stairs.*)

CHICO: Well, it's better to have loft and lost, then never to have loft at all.

GROUCHO: (*Patting him on the shoulder*) Nice work!

(*Resume on* BUTCH.)

BUTCH: Beat it, or I'll t'row you out. (*He runs off.*)

(*Camera pans with* BUTCH *as, having come down the stairs, he chases the others across the barn and round one of the posts supporting the gallery. Hens scatter, clucking, and the cow moos as he trips over a bale of straw, while* GROUCHO *starts up a ladder. In a longer shot,* GROUCHO *and* CHICO *climb the ladder to the loft.* BUTCH *pokes* CHICO *from below with a pitchfork and follows them up. They leap over the edge on to a pile of hay and*

78

BUTCH *starts back down the ladder.*
At the bottom, we follow BUTCH *as he comes down and throws himself into the pile of hay.*
Meanwhile, up in the loft, MARY *runs across and pulls frantically at the locked door.*
CHICO *emerges from the pile of hay and starts up the ladder again, pursued by* BUTCH.
At that moment the door opens and HARPO *runs in. We follow him as he runs across the stable, seizing a pitchfork.* BUTCH *laughs off-screen, and* CHICO *shouts:*)

CHICO: (*Off*) Take your face out of my foot!

BUTCH: (*Off*) I gotcha! Now I gotcha!

(HARPO *now arrives at the bottom of the ladder and jabs* BUTCH *in the backside with the pitchfork.* BUTCH *comes down the ladder and advances threateningly on* HARPO, *who jabs him in the chest.* BUTCH *puts up his hands while* CHICO *descends from the ladder.*)

CHICO: (*Tweaking his face*) So, thought we were afraid, hey? Thought we were afraid, did ya!

(*A closer shot as* BUTCH *seizes the pitchfork and breaks it slowly into pieces.*
At that moment, ZEPPO *comes in through the door and looks round.*)

BUTCH: (*Off*) Now I'm goin' to give it to you guys right!

(*Camera pans as* ZEPPO *runs across the stable.*
Arriving at the bottom of the ladder, he knocks out BUTCH.
Animal noises off.
A closer shot as MARY *screams from the loft;* ZEPPO *looks up and runs off, while* CHICO *and* HARPO *seize* BUTCH's *feet.*
Camera follows ZEPPO *from below as he runs up the stairs and along the gallery.*
We see MARY *locked in the loft as* ZEPPO *bursts in through the door.*
Down below, HARPO *and* CHICO *hide behind the barn door as* BRIGGS *bursts in with* SHORTY *and* SPIKE, *to find* BUTCH *laid out cold.*)

BRIGGS: (*Bending over him*) Butch! Butch, what happened? (*Looking up.*) Hey!

(Up in the gallery, ZEPPO *and* MARY *turn and look round, then we cut back to the barn floor.)*

BRIGGS: You get out of that loft!

(Seen from below, ZEPPO *vaults over the edge of the gallery to the top of the stairs.*

In a long shot, he leaps from the head of the stairs and lands on BRIGGS. *They roll over in the hay.* MARY *screams off.*

Resume on the scene by the door as SHORTY *and* SPIKE *lean over* BUTCH's *recumbent figure.)*

SHORTY: What's happened, old man?

SPIKE: Come out of here. Come out of here, Butch.

(As they pull him up from the floor, HARPO *and* CHICO *emerge from behind the door and knock them out.*

We see ZEPPO *and* BRIGGS *fighting.* ZEPPO *hits* BRIGGS . . . BRIGGS *lands on the hay pile;* ZEPPO *follows. They roll over and vanish, as* GROUCHO *rises from the hay.)*

GROUCHO: Where's all those farmers' daughters I've been hearing about for years? *(He disappears into the hay again.)*

(Resume on ZEPPO *and* BRIGGS *fighting.* BRIGGS *hits* ZEPPO . . . ZEPPO *lands on the hay pile;* BRIGGS *follows, and they roll over hitting one another.* GROUCHO *rises from the hay behind them.)*

Hey, why don't you boys fight over there? You wanna break my glasses? *(He gets up and goes off.)*

(We see BRIGGS's *three henchmen laid out on the floor.* CHICO *is standing by a wagon wheel fixed to the wall behind.)*

CHICO: Come on, folks, step right up. Only ten cents a chance.

(HARPO enters and gives him a coin.)

Attaboy. Here you are. *(He spins the wheel.)* Ten cents gets you . . . look at that. The only game in the stable. *(The wheel stops.)* Let's see. Number sixteen wins. The lucky number There you are, young man.

(He hands HARPO *an iron bar.* HARPO *coshes* SPIKE *as he sits up groggily, and he falls back on the floor again.)*

(Taking back the bar) Sorry you didn't get a better one.

(We see ZEPPO *and* BRIGGS *still fighting, then cut back to the wagon wheel.* CHICO *spins it a second time.)*

Here we go. Let's see what comes up. *(The wheel stops.)*

Well, well, if he isn't the lucky guy . . . Double O, two shots
for the price of one.
(*He hands the iron bar to* HARPO, *who coshes* SHORTY *as he
rises.*)
Folks, this is the best game in all . . .
(HARPO, *carried away, hits him too and he falls.*
We return to ZEPPO *and* BRIGGS *fighting.*
Then camera pans with GROUCHO *as he goes across to the cow
and its suckling calf.*)
GROUCHO: You're a mother, you understand. How would you
like to have somebody steal one of your heifers? I know,
heifer cow is better than none, but this is no time for puns.
(*Pointing*) Get in that battle over there. (*He runs off.*)
(ZEPPO *knocks down* BRIGGS *at the bottom of the stairs* . . .
While GROUCHO *starts a running commentary, standing in an
old buggy and talking into a carriage lamp.*)
Well, here we are again at the ringside and, folks, it looks
like a great battle. Now the boys are locked in the centre of
the ring. Oh, baby, what a grudge fight!
(*Sounds of punching.* GROUCHO *leaps up and down in the
buggy.*)
Zowie! Zowie! Zowie! That makes three zowies, and a man
gets a base on balls.
(*Dust showers down on him from the canopy of the buggy.*)
Ending of the first inning, no runs, no errors, but plenty of
hits. Whee! (*He steps out of the buggy.*)
(*Resume on the other two as the fighting continues.* ZEPPO *hits*
BRIGGS, *who grunts with pain.*
GROUCHO *is now seen perched on a crossbeam up by the gallery.*
He talks into a watering can.)
This programme is coming to you through the courtesy of
the Golden Goose Furniture Company with three stores –
125th Street, 125th Street and 125th Street. You furnish the
girl, we tar and feather your nest. Look for our
advertisement in today's ash can.
(*He resumes his commentary, to sounds of fighting off-screen.*)
Now the boys are at it in the centre of the ring. Oh! That one
hurt! (*Waving the watering can.*) Come on, you palookas, stop

stalling. Oh, mama, if I only had my youth again. Wheee!
(*He steps along the beam.*)
(*Down below,* BRIGGS *hits* ZEPPO, *and the fight continues.
We see* HARPO *sitting backwards on a horse. Hand thrust in
shirt-front à la Napoleon, he watches the fight through an old
bottle used as a telescope, and points fiercely, directing the battle.
The horse whinnies.
Resume on the fight.* BRIGGS *hits* ZEPPO *again.*

CHICO *is seen sitting on a cow. He sounds its bell and calls out.*)

CHICO: Round two.
(BRIGGS *and* ZEPPO *grapple by the staircase . . .
While* GROUCHO *continues his commentary, perched up in the
roof.*)

GROUCHO: (*Into the watering can*) Both boys are fiddling in the
middle of the ring, and I don't think much of the tune.
(*The cows moo.*)
Briggs is bobbing and weaving. It's nice work if you can get
it. Now they're trying – very trying.
(*Sounds of punching off.*)
I copped that one from an almanac. Now they're in the
centre of the ring and the crowd rrroars!
(*Shot of a cow. It moos loudly.*
BRIGGS *raises a chair above his head . . .
Camera pans with* ZEPPO *as he falls across the floor.*
BRIGGS *advances with the chair raised, and we cut to a shot of
the scene as he brings it down on* ZEPPO.
At that moment HELTON *comes in through the door.*
BRIGGS *picks up* ZEPPO *and hits him.* ZEPPO *hits* BRIGGS . . .
*Camera pans as he falls backwards . . .
And lands on his back amid a pile of old chairs.
Meanwhile* MARY *rushes down the staircase and into* HELTON'*s
arms, watched by* ZEPPO.)

MARY: Oh, Dad!

HELTON: Are you all right, honey?
(*Beside them* HARPO *emerges from the hay pile, clutching the
calf. Its bell rings.
Seen in closer shot,* HARPO *gleefully kisses the calf.*)
(*Off*) Good boy . . .

(*Camera pans to show him shaking* ZEPPO *by the hand.*)
Remember, old Joe Helton . . .
(*Shot of the scene.*)
. . . never forgot a friend.

ZEPPO: Well, this was one job that certainly was a pleasure.

HELTON: Ah! (*He laughs.*)

(ZEPPO *and* MARY *exit arm in arm, to a chorus of cowbells and animal noises.* HELTON *turns to find* GROUCHO *by the hay pile, pitching hay in the air.*)
What are you doing?

GROUCHO: I'm looking for a needle in a haystack.

(*Fade out to the music of* 'Sugar in the morning . . .')

Duck Soup

CAST

RUFUS T. FIREFLY	Groucho
PINKY	Harpo
CHICOLINI	Chico
BOB ROLAND	Zeppo
MRS TEASDALE	Margaret Dumont
VERA MARCAL	Raquel Torres
TRENTINO	Louis Calhern
LEMONADE VENDOR	Edgar Kennedy
ZANDER	Edmund Breese
SECRETARY	Verna Hillie
AGITATOR	Leonid Kinsky
JUDGE	George MacQuarrie
SECRETARY OF WAR	Edwin Maxwell
PROSECUTOR	Charles B. Middleton
MINISTER OF FINANCE	William Worthington

Directed by	Leo McCarey
Screenplay by	Bert Kalmar and Harry Ruby
Additional dialogue by	Arthur Sheekman and Nat Perrin
Director of photography	Henry Sharp
Art direction	Hans Dreier and Wiard B. Ihnen
Edited by	LeRoy Stone
Music and lyrics by	Bert Kalmar and Harry Ruby
Musical director	Arthur Johnstone
Running time	68 or 70 minutes
Released by	Paramount, 17 November 1933

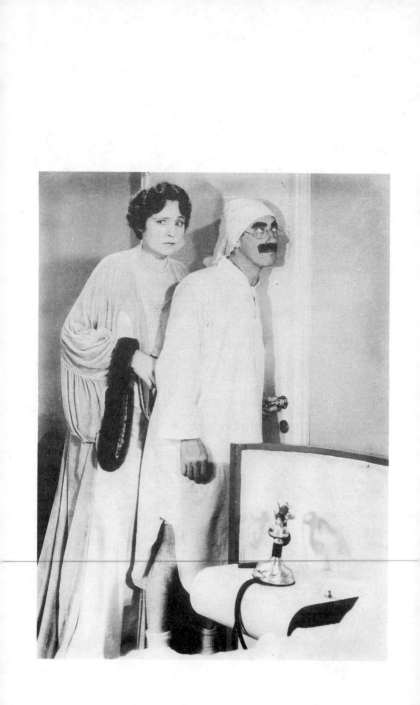

*Music as the credits come up over a shot of some ducks swimming in a
cauldron over a fire, then fade in to a flag waving from a mast. The
word* FREEDONIA *appears over it, then we wipe to a shot of
Freedonia itself – a small Ruritanian town with steeply pitched roofs
and church steeples.*

*The music ends as a diagonal wipe transports us to the council chamber
of the Freedonian government where the president,* ZANDER, *and his
cabinet are in session. Camera follows* ZANDER *as he walks across to*
MRS TEASDALE *on the left..*

ZANDER: Mrs Teasdale.
MRS TEASDALE: Yes, Your Excellency?
ZANDER: I again ask you to reconsider.
 (*Shot of* MRS TEASDALE *and a minister.*)
MRS TEASDALE: (*Decisively*) Gentlemen, I've already loaned
 Freedonia more than half the fortune my husband left me.
 (*We lose the minister as she walks to the right.*)
 I consider that money lost, and now you're asking for
 another 20 million dollars.
 (*The cabinet stands in consternation as she walks away to the
 window.*)
A MINISTER: (*Following*) But it would only be for a few months
 to meet this present emergency.
 (*They are now seen across the council table; camera pans as they
 pursue* MRS TEASDALE.)
 With 20 million dollars in the treasury, we can announce an
 immediate reduction in taxes. (*They stop.*) That's all the
 people are asking for.
MRS TEASDALE: I'm sorry, but I'm inclined to agree with the
 people. The government has been mismanaged.
ZANDER: (*Starting forward*) What?
 (*A longer shot of the group.*)

MRS TEASDALE: I will lend the money, but only on condition that
His Excellency withdraw and place the government in new
hands.
(*As she speaks, the other members of the council get up from their
places and gather round, and we cut in to a medium shot.*)
ZANDER: You ask me to give up my office?
MRS TEASDALE: Yes, Your Excellency. In a crisis like this I feel
Freedonia needs a new leader. (*Dramatically*) A progressive,
fearless fighter, a man like Rufus T. Firefly.
(*Back to the longer shot.*)
A MINISTER: Rufus T. Firefly?
MRS TEASDALE: I will lend the money . . .
(*Back to the previous shot again.*)
. . . to Freedonia only if Firefly is appointed leader.
(*Music as we dissolve to a newspaper headline which reads:*
FIREFLY APPOINTED NEW LEADER OF
FREEDONIA.
Dissolve again to a picture of FIREFLY, *with cigar.*
Then to another newspaper which reads: MAMMOTH
RECEPTION ARRANGED TO WELCOME
NATION'S LEADER TONIGHT: SELECTION OF
RUFUS T. FIREFLY GREETED WITH CHEERS OF
FREEDONIANS. Rufus T. Firefly will take over the reigns of
the Freedonian government immediately. Firefly's sponsor,
it was learned, is Mrs Gloria Teasdale, wealthy widow of the
late Chester V. Teasdale, and from all reports the new leader
will execute his duties with an iron hand . . .'

The music fades as we dissolve to the ballroom where the reception for
FIREFLY *is being held. Guests in evening dress throng the floor. There
is a fanfare of trumpets.*
*After another dissolve, we see the main staircase with the entrance to
the ballroom at the top, flanked by guards, and the trumpeters in the
background. Camera tracks in as a* LACKEY *enters.*

LACKEY: (*Announcing*) The Honorable Secretary of Finance and
party.
(*The* LACKEY *exits and the* MINISTER OF FINANCE *and his*

party enter and start down the stairs. Track in again as the
LACKEY *reappears; there is another fanfare.*)
His Excellency, Ambassador Trentino of Sylvania.
(TRENTINO *and his party enter, bowing; camera pans as they*
come down and meet MRS TEASDALE *on the staircase.*)

MRS TEASDALE: Ambassador!

TRENTINO: Mrs Teasdale!
(*Music over a low-angle shot of the two of them. One of*
TRENTINO'*s aides bows and exits.*)

MRS TEASDALE: It was so good of you to come. I am anxious for
you to meet the new leader of our country.

TRENTINO: (*Clasping her hand*) No matter who rules in
Freedonia, Mrs Teasdale, to me you will always be the first
lady of the land.
(*He looks round as* VERA MARCAL *passes up the staircase; she*
halts.)

MRS TEASDALE: Oh, permit me. This is Miss Vera Marcal.
Ambassador Trentino.
(TRENTINO *kisses her hand with an air of complicity.*)

TRENTINO: Miss Marcal needs no introduction. I've seen her
dance many times at the theatre.

VERA: Thank you.
(*Seen from below, the trumpeters sound another fanfare and the*
LACKEY *re-enters.*)

LACKEY: The Honorable Pandooh of Mufhtan.
(*Resume on the trio, with the entrance in the background.*
Oriental music as the Pandooh appears, wearing a turban.)

MRS TEASDALE: I must greet His Honour.
(*She goes up the stairs to meet him, while* TRENTINO *takes* VERA
by the arm and walks her down the stairs towards camera.
We look down on the guests in the ballroom.
Then resume on TRENTINO *and* VERA *as they sit down on the*
edge of the staircase.)

TRENTINO: (*In a half-whisper*) What have you found out?

VERA: (*Also half whispering*) Nothing. I've been waiting to hear
from you.

TRENTINO: I've given up the idea of a revolution. I have a better
plan.

(*Music over a closer shot of the two of them.*)

TRENTINO: I can gain control of Freedonia much easier by
marrying Mrs Teasdale.

VERA: (*Laughing*) Maybe that's not going to be so easy.

TRENTINO: Eh?

VERA: Oh, from what I hear . . . You see, Mrs Teasdale is rather
sweet on this Rufus T. Firefly.

(*The Pandooh passes on the stairs behind them.*)

TRENTINO: Oh! Well, that's where you come in.

VERA: Oh!

TRENTINO: I'm going to place him in your hands.

VERA: (*With relish*) Yes?

TRENTINO: (*Leaning towards her*) I don't have to tell you what to
do . . .

VERA: No.

TRENTINO: Or how to . . . Careful.

(*Music over a shot of the scene.* TRENTINO *gets up as* MRS
TEASDALE *and* BOB *enter down the stairs.*)

MRS TEASDALE: I want you to meet His Excellency's secretary,
Bob Roland – Ambassador Trentino.

TRENTINO: How do you do, sir.

(*They shake hands.*)

BOB: How do you do?

MRS TEASDALE: Miss Marcal.

(*We now see the group from below.* BOB *bows to* VERA *and smiles.*)

BOB: We've met.

MRS TEASDALE: Of course.

TRENTINO: (*Acidly*) Well, I hope His Excellency gets here soon.

BOB: (*Turning to him*) His Excellency makes it a point always to be
on time. As long as I've known him, he's never been late for
an appointment. (*He sings:*)

    'His Excellency is due

    To take his station,

    Beginning his new administration

    He'll make his appearance when . . .'

(*He turns and points.*)

    'The clock on the wall . . .'

(*Camera pans to show the clock on the wall; it says just on ten.*)

(*Singing, off*) '. . . strikes ten.'
MRS TEASDALE: (*Singing, off*) 'When the clock on the . . .'
　　　(*Camera pans back to the group.*)
　　　(*Singing*) '. . . wall strikes ten,
　　　　All you loyal ladies and you patriotic men . . .'
　　　(*We look down on the whole ballroom, with* MRS TEASDALE *on
　　　the stairs in the background. Music.*)
　　　(*Singing*) Let's sing the national anthem when
　　　　The clock on the wall strikes ten.
　　　(*Seen from below, the clock strikes ten. There is a roll of drums
　　　off-screen.*
　　　*A long shot shows another entrance at the side of the ballroom,
　　　flanked with banners. Two trumpeters step forward and sound a
　　　fanfare, while guards with plumed helmets march into the
　　　ballroom. The guests all sing, accompanied by music.*)
GUESTS: (*Singing, off*)
　　　　His Excellency is due
　　　　To take his station,
　　　　Beginning his new administration.
　　　　He'll make his appearance when
　　　　The clock on the wall strikes ten.
　　　(*The guards halt and face one another in two lines, then a troop
　　　of ballet dancers enters, scattering flowers. Camera tracks back.*)
　　　(*Singing, off*) We'll give him a rousing cheer
　　　　To show him we're glad he's here.
　　　(*A very high-angle shot shows the guards and ballet girls flanking
　　　the staircase which leads up to the entrance.*)
　　　(*Singing, off*) Hail, hail Freedonia!
　　　(*The trumpeters step forward and sound a fanfare while the ballet
　　　girls kneel and the guards draw their swords.*
　　　*We see them again in a general shot as they stretch out their arms
　　　and swords towards the entrance.*)
　　　(*Singing, off*) Hail, hail Freedonia!
　　　　Land of the brave and free!
　　　(*The music stops.* TRENTINO, MRS TEASDALE, VERA *and* BOB
　　　stand with heads respectfully bowed, waiting for FIREFLY's
　　　entrance. Nothing happens. They straighten up and TRENTINO
　　　looks round.

The guards and ballet girls are still posed in welcome on the staircase.

Standing by the window, a row of trumpeters raise their trumpets and sound a fanfare. The music starts again.

TRENTINO, MRS TEASDALE, VERA *and* BOB *bow their heads again.)*

(Singing, off) Hail, hail . . .

(Resume on the guards and ballet girls, still posed in welcome.)

(Singing, off) . . . Freedonia,
    Land of the brave and free.

(The music stops again as we cut to FIREFLY's *bedroom, where he is lying asleep in bed, beneath the Freedonian flag. An alarm clock rings loudly.*

FIREFLY *wakes and leaps up in bed. He pulls off his nightshirt, revealing his clothes underneath, while the guests start singing again off-screen.)*

(Singing, off) Hail, hail, Freedonia.

(A long shot of FIREFLY *as he slides down a pole at the end of the bed and disappears from view.)*

(Singing, off) Land of the . . .

(Down in the ballroom, the guards and ballet girls are still gazing expectantly towards the entrance as FIREFLY *comes sliding down the pole in the foreground and starts towards them.)*

(Singing, off) . . . brave and free.

(The music stops.

FIREFLY *approaches one of the files of guards. He peers up the staircase, following their gaze, then crosses to the guards on the other side.*

He tugs at the nearest guard's cuff, seen in medium close-up.)

FIREFLY: *(In an undertone)* You expecting somebody?

GUARD: *(Out of the side of his mouth)* Yes.

*(*FIREFLY *stands in line, his arm outstretched like the rest of them.*

A medium show now shows FIREFLY, *the guards and ballet girls, all gazing expectantly towards the entrance. The music starts again.)*

GUESTS: *(Singing)* Hail, hail, Freedonia.
    Land . . .

(*We see them from another angle as* MRS TEASDALE *enters in the background.*)
(*Singing*) . . . of the brave and free.
(*The music ends.* MRS TEASDALE *spots* FIREFLY *and comes down the steps towards him.*)

MRS TEASDALE: Oh, Your Excellency!
(*The guards retract their swords, the ballet girls their arms, and we cut to another shot of the group.*)
We've been expecting you. (*She gives him her hand; pompously*) As chairwoman of the reception committee, I extend the good wishes of every man, woman and child of Freedonia.
(*She and* FIREFLY *are seen from a low angle.*)

FIREFLY: Never mind that stuff. Take a card.
(*He fans out a pack of cards.*)

MRS TEASDALE: A card? What'll I do with a card? (*She takes it.*)

FIREFLY: You can keep it. I've got fifty-one left. Now, what were you saying?

MRS TEASDALE: (*Pompously*) As chairwoman of the reception committee, I welcome you with open arms.

FIREFLY: Is that so? How late do you stay open?
(*She looks at him dubiously but continues in the same tone.*)

MRS TEASDALE: I've sponsored your appointment because I feel you are the most able statesman in all Freedonia.

FIREFLY: Well, that covers a lot of ground. (*He looks her up and down.*) Say, you cover a lot of ground yourself. You'd better beat it. I hear they're going to tear you down and put up an office building where you're standing. You can leave in a taxi. If you can't leave in a taxi you can leave in a huff. If that's too soon, you can leave in a minute and a huff. You known you haven't stopped talking since I came here? You must have been vaccinated with a phonograph needle.

MRS TEASDALE: (*Grandiose*) The future of Freedonia rests on you. Promise me you'll follow in the footsteps of my husband.
(*Close-up of* FIREFLY.)

FIREFLY: (*To camera*) How do you like that? I haven't been on the job five minutes and already she's making advances to me.

(*Resume on the two of them.*)

Not that I care, but where is your husband?

MRS TEASDALE: (*Mournful*) Why, he's dead.

FIREFLY: I'll bet he's just using that as an excuse.

MRS TEASDALE: (*Proudly*) I was with him to the very end.

FIREFLY: Huh! No wonder he passed away.

MRS TEASDALE: (*Dramatically*) I held him in my arms and kissed him.

FIREFLY: Oh, I see. Then it was murder. Will you marry me? Did he leave you any money? Answer the second question first.

MRS TEASDALE: He left me his entire fortune.

FIREFLY: Is that so? Can't you see what I'm trying to tell you? I love you.

(*Camera pans as he clasps her hands and circles round her.*)

MRS TEASDALE: (*With a bashful smile*) Oh, Your Excellency!

FIREFLY: You're not so bad yourself. (*He works his eyebrows.*)

(*We cut to a medium shot as* TRENTINO *strides up to them.*)

MRS TEASDALE: Oh, I want to present to you Ambassador Trentino of Sylvania . . .

(FIREFLY *offers him a card; he refuses.*)

. . .

Having him with us today is indeed a great pleasure.

(*Camera tracks in on them.*)

TRENTINO: Thank you, but I can't stay very long.

FIREFLY: (*Turning his back*) That's an even greater pleasure.

(*Shot of* FIREFLY *and* TRENTINO.)

Now, how about lending this country 20 million dollars, you old skinflint? (*He puffs at his cigar.*)

TRENTINO: 20 million dollars is a lot of money. I should have to take that up with my Minister of Finance.

FIREFLY: Well, in the meantime, could you let me have twelve dollars until pay day?

TRENTINO: Twelve dollars?

FIREFLY: Don't be scared. You'll get it back. I'll give you my personal note for ninety days. If it isn't paid by then, you can keep the note.

TRENTINO: Your Excellency, haven't we seen each other somewhere before?

96

FIREFLY: I don't think so. I'm not sure I'm seeing you now. It must be something I ate.

(*A warning hand is laid on his shoulder; camera pans to include* MRS TEASDALE.)

TRENTINO: (*Starting forward, indignant*) Look here, sir, are you trying to . . .

(FIREFLY *looks round furtively.*)

FIREFLY: Don't look now, but there's one man too many in this room . . . (*He taps* TRENTINO *on the chest.*) . . . and I think it's you.

(*Cut to a longer shot as* VERA *enters in the background.*)

MRS TEASDALE: (*To* TRENTINO) Oh, I'm so sorry.

(TRENTINO *exits with a baffled bow to* MRS TEASDALE. FIREFLY *bows back.*)

(*To* FIREFLY) I want you to meet a very charming lady.

FIREFLY: And it's about time.

(*He makes off up the steps.*)

MRS TEASDALE: Just a moment.

(*He stops next to* VERA, *who laughs nervously.*)

I want to present Miss Vera Marcal.

(*Shot of the three of them.*)

FIREFLY: Go ahead, I can take it.

MRS TEASDALE: (*With a laugh*) Oh, you don't understand. This is Vera Marcal, the famous dancer.

FIREFLY: Is that so?

VERA: Umm.

FIREFLY: Can you do this one?

(*He dances, kicking up his legs. There is general laughter as we cut to a closer shot. The guests watch in the background.*)

I danced before Napoleon. No, Napoleon danced before me. In fact he danced two hundred years before me. Here's one I picked up in a dance hall.

(*Resume on the previous shot as* FIREFLY *dances, flamenco style. The two women laugh.*

FIREFLY *is seen in medium close-up; then camera pans to include* MRS TEASDALE.)

(*Pointing at her*) Here's another one I picked up in a dance hall.

MRS TEASDALE: (*Indignant*) Oh! (*She exits.*)
   (VERA *enters, lays her hands on* FIREFLY's *shoulders and murmurs suggestively:*)
VERA: Perhaps we get a chance to dance together, huh?
FIREFLY: I could dance with you till the cows come home.
VERA: Yes?
FIREFLY: On second thoughts, I'd rather dance with the cows till you came home.
VERA: (*Starting back*) Huh!
   (*The group are seen from a low angle as* VERA *flings off in a huff.*)
FIREFLY: Where's my secretary?
BOB: (*Loudly, appearing on the right*) Here I am.
   (FIREFLY *nearly falls over and turns to hide behind* MRS TEASDALE.)
MRS TEASDALE: Good heavens, Your Excellency!
   (FIREFLY *recovers himself and strides to and fro.*)
FIREFLY: Er . . . take a letter.
BOB: Who to?
FIREFLY: To my dentist.
   (*Medium close-up of* FIREFLY.)
   Er . . . 'Dear Dentist: Enclosed find cheque for five hundred dollars. Yours very truly.' Send that off immediately.
BOB: (*Off*) I'll . . . er . . . I'll have to enclose the cheque first.
FIREFLY: You do and I'll fire you.
   (*Resume on the group, with the guests watching in the background.* BOB *goes off.*)
MRS TEASDALE: Your Excellency, the eyes of the world are upon you . . .
   (FIREFLY *starts hopping to and fro on one leg.*)
   . . . Notables from every country are gathered here in your honour. This is a gala day for you.
FIREFLY: Well, a gal a day is enough for me. I don't think I could handle any more.
   (*A closer shot of him and* MRS TEASDALE.)
MRS TEASDALE: If it's not asking too much . . . (*Music; she sings:*)
      For our information,
      Just for illustration,

Tell us how you intend
To run the nation.
(*Camera pans as* FIREFLY *steps forward, smoothing his hair, then follows him as he lopes to and fro, singing to the guests who surround him.*)

FIREFLY: (*Singing*) These are the laws of my administration.
No one's allowed to smoke . . .
(*In the ear of a blond woman*) Or tell a dirty joke.
And whistling is forbidden.
(*He whistles and conducts the guests as they sing.*)

GUESTS: (*Singing*) We're not allowed to tell a dirty joke.
Hail, hail Freedonia.

FIREFLY: (*Singing*) If chewing gum is chewed
The chewer is pursued,
And in the hoose-gow hidden.
(*He makes chewing motions.*)

GUESTS: (*Singing*) If we choose to chew, we'll be pursued.
(*Pan as* FIREFLY *moves to another group of guests and addresses a grey-haired lady.*)

FIREFLY: (*Singing*) If any form of pleasure is exhibited.
Report to me and it will be prohibited.
(*Camera follows him from a high angle as he moves past some more guests and up to a girl.*)
(*Singing*) I'll put my foot down,
So shall it be.
This is the land of the free.
(*He takes the girl in his arms and goes on singing.*)
The last man nearly ruined this place,
He didn't know what to do with it.
If you think this country's bad off now,
Just wait till I get through with it.
(*He releases the girl.*
We now see him with a group of generals and ministers behind him. Music as he dances a hornpipe, then cut to show him and a general.)
(*Wagging a finger at the general*) The country's taxes must be fixed,
And I know what to do with it.

(We follow him to a group on the left.)
 If you think you're paying too much now,
 Just wait till I get through with it.
(Another shot of FIREFLY *and the guests. He produces a piccolo and circles round, playing it. Everyone cheers and waves. We see* FIREFLY *and a minister.* FIREFLY *leans on one of the guard's trumpets as he sings.)*
(Singing) I will not stand for anything
 That's crooked or unfair.
 I'm strictly on the up and up,
 So everyone beware.
 If anyone's caught taking graft
 And I don't get my share,
 We stand 'em up against the wall . . .
(He aims with the trumpet.)
 And pop goes the weasel!
(We see him again with the guests. Camera pans as he dances round with the trumpet, singing 'Ah-ah-ah' in accompaniment to the guests.)
GUESTS: *(Singing)* So everyone beware,
 Who's crooked or unfair,
 No one must take a bit of graft
 Unless he gets his share.
(In a long shot of the scene, he goes up to a couple standing on the steps, the woman talking to a second man. Cut to show the four of them as FIREFLY *sings, gesturing from one to the other.)*
FIREFLY: *(Singing)* If any man should come between
 A husband and his bride,
 We find out which one she prefers
 By letting her decide.
 If she prefers the other man,
 The husband steps outside.
 We stand him up against the wall,
 And pop goes the weasel!
(Camera pans with him as he lopes along, rolling up his trousers. We see him again as he stands between two lackeys and sings 'Ah-ah-ah' again, along with the guests.)

GUESTS: (*Singing*) The husband steps outside,
    Relinquishes his bride.
    (FIREFLY *and the guests continue to sing, in a long shot of the scene.*)
FIREFLY: (*Singing*) Ah-ah-ah . . .
GUESTS: (Simultaneously) They stand him up against the wall,
    And take him for a ride.
    (*As they finish, resume on* FIREFLY *and the lackeys.* FIREFLY *stands with his mouth still open as* MRS TEASDALE *enters.*)
MRS TEASDALE: You have an appointment at the House of
    Representatives. (*She looks down.*) Good heavens! You can't
    go with your trousers up.
FIREFLY: I can't, eh? Well, they'll never catch me any other way.
    My car! His Excellency's car!
    (*A* LACKEY *is seen from below.*)
LACKEY: His Excellency's car!
    (*Then a trumpeter from a similar angle. He sounds a fanfare.*
    ANOTHER LACKEY *takes up the cry.*)
ANOTHER LACKEY: His Excellency's car!
    (*Another trumpeter sounds a fanfare.*
    Outside the palace, the guards stand in line at the gate.)
GUARDS: His Excellency's car!
    (*Another fanfare. In a closer shot, the guards stand aside while*
    PINKY *drives in through the gate on a motorcycle and side-car*
    and exits in the foreground.
    High-angle shot of the palace steps. The trumpets sound again as
    PINKY *drives up on the motorcycle and squeals to a halt, with the*
    Freedonian flag flying from the side-car.
    We now look up the palace steps to the entrance. In the
    foreground, PINKY *crouches down by the motorcycle and takes a*
    photograph as FIREFLY *comes down flanked by two guards, who*
    help him into the side-car. The trumpeters sound another fanfare
    at the top of the steps.
    PINKY *puts away his camera and gets back on his motorcycle as*
    FIREFLY *orders him:*)
FIREFLY: I'm in a hurry. To the House of Representatives. Ride
    like fury. If you run out of gas, get ethyl. If Ethyl runs out,
    get Mabel. Now, step on it!

(*In a high-angle shot the guards salute as* PINKY *roars off on the motorcycle – leaving* FIREFLY *and the side-car behind.*
FIREFLY *looks after him for a moment, then gets out.*
We see him from below, with the guards still saluting.)
(*Nonchalantly*) Well, it certainly feels good to be back again.
(*Fade out.*)

Fade in to a flag waving from a mast. Music. The word SYLVANIA *appears over it, then we wipe to a shot of Sylvania itself. It is another Ruritanian town, of more southern aspect than Freedonia.*
The music ends as a diagonal wipe transports us to TRENTINO's *office.* TRENTINO *is seated at his desk in close-up, holding a newspaper.*

AGITATOR: (*Off*) I have failed, Ambassador.
TRENTINO: I know it, I know it, you idiot!
    (*Close-up of the* AGITATOR, *leaning over* TRENTINO's *desk with a cringing expression.*)
AGITATOR: I'm sorry.
TRENTINO: (*Off*) You have muddled everything.
    (*We now see him at his desk in the foreground, with the* AGITATOR *beyond him.*)
    If you'd started the revolution as I planned, during the turmoil I could have stepped in and placed Freedonia under the Sylvanian flag – our flag.
    (*Close-up of the* AGITATOR, *leaning over the desk.*)
AGITATOR: But Firefly blocked us. Your Excellency . . .
    (*Resume on* TRENTINO *from his point of view.*)
    (*Off*) . . . you have no idea how popular he is in Freedonia.
TRENTINO: Oh, yes, I've known of that too. That's why I have two spies shadowing him. I want to find out something about him – something to disgrace him, to discredit him with the people.
    (*He turns as the door opens off-screen and we cut to* TRENTINO's SECRETARY, *who has come in through the door.*)
SECRETARY: Ambassador, Chicolini and Pinky are here.
    (*Resume on* TRENTINO *at his desk, with the* AGITATOR *in back view.*)

TRENTINO: Ah, those are my spies. Show them in. (*To the* AGITATOR) Wait outside.

(*The* AGITATOR *hurries off in the background and we cut back to the* SECRETARY *as she opens the door, revealing* PINKY *in disguise.*

We see CHICOLINI *and* PINKY *standing in the doorway, both wearing bearded masks and hats. The eyes on* PINKY's *mask whirl round.* CHICOLINI *removes his mask and grins, then spins* PINKY *round to reveal his face on the other side.*)

CHICOLINI: We fool you good, heh?

(*Shot of* TRENTINO.)

TRENTINO: (*Genially*) Gentlemen! (*He starts forward.*)

(*Resume on the door, which the* SECRETARY *is holding open.* TRENTINO *advances towards* CHICOLINI *and* PINKY *with open arms, but they suddenly dive past him to the desk as a bell rings.*

At the desk, PINKY *answers first one phone, then the other, but the bell goes on ringing.*)

Gentlemen, what is this?

(*A closer shot excludes him as* CHICOLINI *replies:*)

CHICOLINI: Sssh! This is spy stuff!

(PINKY *listens to both phones at once but the bell still goes on ringing. Finally he gives a grin and pulls a large alarm clock out of his pocket.* CHICOLINI *laughs.*)

SECRETARY: (*Off*) A telegram for you sir.

(*As she finishes, we see her and* TRENTINO.)

TRENTINO: Oh!

(CHICOLINI *and* PINKY *rush round beside him.* PINKY *grabs the telegram, looks at it, then screws it up and throws it on the floor in a rage.*)

CHICOLINI: He gets mad because he can't read.

(*The* SECRETARY *exits and* PINKY *leers after her.*)

TRENTINO: Oh, I see. Well, gentlemen, we have serious matters to discuss.

(*Camera pans with them to the desk, then cuts to show them from a high angle.*)

So please be seated.

(CHICOLINI *and* PINKY *slide under* TRENTINO *as he sits down.*

PINKY *whistles while* CHICOLINI *sings:*)

CHICOLINI: Rock-a-bye . . .

(*In a medium shot of the group,* PINKY *continues to whistle and puts his feet up on the desk while the other two get up again.*)

TRENTINO: Gentlemen! Gentlemen! Now, about that information I asked you to get.

(CHICOLINI *reaches in his pocket.*)

CHICOLINI: Wait, wait, wait, wait. Here, have a cigar.

(*We see his hands as he holds out the charred butt of a cigar.* TRENTINO'*s hand takes it from him.*

Seen from below TRENTINO *looks at the butt with distaste.*)

(*Off*) That's a good quarter cigar.

(*Back to the group.*)

I smoked the other three-quarters myself.

TRENTINO: Yes. Well, no thank you. I have one of my own.

(*He throws down the butt and produces a cigar from a box on the desk.* PINKY *leaps up and grabs it in his mouth.*)

Here, try one of these.

(*Shot of* PINKY *and* CHICOLINI. PINKY *tries to light the cigar with the telephone receiver.*)

CHICOLINI: Aw, 'at's-a no good.

(*He takes out a lighter but finds that it does not work.*

Resume on all three of them as PINKY *pulls a blowlamp out of his pocket. It ignites with a roar, and he lights his own cigar, then* TRENTINO'*s.*)

'At's-a good, all right. 'At's-a fine. 'At's-a good.

(PINKY *blows out the flame.*

In another shot of the group camera pans, excluding CHICOLINI, *while* PINKY *puts the blowlamp down on the desk behind* TRENTINO. *The Sylvanian Ambassador turns to* CHICOLINI, *holding his cigar behind his back.*)

TRENTINO: Now, let's concentrate. Have you been trailing Firefly?

(PINKY *opens a drawer in the desk and snips the end off* TRENTINO'*s cigar with a pair of scissors; it falls into the drawer. Camera pans to include* CHICOLINI *again.*)

CHICOLINI: (*Laughing*) Have we been trailing Firefly? Why, my partner – he's got a nose just like a bloodhound.

TRENTINO: (*Turning to look at* PINKY) Really?

CHICOLINI: Yeah, and the rest of his face don't look so good either.
(*The three of them are seen standing in a row behind the desk.*
TRENTINO *tries to puff on his truncated cigar, then looks
suspiciously at* PINKY.)
Look. We find out all about this Firefly. (*He pulls out a letter.*)
Here, look at this.
(TRENTINO *grabs it and sits down.*)

TRENTINO: Ah very good, very good. Wait a minute. We must not
be disturbed.
(*Close-up of his hand pressing a buzzer on the desk.*
The trio are seen from the side as the SECRETARY *enters in the
background and comes up to the desk.*)

SECRETARY: Yes, sir?

TRENTINO: Oh . . . This is a very important conference, and I do
not wish to be interrupted.
(*Shot of* TRENTINO, PINKY *and the* SECRETARY.)

SECRETARY: Yes sir.
(*She sees* PINKY *leering at her and backs away nervously.* PINKY
starts to follow, but CHICOLINI *restrains him.*)

CHICOLINI: Ah-ah! Ah-ha! (*He snaps his fingers.*)
(*Resume on the three of them beyond the desk.* TRENTINO *gets up
in exasperation.*)

TRENTINO: Gentlemen, we are not getting anywhere. (*He puts his
cigar in the ashtray.*)
(*Close-up of* PINKY'S *hand as he balances the cigar on the end of
the buzzer board.*
PINKY *hits the cigar in the air with a ruler and belts it across the
room.*
We see the others as PINKY *runs to first base by the door, then back
to the desk. He throws himself down on the carpet and* CHICOLINI
stands over him.)

CHICOLINI: You're out!
(*He goes back to the other side of* TRENTINO. PINKY *tries to press
the buzzer, but* TRENTINO *raises a finger.*)

TRENTINO: (*To* PINKY) Ah-ah-ah! (*To both of them*) Now,
gentlemen, please! Will you tell me what you found out about
Firefly?

(*Shot of him and* CHICOLINI.)

CHICOLINI: Well, you remember you gave us a picture of this man and said follow him?

TRENTINO: Oh, yes.

CHICOLINI: Well, we get on the job right away . . . (*He gestures dramatically.*) . . . and in one hour . . . even in less than one hour . . .

TRENTINO: (*Excitedly*) Yes?

CHICOLINI: . . . we lose-a da picsh . . .

(TRENTINO *sighs.*)

. . . Dat'sa pretty quick work, huh?

TRENTINO: But I asked you to dig up something I can use against Firefly. Did you bring me his record?

(*Resume on the three.* PINKY *gets out a gramophone record from under his coat and hands it to* TRENTINO. *The* AMBASSADOR *gets up, at his wits' end.*)

No, no!

(*He throws the record over his shoulder.* PINKY *pulls out a gun. We see the record flying through the air. A shot rings out and it disintegrates.*

Back to the group as CHICOLINI *rings a handbell which he has found on the desk and hands* PINKY *a cigar from the box.*)

CHICOLINI: And da boy gets a cigar.

(*He slams the lid on* TRENTINO's *fingers.*)

TRENTINO: Oww!

(*He shakes his fingers;* PINKY *commiserates.*)

Now, Chicolini . . .

(*Shot of* CHICOLINI *and* TRENTINO. TRENTINO *sits down.*)

(*Wagging a finger*) . . . I want a full detailed report of your investigation.

(PINKY *is partly visible to the right.*)

CHICOLINI: All right, I tell you. Monday we watch Firefly's house, but he no come out. He wasn't home. Tuesday we go to the ball game, but he fool us. He no show up. Wednesday he go to the ball game, and we fool him. We no show up. Thursday was a double header. Nobody show up. Friday it rained all day. There was no ball game so we stayed home and we listened to it over the radio.

TRENTINO: (*Exasperated*) Then you didn't shadow Firefly?

CHICOLINI: Oh, sure we shadow Firefly. We shadow him all day.

TRENTINO: But what day was that?

CHICOLINI: Shadderday.

(*Cut to include* PINKY. TRENTINO *clutches his head in his hands.*)

(*Laughing*) 'Ats-a some joke, eh, boss?

(PINKY *snips at* TRENTINO's *hair, which is standing up between his fingers.*

Resume on TRENTINO *and* CHICOLINI.)

TRENTINO: Now, will you tell me what happened on Saturday?

CHICOLINI: I'm glad you asked me. We follow this man down to a roadhouse and at this roadhouse he meet a married lady.

TRENTINO: A married lady?

CHICOLINI: Yeah. I think it was his wife.

TRENTINO: Firefly has no wife.

CHICOLINI: No?

TRENTINO: No.

CHICOLINI: Den you know what I think, boss?

TRENTINO: What?

CHICOLINI: I think we follow da wrong man.

(*We see the three of them again, facing camera.* TRENTINO *gets up.*)

TRENTINO: Oh, gentlemen, I am disappointed.

(*They hang their heads.*)

I entrusted you with a mission of great importance . . .

(*They look up eagerly.*)

. . . and you failed.

(*They hang their heads again.*)

However . . .

(*They look up again.*)

. . . I am going to give you one more chance.

(*A closer shot of the three of them, from the side.* TRENTINO *bends over, looking in a drawer, and* PINKY *cuts off his coat tails.*)

I have credentials here that will get you into any place in Freedonia. If I can only . . . Ah, here we are.

(*He straightens up and hands* CHICOLINI *a document.*

Shot of TRENTINO *and* PINKY.)
Now, are you sure that you can trap Firefly?
(PINKY *nods and pulls out a mousetrap.*
We see PINKY'*s hands with the mousetrap. It snaps shut.*
Back to TRENTINO *and* PINKY. TRENTINO *sighs in despair.*
We see the three of them from the side again. TRENTINO *turns*
towards CHICOLINI *in the background, while* PINKY *picks up a*
paste pot.)
Remember, this time . . .
(PINKY'*s hand dips the brush in the paste.*)
(*Off*) . . . I expect results.
(*Resume on the group as* TRENTINO *bends over, shaking hands*
with CHICOLINI.)
Goodbye, and good luck.
(PINKY *smears paste on the seat of* TRENTINO'*s trousers.*)
CHICOLINI: Okay, Cap. Come on, Pinky.
(*He goes off, while* PINKY *waves to* TRENTINO.
Another shot looking towards the door. TRENTINO *sits on the*
desk with his hand outstretched.)
TRENTINO: Goodbye.
(PINKY *shakes his hand and exits, leaving* TRENTINO'*s fingers*
caught in the mousetrap. TRENTINO *gets up with an agonized*
expression – and the newspaper stuck to his backside. He groans
and tries to remove his fingers from the trap. Fade out.)

Fade in to a sign on a door which reads:
'FREEDONIA CHAMBER OF DEPUTIES.
In Conference – Do not disturb under any circumstances.'

A ball is heard bouncing off-screen.
Dissolve to the interior of the Chamber of Deputies, where FIREFLY *is*
standing at his desk at the end of the council table, playing 'jacks'.
BOB *is sitting beside him.*
Dissolve to show the council table from above. The ministers watch
transfixed on either side while FIREFLY *plays at the far end. He misses*
the ball and throws the jacks on the floor.
Camera tracks in.

DUCK SOUP

FIREFLY: All right, the meeting is called to order.
> (*He bangs a gavel on the table and the* MINISTER OF FINANCE *gets up.*)

MINISTER OF FINANCE: Your Excellency, here is the Treasury Department's report. (*He hands it up to* FIREFLY.) I hope you'll find it clear.

FIREFLY: Clear? Huh! Why, a four-year-old child could understand this report.
> (*Shot of him and* BOB.)

Run out and find me a four-year-old child. I can't make head or tail out of it. (*He hands the report to* BOB.)
> (*Seen from the end of the table, the ministers look towards* FIREFLY *in the background.*)

And now, members of the cabinet . . . (*He bangs the gavel.*)
. . . we'll take up old business.
> (*The* MINISTER OF COMMERCE *gets up.*)

MINISTER OF COMMERCE: I wish to discuss the tariff.

FIREFLY: Sit down. That's new business. No old business? Very well
. . . (*He bangs the gavel*) . . . then we'll take up new business.
> (*The* MINISTER OF COMMERCE *gets up again.*)

MINISTER OF COMMERCE: Now, about that tariff.
> (FIREFLY *and* BOB *are seen from above, with the ministers in the foreground.*)

FIREFLY: Too late. That's old business already. Sit down.
> (*The* MINISTER OF WAR *gets up.*)

MINISTER OF WAR: Gentlemen, as your Secretary of War, I . . .

FIREFLY: The Secretary of War is out of order . . .
> (*A closer shot of* FIREFLY *and* BOB.)

Which reminds me, so is the plumbing. (*To* BOB) Make a note of that . . . Never mind, I'll do it myself.
> (*He picks up a long, wavy quill and starts to write.*)

MINISTER OF LABOUR: (*Off*) The Department of Labour wishes to report that . . .
> (*Cut to include the ministers again.*)
> (*Standing*) . . . the workers of Freedonia are demanding shorter hours.

FIREFLY: Very well, we'll give them shorter hours. We'll start by cutting their lunch hour to twenty minutes. And now,

gentlemen, we've got to start looking for a new Treasurer.
(*The* MINISTER OF LABOUR *sits down, bewildered.*)
ANOTHER MINISTER: (*Getting up*) But you appointed one last
week.
FIREFLY: That's the one I'm looking for.
(*A reverse shot down the table shows the ministers facing camera.*)
MINISTER OF WAR: (*Rising*) Gentlemen! Gentlemen! Enough of
this. How about taking up the tax?
(*Resume on* FIREFLY *and* BOB.)
FIREFLY: (*Removing his cigar*) How about taking up the carpet?
(*He puts his feet up on the desk.*)
(*We see the* MINISTER OF WAR *again, standing, with some other
ministers sitting behind.*)
MINISTER OF WAR: I still insist we must take up the tax.
(*Back to* FIREFLY *and* BOB.)
FIREFLY: (*Leaning towards* BOB) He's right. You've got to take up
the tacks before you can take up the carpet.
(*The ministers are seen from a high angle.*)
MINISTER OF WAR: I give all my time and energy to my duties and
what do I get?
(*Close-up of* FIREFLY.)
FIREFLY: You get awfully tiresome after a while.
(*A closer shot of the* MINISTER OF WAR.)
MINISTER OF WAR: Sir, you try my patience!
(*Back to* FIREFLY *and* BOB. FIREFLY *gets up and leans
forward.*)
FIREFLY: I don't mind if you do. You must come over and try mine
some time.
(*We see the* MINISTER OF WAR *again.*)
MINISTER OF WAR: (*Waving his arms*) That's the last straw! I
resign. I wash my hands of the whole business.
(*In a shot of the scene, the* MINISTER OF WAR *exits in
indignation.*)
FIREFLY: A good idea. You can wash your neck, too.
(*Fade out.*)

Fade in to the street outside the Chamber of Deputies, where
CHICOLINI *is seen by a peanut stand on a barrow.*

CHICOLINI: Peanuts!

(PINKY *enters from the left, and we cut to medium close-up as he comes up behind the cart and starts stuffing his pockets full of peanuts.* CHICOLINI *turns to face camera, daubing mustard on a frankfurter.*

As CHICOLINI *is about to put the frankfurter in his mouth,* PINKY *snips the end off with his scissors.*

CHICOLINI *throws away the frankfurter in disgust, seen in the medium close-up again.*

Hey, come here. (*He pushes* PINKY.)

(*Shot of the scene.*)

Just the guy I want to see. What do you find out about this guy, Firefly? You find outa something? You no find out something? You spy on him? You no spy on him?

(PINKY *gives him his leg.* CHICOLINI *thrusts it aside, then we cut in on the two of them.*)

What's-a matter? All the time I talk to you, you no say nothin'. What's-a matter you no speak?

(PINKY *puts a peanut in his mouth. He crunches the shell and splutters.*)

Stop it! Whata you find? Eh? Whata you find?

(PINKY *produces a handful of peanuts;* CHICOLINI *knocks them out of his hand.*)

'At's-a no good.

(*A longer shot includes a* LEMONADE VENDOR *standing by his cart on the right.*)

(*Pushing* PINKY) Hey, come here. You acta crazy, what's-a matter for you? What you make da face like this? (*He grabs* PINKY's *face and shakes it.*) What's-a matter for you?

(PINKY *gets angry. In a closer shot of the group, he aims at* CHICOLINI *with one fist and starts swinging the other.*)

Aw, come on, you wanna fight? You wanna fight? Come on, I give you fight.

(*Back to the scene as the* VENDOR *watches between the other two while* CHICOLINI *swings back his fist.*)

Come on. I give you fight. Come on.

(PINKY *kicks him in the pants, and we cut back to the closer shot again.*)

(Angry) Hey, upstairs this time, no downstairs.
(PINKY takes aim and starts swinging his fist again.
Resume on the scene as the VENDOR turns to serve a customer in the background.)
Come on.
(PINKY kicks him in the pants again. CHICOLINI pushes him angrily back into the customer.)
What you think you are, eh?
(PINKY thrusts his hand into the customer's pocket.
A closer shot excludes CHICOLINI as the customer turns in amazement, then wrestles free and goes off leaving PINKY with his handkerchief. He comes back and grabs the handkerchief, then goes off again indignantly. The VENDOR, who has been watching curiously, now finds PINKY's hand in his pocket. He slaps the hand away as CHICOLINI appears in the background.
Back to the scene again.)

VENDOR: *(Angrily)* Hey, what's the idea of fightin' in front of my place and driving my customers away?
(PINKY sits down on the wheel of the VENDOR's cart.)

CHICOLINI: Hey, mister, you got a mistake some place. I no fight.
(Seen in a closer shot again, PINKY produces his scissors and snips off the VENDOR's pocket which is still hanging out of his trousers. The VENDOR does not notice.)
You understand? This guy he's-a working for me. I ask him something and he no tell me nothing. I ask him why he no speak, and alla time he no speak.
(PINKY starts happily filling the amputated pocket with peanuts.)
And what do you think he do? He make a fight and go like-a dis. *(He kicks the VENDOR in the pants.)*
(Camera pans, excluding PINKY.)

VENDOR: Hey, what's the idea?

CHICOLINI: Aw, 'at's-a not my idea, 'at's his idea. Alla time I say something he no say nothing. Every time I speak . . .

VENDOR: Will you shut up?
(Resume on the group. The VENDOR turns back to PINKY.)
Say, listen, what are you doing around here?
(PINKY leans against him, sounding one of the horns which is stuck in his belt.

Shot of PINKY *and the* VENDOR.)
(*Pushing him away*) Who are you?
(PINKY *leans against him again. Sound of horn.*)
Hey, can't you say . . .
(*Two horns sound.*)
(*Pushing him away*) Can't you say anything?
(*Back to the group.*)
CHICOLINI: No, he no say nothin'. He . . .
VENDOR: Aw, shut up!
CHICOLINI: I am shut up, but Mister . . .
(*A closer shot of all three.*)
. . . you no understand. Look, he's a spy and I'm a spy. He works for me. I want him to find out something, but he no find out what I want to find out . . .
(*The* VENDOR *runs his hand wearily over his face.*)
Now, how am I gonna find out what I want to find out if he don't find out what I gotta find out?
VENDOR: (*Desperate*) Will you quit annoying me?
CHICOLINI: All right, I quit.
(*Shot of the scene.*)
All you gotta do is to make him stop doing this.
(*He kicks the* VENDOR *in the pants.*)
VENDOR: Ugh! Ohhh!
(*He clutches the air behind him and* PINKY *gives him his leg. We see the three of them in medium close-up.*)
(*Advancing on* PINKY) Now, just for that I'm gonna tear you limb from limb, limb . . . Ugh!
(*He advances on* PINKY, *hands clawing the air;* PINKY *grabs his hand and starts shaking it violently, grinning from ear to ear. Both their hats fall off.*
Back to the scene as they both bend down and reach for their hats. The VENDOR *grunts.*
They put on their hats and the VENDOR *turns grimly to* CHICOLINI.)
In fact I'll do the same . . .
(CHICOLINI *points dumbly at the grinning* PINKY – *they have on the wrong hats. The* VENDOR *takes off* PINKY's *hat with a sigh, hands it to* PINKY *and reaches for his own.* PINKY *drops it*

on the ground.
Resume on the scene: PINKY *and* CHICOLINI *watch as the*
VENDOR *bends to pick up his hat. Then we cut back to the closer*
shot again.)
Ohhh!
(*As* CHICOLINI *addresses him, the* VENDOR *puts on his hat;*
PINKY *standing behind him, swaps it neatly for his own, which*
he puts on the VENDOR's *head.*)
CHICOLINI: Now, you see, I no say one thing, mister, before
   when you . . .
VENDOR: No! . . . (*He breathes heavily, and clutches the air*
   desperately.)
CHICOLINI: No, I no say . . .
   (*The* VENDOR's *groping hand finds* PINKY's *leg again; he thrusts*
   aside the leg, whips off his hat in a rage and finds it's the wrong one.)
VENDOR: Doh!
   (*He throws down the hat and reaches for his own;* PINKY *takes it*
   off and throws it on the ground.
   In another medium shot, the VENDOR *bends down to retrieve his*
   hat; PINKY *kicks it across to* CHICOLINI. *The* VENDOR *goes*
   after it and CHICOLINI *kicks it back to* PINKY, *who picks it up.*
   PINKY *brushes off the hat with an indignant expression.*
   Resume on the scene. PINKY *holds out the hat and the* VENDOR
   reaches for it. PINKY *drops it on an elastic and it goes up and*
   down like a yo-yo. Breathing heavily, the VENDOR *reaches for*
   the hat again and catches it. PINKY *puts his foot in the hat as it*
   hangs from the VENDOR's *hand. The* VENDOR *whips it away but*
   PINKY *knocks it to the ground again.* CHICOLINI *picks it up and*
   puts it on top of his own, while the VENDOR *reaches for* PINKY,
   who makes a 'pax' sign with both hands. The VENDOR *bends*
   down for his hat, can't find it, mops his brow, then finds it's on
   CHICOLINI. PINKY *puts on his own hat.*
   In a closer shot again the VENDOR *grabs his hat from*
   CHICOLINI *and puts it on with* CHICOLINI's *underneath.*
   PINKY *gives* CHICOLINI *his hat and takes the* VENDOR's,
   leaving the VENDOR *with* CHICOLINI's. *The* VENDOR, *who has*
   not noticed this last manoeuvre, looks from PINKY *to* CHICOLINI
   in bewilderment. PINKY *makes a crease in the* VENDOR's *hat,*

puts it on again, and sticks out his tongue, goggle-eyed. The
VENDOR *turns back to him and gets a fright.*
Back to the scene as the hat business continues. The hats get
passed round and round until the VENDOR *ends up with his own.*
He then finds he's holding PINKY's *leg, then* CHICOLINI's.)
(*Spluttering*) Aw now, now, I'm goin' to get you . . .
(*He chases* CHICOLINI *off while* PINKY *pulls out his horn.*
PINKY *is seen siphoning lemonade into the horn from the vat on*
the VENDOR's *cart, then we cut to a longer shot as he puts the*
horn back in his belt. The VENDOR *reappears.*)
What are you doin'?
(*Seen in the closer shot,* PINKY *leans against the* VENDOR *and*
the horn squirts lemonade in his face.)
Aw!
(*Another shot of the two of them.*)
(*Going for* PINKY) Why, you . . .
(PINKY *leans against him again. Sound of the horn. The*
VENDOR *splutters in the shower of lemonade, then starts roaring*
with laughter.
Back to the scene as PINKY *joins in, shaking with silent laughter,*
then cut back to the two of them. While PINKY *laughs with his*
head thrown back, the VENDOR *grabs the horn and squirts*
lemonade down inside his trousers. He goes off as the smile freezes
on PINKY's *face.*
PINKY *shifts uncomfortably from one leg to the other, then goes*
off whistling, with a pained expression.
We now see CHICOLINI *by the peanut stand, as the* VENDOR
rushes up to him.)
I'll teach you to kick me!
CHICOLINI: You don't have to teach me. I know how.
(*He kicks the* VENDOR, *whose hat flies off.* PINKY *enters from*
the right and catches it.)
VENDOR: Ohhh!
(*He grabs* CHICOLINI *and shakes him, while* PINKY *puts his hat*
over the flame in the warming cabinet on the peanut cart.
Shot of PINKY *and the hat as it bursts into flames. Camera pans*
to include the VENDOR, *who is throttling* CHICOLINI.)
CHICOLINI: (*Off*) Stop it now. Look out!

(PINKY *whistles and taps the* VENDOR *on the back; he turns and sees the hat.*
Shot of the scene. The VENDOR *runs his hands over his head and groans, while* PINKY *points at the burning hat, grinning.*)
Oh, 'at's-a good, eh?
(*Fade out.*)

Fade in to the same street from a low angle, with CHICOLINI *and his peanut stand. Two girls pass across the scene.*

CHICOLINI: (*Shouting*) Peanuts!
(FIREFLY *appears on the balcony in the background.*)
FIREFLY: Hey!
(CHICOLINI *throws him up a bag of peanuts, and we cut to a low-angle shot of him leaning on the balcony.*)
Do you want to be a public nuisance?
(*Reverse shot of* CHICOLINI *from* FIREFLY'*s point of view.*)
CHICOLINI: (*Looking up*) Sure. How much does the job pay?
(*Back to* FIREFLY.)
FIREFLY: I've got a good mind to join a club and beat you over the head with it.
(*Resume on* CHICOLINI.)
CHICOLINI: (*Shouting*) Peanuts . . . to you!
(*Camera on* FIREFLY *again.*)
FIREFLY: Have you got a licence?
CHICOLINI: Licence? . . .
(*Resume on him; he points to a dog sitting on the ground behind him.*)
No, but my dog – he's-a got millions of 'em. Believe me, he's some smart dog. You know, he went with Admiral Byrd to the pole?
(*Another shot of* FIREFLY.)
FIREFLY: I'll bet the dog got to the pole first.
(*Back to* CHICOLINI.)
CHICOLINI: You win!
(FIREFLY *beckons.*)
FIREFLY: Come on up here. I want to scare the cabinet.
(*In a long shot of the scene,* FIREFLY *leaves the balcony.*)

Dissolve to the interior of the Chamber of Deputies, where FIREFLY *and* CHICOLINI *approach the former's desk from either side as a phone rings.* CHICOLINI *rushes to answer it.*

CHICOLINI: Hello. Hello. No. No, he's not in. All right, I'll tell him. Goodbye.
  (*The two of them are seen in medium close-up.*)
  That was for you.
FIREFLY: (*Shelling a peanut*) I'm sorry I'm not in. I wanted to have a long talk with you. (*He sits down.*) Now listen here. You give up that silly peanut stand and I'll get you a soft government job. Now, let's see . . .
  (*A longer shot of the two of them.*)
  (*Getting up again*) How would you like a job in the mint?
CHICOLINI: (*Reflecting*) Mint? No, no, I no like-a-mint. Uh . . . what other flavour you got?
  (*The phone rings and* CHICOLINI *beats* FIREFLY *to it again.*)
  Hello, hello.
  (*They are seen in a closer shot.*)
  (*Into the phone*) No, not yet. All right, I tell him. Goodbye, thank you. (*To* FIREFLY) That was for you again.
FIREFLY: I wonder whatever became of me . . .
  (*Shot of the scene as* FIREFLY *searches round the desk.*)
  I should have been back here a long time ago. Now, listen here. I've got a swell job for you . . . (*He climbs on to his presidential chair.*) . . . but first I'll have to ask you a couple of . . .
  (*Back to medium close-up.*)
  . . . important questions. (*He perches on the back of the chair.*) Now, what is it that has four pairs of pants, lives in Philadelphia, and it never rains but it pours? (*He leers at camera.*)
CHICOLINI: 'At's-a good one. I give you three guesses.
FIREFLY: Now lemme see. Has four pair of pants, lives in Philadelphia. Is it male or female?
CHICOLINI: No, I don't think so.
FIREFLY: Is he dead?
CHICOLINI: Who?

FIREFLY: I don't know. I give up.

> (*He gets down from the chair, puffing on his cigar.*)

CHICOLINI: I give up, too. Now, I ask you another one. What is
it got a big black moustache, smokes a big black cigar and is
a big pain in the neck?

FIREFLY: Now, don't tell me. (*Pondering*) Has a big black
moustache, smokes a big black cigar and is a big pain in
the . . .

> (*The penny drops.*)

CHICOLINI: Uh . . .

FIREFLY: (*Turning to* CHICOLINI) Does he wear glasses?

CHICOLINI: (*Laughing*) 'At's-a right. You guess it quick.

FIREFLY: Just for that you don't get the job I was going to give
you.

CHICOLINI: What job?

FIREFLY: Secretary of War.

CHICOLINI: All right, I take it.

FIREFLY: Sold!

> (*They shake hands. At that moment the phone rings again.*
> *Shot of the scene as they both dive for the phone.* PINKY *enters in*
> *the background and beats them to it.*
> *In a closer shot of the three of them,* PINKY *answers the phone*
> *and carries on a conversation, using his horns. He asks a*
> *question.*
> *Cut to exclude the others.* PINKY *shakes his head, asks another*
> *question, laughs, then growls and slams down the phone*
> *indignantly.*
> *Resume on the group as* PINKY *whistles and gestures to*
> FIREFLY, *indicating the call was for him.*)

You know, I'd be lost without a telephone.

> (PINKY *gestures as if to say 'Don't mention it', and turns to go,*
> *but* FIREFLY *stops him.*)

Hey, don't go away. I want to talk to you. (*To* CHICOLINI)
Now, where were we? Oh, yes.

> (*Camera pans as he conducts* CHICOLINI *to the door.*)

Now that you're Secretary of War, what kind of an army do
you think we ought to have?

> (*We see the two of them at the door.*)

CHICOLINI: Well, I tell you what I think. I think we should have a standing army.

    (*Resume on* PINKY. *He sits at* FIREFLY's *desk and starts writing with the quill. The long plume tickles his nose.*)

FIREFLY: (*Off*) Why should we have a standing army?

    (*Resume on him and* CHICOLINI.)

CHICOLINI: Because then we save money on chairs.

    (FIREFLY *exits with* CHICOLINI *and boots him downstairs, off-screen; there is a loud crash;* FIREFLY *reappears.*)

FIREFLY: Peanuts!

    (*Camera tracks with him as he comes back to* PINKY, *humming, and we cut in on the two of them.*)

Scat!

    (*He takes* PINKY's *place at the desk and starts writing.* PINKY *snips the top off the plume with his scissors.*)

    (*Looking up*) Say, who are you, anyway?

    (PINKY *pulls up his coat sleeve, and we see . . .*

    PINKY's *face tattooed on his arm.*

    Resume on PINKY *and* FIREFLY.)

I don't go in much for modern art. Have you got anything by one of the old masters?

    (PINKY *pulls up his other sleeve; oriental music is heard.*

    Close-up of a girl tattooed on his arm. She does a belly dance in time to the music as PINKY *flexes his muscles.*)

    (*Off*) Not bad!

    (*The music stops, and we resume on* PINKY *and* FIREFLY.)

You don't happen to have her telephone number?

    (PINKY *drops his collection of horns and pulls up his shirt.*

    FIREFLY *copies the number off* PINKY's *side, seen in a medium shot.*)

Say, you could be a big help to me. Where do you live?

    (PINKY *starts to pull open his shirt.*

    A closer shot of the two of them as PINKY *displays a picture of a dog kennel tattooed on his chest.* FIREFLY *leans forward to look.*)

Well, it's not much of a place, but it's home.

    PINKY *beckons him closer, and he leans forward.*)

Meow!

(*A dog's head appears at the kennel door, seen in close-up, and barks loudly.*

Resume on PINKY *and* FIREFLY, *who leap back in alarm.*)

(*Recovering*) Well, I know one thing. I bet you haven't got a picture of my grandfather.

(PINKY *takes off his coat, bends over and starts to pull out his shirt.*)

(*Restraining him*) Ah-ah! Not now. Some other time.

(*Seen in close-up*, PINKY *picks up his collection of horns.*

Camera pans with him to the door, where he exits with a merry wave.

We look towards the doorway as BOB *enters, reaches up to take off his hat and finds it has been cut in half; he throws it out of the door.*

Camera pans as he moves across to FIREFLY.)

BOB: (*Loudly*) Your Excellency.

(FIREFLY *leaps up with a start and salutes, then bangs the gavel on his desk.*)

FIREFLY: Quiet!

(*Shot of him and* BOB, *who puts a letter on the desk.*)

BOB: This letter is the work of Trentino. The man is trying to undermine you. Now, what are you going to do about it?

(FIREFLY *picks up the letter.*)

FIREFLY: I've got a good mind to ring his doorbell and run.

BOB: We've got to get rid of that man at once. Now, I've got a plan. You say something to make him mad, and he'll strike you . . . (*He bangs his fist in his palm.*) . . . and we'll force him to leave the country. (*He walks round behind* FIREFLY's *chair.*)

FIREFLY: That's a swell plan. Why couldn't you arrange for me to strike him?

(*We see the two of them facing one another across the chair.*)

BOB: Ambassador Trentino is a very sensitive man. Perhaps if you insult him – he's very easy to insult. Why, I said something to Vera Marcal in his presence once and he slapped my face.

FIREFLY: Why didn't Vera slap your face?

BOB: She did.

FIREFLY: What'd you say to her?

(BOB *leans forward and whispers in* FIREFLY's *ear.* FIREFLY *slaps his face.*)

You ought to be ashamed of yourself! Where did you hear
that story?

BOB: Why, you told it to me.

FIREFLY: Oh, yes. I remember. I should have slapped Mrs
Teasdale's face when she told it to me. Where is Trentino?

BOB: At Mrs Teasdale's tea party.

FIREFLY: Was I invited?

BOB: No.

FIREFLY: Take a letter.

*(In a medium shot of the two of them, BOB sits at the desk while
FIREFLY paces to and fro, dictating.)*

(Clearing his throat) 'You are cordially invited to attend my
tea party.' Er . . . sign Mrs Teasdale's name and tell her I
accept. Come on, let's go.

(They make for the door.)

*Outside the palace, camera pans with PINKY as he drives up on the
presidential motorcycle and halts at the bottom of the steps with a
squeal of brakes.*
*A closer shot, with PINKY in the foreground. The trumpeters step
forward in the background and sound a fanfare, as FIREFLY comes
out of the palace and down the steps.*

FIREFLY: I've got an appointment to insult Ambassador Trentino
and I don't want to keep him waiting. Step on it! . . .

*(As he climbs into the side-car, PINKY roars off on the
motorcycle, leaving him standing.)*

(Chin on fist) This is the fifth trip I've made today and I
haven't been anywhere yet.

(Fade out.)

*Fade in to the grounds of MRS TEASDALE's residence. Elegantly
dressed guests are wandering to and fro. In the foreground,
TRENTINO is sitting at a table with a sunshade. There is gay music as
VERA approaches from the background, and we cut to a closer shot as
she comes up some steps behind TRENTINO.*
She sits down at the table.

VERA: You don't seem to be making much progress with Mrs Teasdale, huh?

TRENTINO: (*Despairing*) How can I? Every time I get her in the right mood to say 'Yes', Firefly pops in.

VERA: Well, this is your opportunity. He won't be here today.

TRENTINO: Are you sure?

VERA: Positive. I helped Mrs Teasdale with the . . . invitations.

(*She makes the motions of tearing an invitation up and throwing it away.*)

TRENTINO: Oh!

(*We look towards the end of the garden as a* LACKEY *appears at the top of some steps.*)

LACKEY: His Excellency . . .

(*Shot of the lawn with the guests sitting at umbrella tables laid out on either side.*)

(*Off*) . . . Rufus T. Firefly!

(*Music as the guests all rise and sing.*)

GUESTS: Hail . . .

(FIREFLY *appears at the end of the garden and comes past the* LACKEY.)

(*Singing, off*) . . . hail, Freedonia!

(*Seen from above,* FIREFLY *passes one of the tables. He picks up a doughnut from a guest's plate and walks on, camera tracking ahead of him.*)

(*Singing*) Land of the brave . . .

(FIREFLY's *hand dunks the doughnut in someone's coffee.*)

(*Singing, off*) . . . and . . .

(*Resume on* FIREFLY *and the guests. Camera tracks on again as he walks forward, eating the doughnut.*)

(*Singing*) . . . free!

(*The music ends.*

We now see TRENTINO, *seated alone with* MRS TEASDALE *in a corner of the garden.*

Resume on the guests as FIREFLY *goes off in the foreground.*

TRENTINO *meanwhile clasps* MRS TEASDALE's *hand.*)

TRENTINO: Gloria, I've waited for years. I can't be put off any longer. I love you! I want you! Can't you see I'm at your feet? (*He goes down on one knee.*)

(*They are seen in a medium shot as* FIREFLY *enters behind* TRENTINO.)

FIREFLY: When you get through with her feet, you can start on mine!

(TRENTINO *turns with a sigh, and we cut in on the group.*)

If that isn't an insult, I don't know what is! Gloria, I love you!

(*He dives for* MRS TEASDALE, *knocking* TRENTINO *out of the way.*

In a closer shot, FIREFLY *pushes* TRENTINO *off and kneels at* MRS TEASDALE's *feet.*)

I realize how lonely you are . . .

(*Cut to include* TRENTINO *again.*)

TRENTINO: (*To* MRS TEASDALE) Can't we go some place where we can be by ourselves?

FIREFLY: (*Pointing at* TRENTINO) What can this mug offer you? Wealth and family?

(*Resume on just the two of them.*)

I can't give you wealth, but – uh – we can have a little family of our own.

MRS TEASDALE: (*Melting*) Oh, Rufus!

FIREFLY: All I can offer you is a roofus over your head.

MRS TEASDALE: Your Excellency, I really don't know what to say.

FIREFLY: I wouldn't know what to say either if I was in your place.

(*We see* TRENTINO *again as* FIREFLY *turns towards him.*)

Maybe you can suggest something. As a matter of fact, you do suggest something. (*He stands on the bench.*) To me you suggest a baboon.

TRENTINO: What?

(*The group is seen from below.*)

FIREFLY: (*Standing over* TRENTINO) I . . . I'm sorry I said that. It isn't fair to the rest of the baboons.

TRENTINO: (*Furious*) This man's conduct is inexcusable. Why I'll . . .

MRS TEASDALE: Oh, gentlemen, gentlemen!

TRENTINO: I did not come here to be insulted!

(*He starts out and* FIREFLY *goes after him.*)

MRS TEASDALE: Oh!

(*Camera tracks with* TRENTINO *as he strides across the garden, pursued by* FIREFLY. *The guests gather round in the background.*)

FIREFLY: That's what you think!

TRENTINO: You swine!

FIREFLY: Come again?

TRENTINO: You worm!

FIREFLY: Once more?

TRENTINO: You upstart!

(MRS TEASDALE *enters.*)

FIREFLY: That's it!

(*He slaps* TRENTINO's *face with his gloves;* MRS TEASDALE *gasps.*)

Touché! (*He hands* TRENTINO *his card.*)

MRS TEASDALE: Oh!

TRENTINO: (*Tearing up the card*) Mrs Teasdale, I'm afraid this regrettable occurrence may plunge our countries into war.

(FIREFLY *starts fencing with* MRS TEASDALE's *parasol.*)

MRS TEASDALE: Oh, this is terrible!

TRENTINO: I've said enough. I'm a man of few words.

FIREFLY: I'm a man of one word. Scram!

(TRENTINO *exits.*)

The man doesn't live who can call a Firefly an upstart. Why, the *Mayflower* was full of Fireflys, and a few horseflies, too. The Fireflys were on the upper deck and the horseflies were on the Fireflys. (*He kisses* MRS TEASDALE's *hand.*) Good day, my sweet.

(*He starts out, but she grabs him.*)

MRS TEASDALE: Oh, Your Excellency, I must speak to you!

FIREFLY: I'll see you at the theatre tonight. I'll hold your seat till you get there. After you get there, you're on your own.

LACKEY: (*Off*) His Excellency's car!

FIREFLY: (*Shouting*) His Excellency's car.

(*He tucks* MRS TEASDALE's *parasol under his arm and goes off. At the entrance to the garden,* PINKY *is on the motorcycle, saluting; the motor is running.* FIREFLY *enters from the right.*

Shot of the two of them as PINKY *gestures* FIREFLY *into the side-car.*)
Oh, no, you don't! I'm not taking any more chances. You can only fool a Firefly twice. This time you ride in the side-car.
(PINKY *gets into the side-car, grinning, while* FIREFLY *climbs on to the motorcycle. The engine revs and he leans forward to take the acceleration.*
Resume on the scene as PINKY *roars off in the side-car, leaving the motorcycle standing.*
A reverse shot shows PINKY *speeding up the drive, leaving* FIREFLY *in the foreground; then we cut back to* FIREFLY *leaning forward on the motorcycle. He sighs.*)
This is the only way to travel!
(*Fade out.*)

Fade in to the street where CHICOLINI *has his peanut stand. We see* CHICOLINI *and his dog, then* PINKY *enters in the background.*

CHICOLINI: Hey, Pinky! Come here. Watcha the stand. (*To the dog*) Come on, Pastrom. Come on, come on.
(*He goes off with the dog, while the* LEMONADE VENDOR *comes up and stands by the peanut cart; he is now wearing a straw boater instead of the bowler he had earlier.*
Shot of PINKY *and the* VENDOR, *who is eating peanuts.* PINKY *holds his hand out for some; the* VENDOR *daubs it with mustard, then goes on impassively eating.* PINKY *looks at his hand in disgust, then grins and wipes it on the* VENDOR's *sash. He cuts off the sash with his scissors, throws it aside, and slaps the bag of peanuts from the* VENDOR's *hand. Unruffled, the* VENDOR *picks up another bag from the stand and opens it.* PINKY *begs for a nut; the* VENDOR *looks at him stonily.* PINKY *looks up at the sky; the* VENDOR *does likewise, and* PINKY *slaps the bag from his hand.*
Back to the scene: the VENDOR *begins to get angry as* PINKY *gathers an armful of peanut bags from the cart. He dashes them to the ground, losing his hat, which* PINKY *hides behind his back. The* VENDOR *bends down, searching on the ground, and* PINKY

puts the hat on the flame in the glass cabinet. Then he whistles and taps the VENDOR *on the back.*

The VENDOR *turns as* PINKY *whistles, and sees his hat in flames.)*

VENDOR: (*In despair*) Oooooooh!

(*Resume on the scene as he turns the peanut cart over with a crash.*)

Huh!

(*He exits, satisfied, dusting off his hands.*

We now see him at his lemonade stand, where a queue of customers in Ruritanian dress are waiting to be served. As he starts serving them with a ladle, PINKY *comes up behind him with his trousers rolled up, climbs into the vat of lemonade and paddles in it gleefully with his bare feet. The customers leave in disgust, watched by the bewildered* VENDOR.

In a medium close-up, the VENDOR *turns and sees the grinning* PINKY *in the vat. He groans and clutches his head. Fade out.*)

Fade in to the drawing room of MRS TEASDALE'*s residence.*
VERA *is seated in an armchair with* TRENTINO *standing beside her as* MRS TEASDALE *approaches from the background.*

TRENTINO: Mrs Teasdale. (*He kisses her hand.*) I deeply regret the unfortunate affair with His Excellency, but his attitude left me no alternative.

VERA: Maybe we can still avoid this terrible war.

MRS TEASDALE: Oh, if we only could!

VERA: Oh, yes . . .

(*Cut to exclude her as she finishes.*)

(*Off*) . . . I'll do my best.

(MRS TEASDALE *stands wringing her hands.*)

TRENTINO: Er . . . Mrs Teasdale, I have been recalled by my President.

(*She turns to him in alarm.*)

MRS TEASDALE: Then it is too late?

TRENTINO: Not if His Excellency will listen to reason. I am prepared to pocket my pride and forget about the whole matter, if he is.

MRS TEASDALE: Ambassador, that's wonderful of you, but I'm
    afraid His Excellency won't hear of it.
    (*Shot of* VERA.)

VERA: Oh, perhaps he will listen to you.
    (*Resume on all three.*)

MRS TEASDALE: Do you think so?

VERA: Yes, of course.

MRS TEASDALE: I'll call him. (*She starts off.*)

VERA: Oh!
    (*We move to* FIREFLY's *bedroom, where camera shows some
    crackers strewn on the bed, then pans along to* FIREFLY, *in
    nightshirt and cap, lying in bed eating crackers. The telephone
    rings and he lifts the receiver.
    Back in* MRS TEASDALE's *drawing room, camera tracks in on
    her as she speaks into the phone.*)

MRS TEASDALE: I hate to disturb you. I know you're a very busy
    man, but I must see you at once.
    (*Resume on* FIREFLY.)

FIREFLY: Where are you? Oh! Why not come over here? You can
    come in the back way and no one'll see you. (*A pause.*) Well,
    if you think of it, bring some cheese.
    (*Back to* MRS TEASDALE.)

MRS TEASDALE: But, Your Excellency, you must come over. It's
    a long story. I can't tell it to you over the phone.
    (FIREFLY *replies.*)

FIREFLY: Oh, it's that kind of a story! You ought to be ashamed
    of yourself. I'll be right over. (*He hangs up.*)
    (*Back in the drawing room, we see* VERA *and* TRENTINO.)

MRS TEASDALE: (*Off*) He'll be right over. (*She enters.*) Perhaps
    you'd better wait outside until I've had a chance to talk to
    him.

TRENTINO: Very well. We'll be out of here if you want us.
    (MRS TEASDALE *goes off, while* TRENTINO *takes* VERA's *arm
    and leads her towards the garden in the background.
    Dissolve to the drawing room a little while later.* MRS TEASDALE
    is pacing up and down in agitation. FIREFLY enters unnoticed
    and follows her up and down. Then he sits down in a chair, and
    camera tracks in as she turns and notices him.*)

MRS TEASDALE: Oh!

FIREFLY: How'd you get in here?

MRS TEASDALE: (*Standing over him*) Oh, Your Excellency, I'm so
sorry to have to disturb you. Will you ever forgive me?

FIREFLY: After I leave here tonight, will you ever forgive me? (*He
gets up and hands her an envelope.*) Here are the plans of war.
(*Shot of the two of them.*)
They're as valuable as your life, and that's putting 'em pretty
cheap. Watch them like a cat watches her kittens. Have you
ever had kittens? No, of course not. You're too busy running
around playing bridge. Can't you see what I'm trying to tell
you? (*He puts his arms round her.*) I love you. Why don't you
marry me?

MRS TEASDALE: Why, marry you?

FIREFLY: You take me and I'll take a vacation. I'll need a vacation
if we're going to get married.
(*They stand in a romantic pose, holding hands.*)
Married! I can see you right now in the kitchen, bending
over a hot stove, but I can't see the stove. Come, come, say
the word and you'll never see. . . .
(*Cut to medium shot as they sit down on the sofa.*)
. . . me again . . . Gloria!
(*Then a closer shot as he puts his arms round her.*)

MRS TEASDALE: (*With a happy smile*) Rufus, what are you
thinking of?

FIREFLY: (*Gazing into space*) Oh, I was just thinking of all the
years I wasted collecting stamps.
(*He draws her closer and she laughs.*
We see them in medium close-up as FIREFLY *sits forward.*
(*Bashfully*) Oh . . . er . . . I suppose you'll think me a
sentimental old fluff, but . . . er . . . would you mind giving
me a lock of your hair?

MRS TEASDALE: A lock of my hair? (*She laughs coyly.*) Why, I had
no idea . . .

FIREFLY: I'm letting you off easy. I was going to ask for the whole
wig.
(*We see* VERA *and* TRENTINO *coming in from the garden.*
Then return to FIREFLY *and* MRS TEASDALE – FIREFLY *is*

*sitting on her lap. He sees the others approaching, rises and strides
off.*

Resume on VERA *and* TRENTINO *as* FIREFLY *comes up to them,
followed by* MRS TEASDALE.)

So you've come to ask for clemency.

(MRS TEASDALE *takes him aside.*)

MRS TEASDALE: Your Excellency, the Ambassador's here on a
friendly visit.

(*A closer shot of the four of them.*)

He's had a change of heart.

FIREFLY: A lot of good that'll do him. He's still got the same face.

(TRENTINO *looks indignant and* MRS TEASDALE *sighs.*)

TRENTINO: I'm sorry we lost our tempers. I'm willing to forget if
you are.

FIREFLY: Forget? You ask me to forget? A Firefly never forgets.
Why, my ancestors would rise from their graves and I would
only have to bury them again. Nothing doing. I'm going
back to clean the crackers out of my bed. I'm expecting
company.

(*In a longer shot of the group, he starts to leave, but* MRS
TEASDALE *grabs him by the shoulder.*)

MRS TEASDALE: Please wait!

FIREFLY: Let go of me, you bully! (*He aims a mock punch at her.*)

MRS TEASDALE: Oh!

(FIREFLY *bows stiffly to* TRENTINO, *then we cut back to the
closer shot.*)

TRENTINO: (*Arms folded*) I am willing to do anything to prevent
this war.

FIREFLY: It's too late. I've already paid a month's rent on the
battlefield.

(VERA *comes round and lays a hand on his chest.*)

VERA: Oh, Your Excellency, isn't there something I can do?

FIREFLY: Yes, but I'll talk to you about that later.

MRS TEASDALE: Won't you reconsider? Please relent for my sake.

FIREFLY: Well, maybe I am a little headstrong, but I came by it
honestly. My father was a little headstrong. My mother was a
little Armstrong. The Headstrongs married the Armstrongs
and that's why darkies were born. Heh! (*He sits on the arm of*

a chair; jovially) It was silly of me to lose my temper on
account of that little thing you called me.
(*The group is seen from another angle.*)
TRENTINO: (*Good naturedly*) Little thing I called you? Why, what
did I call you?
FIREFLY: (*With a laugh*) Gosh, I don't even remember what it
was.
(*They all laugh.*)
TRENTINO: Well, do you mean worm?
FIREFLY: No, that wasn't it.
TRENTINO: I know. Swine.
FIREFLY: Huh-uh. No, it was a seven-letter word.
TRENTINO: (*Suddenly remembering*) Oh, yes. Upstart.
FIREFLY: That's it! Upstart!
(*He gets up angrily and slaps* TRENTINO *with his glove.*)
MRS TEASDALE: Oh, please, please!
TRENTINO: Mrs Teasdale, this man is impossible! This is an
outrage. My course is clear. This means war!
MRS TEASDALE: Oh!
TRENTINO: You runt!
FIREFLY: I still like upstart the best.
TRENTINO: I shan't stay here a minute longer.
FIREFLY: Go, and never darken my towels again!
MRS TEASDALE: Oh!
TRENTINO: My hat!
FIREFLY: My towels! (*He exits in the background.*)
MRS TEASDALE: Oh!
(*Fade out.*)

Fade in to TRENTINO's *study.* TRENTINO *is surrounded by
Sylvanian ministers and diplomats.*

TRENTINO: I happen to know that Freedonia's plans of war are in
Mrs Teasdale's possession. I must get hold of them.
AN ATTACHE: Yes, but how?
TRENTINO: We have a weekend guest in Mrs Teasdale's house –
Miss Marcal. Now, gentlemen, do you mind waiting for me
outside? I'll join you in a moment.

ATTACHE: Certainly.

>*(They bow and exit, camera panning away from them as* TRENTINO *picks up the telephone.*
>
>*In* MRS TEASDALE's *bedroom,* MRS TEASDALE *and* VERA *are sitting on the bed in night attire. The telephone rings off-screen.)*

VERA: Excuse me. *(She laughs nervously.)*

>*(Camera tracks ahead of her as she comes into her bedroom and shuts her door, then sits down on the bed and answers the telephone.)*

Hello. Yes, I am alone. No, not yet.

>*(We resume on* TRENTINO, *sitting at his desk.)*

TRENTINO: *(Into the telephone)* But Vera, we've got to work fast. You must get hold of those plans tonight. Chicolini and his partner should be there any minute. Do everything you can to help them.

>*(Back to* VERA.)

VERA: But I must be very careful. There's another guest staying here for the weekend – Firefly . . . I don't know. I think he's asleep.

>*(Outside* MRS TEASDALE's *house,* CHICOLINI *creeps into view, making for the front door.* CHICOLINI *beckons to* PINKY *who follows with a finger to his lips.*
>
>*Seen in a closer shot they shush one another, and creep up to the front door.*
>
>*At the door,* CHICOLINI *looks round nervously.* PINKY *makes a popping noise just behind him;* CHICOLINI *jumps with fright and scolds him.)*

CHICOLINI: Ssh! Ring the bell.

>*(*PINKY *pulls a large handbell from under his coat and rings it, shattering the silence.)*

Ssh! Push the button.

>*(*PINKY *pokes his finger in* CHICOLINI's *navel.*
>
>*In a longer shot,* CHICOLINI *pulls away and presses the buzzer on the door.*
>
>*We now see a hedge in the foreground;* CHICOLINI *and* PINKY *hide behind it as the* BUTLER *comes out of the front door and looks from side to side.* PINKY *dives for the front door, followed by* CHICOLINI, *goes in and slams the door in* CHICOLINI's *face*

while the BUTLER *looks behind the hedge.* CHICOLINI *hides
behind the hedge again as the* BUTLER *goes back to the door,
finds it shut and goes off to the left.*

Cut to show CHICOLINI *as he goes up to the door, rings the bell
and hides behind the hedge again.* PINKY *comes out and looks
over the hedge, whistling.* CHICOLINI *dives for the door behind
him and slams the door in his face.* PINKY *presses the bell and
hides.*

We see PINKY *hiding behind the hedge as* CHICOLINI *comes out
again and looks over it. The* BUTLER *reappears in the
background, goes in and shuts the door in the faces of* PINKY *and*
CHICOLINI.

*As the two of them come back to the hedge, camera shows some
french windows in the background.* VERA *comes out and beckons.
They run towards her and all go into the house.*

Seen from the interior, VERA, PINKY *and* CHICOLINI *enter the
darkened drawing room. Then we cut to a closer shot of the
group.*)

You gotta da plans?

VERA: No, but they're somewheres in the house and you must
find them. Oh, for heaven's sakes, whatever you do, don't
make a sound. If you're found, you're lost.

CHICOLINI: Oh, you crazy. How can I be lost if I'm found?

VERA: Ohhh!

(*She looks anxiously round in the darkness and we cut to a
medium close-up.*)

(*To* PINKY) Got a flashlight?

(PINKY *pulls his blowlamp from under his coat, and it lights
with a roar.* VERA *exits.*)

CHICOLINI: Sssh!

(*Cut to include* VERA *again.*)

VERA: You don't know how serious this is. If they catch you,
you'll be court-martialled and shot.

(PINKY *points an imaginary gun at his temple and fires.*)

MRS TEASDALE: (*Off*) Oh, Vera!

(*Camera pans with* VERA *as she moves across to the piano.*
CHICOLINI *follows her and hides by the piano keyboard.*

VERA: I must go before she looks for me. Now remember,

whatever you do, don't make a sound. (*She goes off.*)

(*We see* PINKY *by a clock standing against the wall. He pulls out his alarm clock, which says twelve o'clock, and sets the other clock to the same time. It starts to strike.* PINKY *puts a finger to his lips and moves on.*

Camera follows PINKY *as he moves past the piano. He sees a china duck on a table and stops.*

The clock is still striking as PINKY *picks up the duck – it turns out to be a music box, which starts to play.* PINKY *puts a finger to his lips.*

In a medium shot, he starts to dance like a mechanical doll, then plucks the strings of the piano, which play with the sound of a harp.

CHICOLINI *hears the noise as he is going up the stairs. He stops and comes back down again, camera panning with him. We return to* PINKY *at the piano as* CHICOLINI *appears; the music continues loudly.*

In a closer shot, CHICOLINI *tries to drag him away. The piano lid falls with a crash on* PINKY'*s hands and he nurses his fingers as* CHICOLINI *leads him off.*

They are seen in back view as they go towards the stairs. Then in a medium close-up.)

CHICOLINI: You stay here, but keep quiet. Remember what she said. If we get caught, we're gonna get – uh – court-plastered.

(*Back to the previous shot as* CHICOLINI *goes off up the stairs. Upstairs in his bedroom* FIREFLY *is lying in bed. The telephone rings and he wakes with a start and answers it.*

MRS TEASDALE *is in her bedroom, sitting on the bed.*)

MRS TEASDALE: (*Into the telephone*) Your Excellency, I'm worried. I can't sleep.

(*In a long shot of* FIREFLY'*s bedroom,* CHICOLINI *quietly opens the door in the foreground while* FIREFLY *replies into the phone:*)

FIREFLY: What? You're worried? You can't sleep? That's fine. Now you woke me up. Now I can't sleep.

(*We see* MRS TEASDALE *again.*)

MRS TEASDALE: It's about those plans. I won't rest until they're back in your hands.

(*At the bottom of the stairs,* PINKY *is listening in on the extension.*
MRS TEASDALE *continues.*)

Won't you please come over and get them?

(*Back to* FIREFLY.)

FIREFLY: Oh, the plans? OK. I'll be right over.

(*A longer shot includes* CHICOLINI, *who comes into the room in the foreground as* FIREFLY *hangs up and gets out of bed. He goes into the bathroom, and* CHICOLINI *leaps across the bed and locks him in.*

We see CHICOLINI's *hand locking the door.* FIREFLY *rattles the handle from inside.*

CHICOLINI *runs back across the room towards us as* FIREFLY *shouts from the bathroom.*)

(*Off*) Let me out!

(*In a reverse shot,* CHICOLINI *exits into the dressing room.*)

(*Off*) Let me out.

(*Down in the hall,* PINKY *hangs up the extension phone; he gets an idea, and camera pans as he starts up the staircase.*

Upstairs, CHICOLINI *comes back into* FIREFLY's *bedroom, dressing himself in* FIREFLY's *nightclothes. There is pounding from the bathroom off-screen.*)

(*Off*) Let me out! Hey, let me out of here, or throw me a magazine.

(*More pounding;* CHICOLINI *puts on a pair of glasses and paints himself a moustache.*)

(*Off*) So that's your game, eh? I'll huff and I'll puff and I'll blow your door in. (*He blows.*)

(*Camera pans with* CHICOLINI *as he goes to the door of the bedroom and exits.*

In the corridor at the top of the stairs, CHICOLINI *appears disguised as* FIREFLY, *and runs across to a door in the background.*

MRS TEASDALE *is pacing nervously to and fro in her bedroom. There is a knock at the door.*)

MRS TEASDALE: Come in.

(CHICOLINI *enters, disguised as* FIREFLY, *complete with a cigar.*

Shot of the two of them as CHICOLINI *comes up to her and slaps his thigh.*)

Oh, Your Excellency! I'm so glad you've come.

CHICOLINI: (*Removing his cigar*) I'm glad I come, too. You gotta da plans?

(*He lopes across the room in front of her, imitating* FIREFLY.)

MRS TEASDALE: Why, Your Excellency! You sound so strange. Why are you talking like that?

CHICOLINI: Oh, well, you see, maybe some time maybe I go to Italy and I'm practising da language.

(*In* FIREFLY'*s bedroom,* PINKY *is also disguising himself as* FIREFLY. *He paints on a moustache, then puts on some glasses and a nightcap. More pounding from the bathroom off-screen.* PINKY *puts a cigar in his mouth and admires the effect in a hand mirror.*)

FIREFLY: (*Off*) I'll see my lawyer about this as soon as he graduates from law school.

(*More pounding. Camera pans with* PINKY *as he goes to the door.*

We return to MRS TEASDALE *and* CHICOLINI.)

MRS TEASDALE: Your dialect is perfect. I could listen to you all night.

(*A closer shot of the two of them.*)

CHICOLINI: 'At's-a all right, but I can't stay here all night. (*In a conspiratorial whisper*) Where's the plans?

MRS TEASDALE: They're in the safe downstairs. I'll write out the combination.

(*Outside,* PINKY *crosses the corridor to* MRS TEASDALE'*s door, skipping as he goes.*

In the bedroom, MRS TEASDALE *goes to look in her dressing table. The door opens off-screen;* CHICOLINI *looks off and dives under the bed . . .*

As PINKY *enters and slams the door. Camera tracks with him as he lopes across the room, cigar in mouth, imitating* FIREFLY'*s walk.*

In a medium shot, MRS TEASDALE *turns to find* PINKY *behind her, ferreting about on the dressing table.*)

Oh, there you are. Here's the combination. Is that clear?

(*She gives him a piece of paper on which she has written the combination, and* PINKY *tucks it in the pocket of his nightshirt. At that moment* CHICOLINI *sticks his head out from under the bed behind them.*

Close-up of CHICOLINI: *he dodges back under the bed again. Resume on* PINKY *and* MRS TEASDALE.)

Is there anything else you want to know?

(PINKY *takes the cigar from his mouth and grins. She looks at him curiously.*)

What's the matter with you? Have you lost your voice?

(PINKY *clutches his horn under his nightgown. It makes a loud burping noise and* MRS TEASDALE *starts back, somewhat embarrassed.*)

Let me get you a glass of water, Your . . .

(*Cut to a medium shot.*)

. . . Excellency.

(*She bows low to him and goes to the back of the room.* PINKY *bows also and loses his nightcap, revealing his blond hair.*

He bends to pick his nightcap up, and comes nose to nose with CHICOLINI *as he sticks his head out from under the bed again. In a closer shot, they exchange glances, as* PINKY *replaces his nightcap, looking alarmed.*

Back to the scene: MRS TEASDALE *turns, holding a glass of water, while* PINKY *makes for the door, and* CHICOLINI *disappears under the bed again.*)

Your Excellency . . .

(*We see them by the door as* MRS TEASDALE *approaches with the glass.*)

. . . here's your water.

(PINKY *exits through the door, head down, flapping his hand at her.*)

What in the world's the matter with him?

(*In a shot from the end of the bed,* MRS TEASDALE *starts taking off her dressing-gown, while* CHICOLINI *crawls out from under the bed. She turns to find him behind her and hastily draws the dressing-gown around her again.*)

Oh! (*Sternly*) Your Excellency, I thought you'd left.

CHICOLINI: Oh, no, I no leave.

MRS TEASDALE: But I saw you with my own eyes.

CHICOLINI: Well, who you gonna believe, me or your own eyes?

MRS TEASDALE: (*Turning round and round*) Oh! Your Excellency, I'm sorry, but this excitement's too much for me. I feel faint. Ohh!

(*She lies back on the bed, clutching at her forehead.*)

CHICOLINI: Wait. I get you a glass of water.

(*In* FIREFLY's *bedroom, there is more pounding at the bathroom door. Then* FIREFLY *finally breaks it open and comes out. He starts towards the bedroom door.*

Out in the corridor, FIREFLY *appears in the foreground, looks to and fro, and makes for* MRS TEASDALE's *bedroom in the background.*

MRS TEASDALE *is lying on her bed in a faint. There is a knock at the door and* CHICOLINI *dives under the bed. Camera pans to include the door as* FIREFLY *enters.*

In a shot across the bed, MRS TEASDALE *is seen stretched out in the foreground while* FIREFLY *comes forward, peering suspiciously round the room. He notices* MRS TEASDALE, *who waves an arm.*)

MRS TEASDALE: (*Feebly*) How about my glass of water?

FIREFLY: I give up. How about your glass of water? (*He goes on peering to and fro.*)

(*Long shot of the stairs from the bottom:* PINKY *comes hurtling down clutching the piece of paper with the combination on it, skids on the marble in his bedsocks, back-pedals wildly and finally runs off in the foreground.*

In the drawing room, PINKY *is reflected in a large mirror in the background as he appears in front of camera and searches to and fro. He spots something on the right and we follow him as he goes up to a radio with a central dial which looks like a safe, standing on a table by the wall.*

Shot of his hands holding the piece of paper with the safe combination written on it: 'TO RIGHT – 5; THEN LEFT – 3; THEN RIGHT – 4'.

Resume on PINKY *as he turns the dial, following the instructions. Suddenly, loud brass-band music starts blaring from the radio.* PINKY *clutches at his ears, then flaps his hands helplessly at the machine.*)

In MRS TEASDALE'*s bedroom, she and* FIREFLY *stand at the door, listening to the noise from down below.*
Back in the drawing room, the radio continues blaring as PINKY *frantically turns the dial. It comes off in his hand. He throws it on the floor, then grabs a cushion and puts it on top of the radio, trying to muffle the sound; it has no effect, and he tries a curtain hanging beside him, then grabs a soda siphon and sprays it all over the radio. The music keeps on blaring. Finally he picks up the radio and runs off.*
PINKY *runs across the drawing room with the radio, throws it into a closet and slams the door on it. It lands with a crash inside, but the music keeps on playing.*
Up in the bedroom, FIREFLY *is listening at the half-open door. He shuts it and turns to* MRS TEASDALE.)
MRS TEASDALE: What's that?
FIREFLY: Sounds to me like mice.
MRS TEASDALE: Mice? Mice don't play music.
FIREFLY: No? How about the old maestro?
MRS TEASDALE: Oh!
　　　(*Resume on* PINKY *in the drawing room. He clutches at his ears, then opens the closet, picks up the blaring radio and brings it out again.*
　　　In a closer shot, he throws the radio on the floor with a crash. Still it plays. He stands flapping his hands in despair, then picks up a pedestal ashtray and starts smashing the thing up. More music. He gathers up the bits and runs off.
　　　We move to the window. PINKY *runs up and throws the radio outside. He shuts the window and the music finally stops.*
　　　Up in the bedroom, MRS TEASDALE *is sitting on the bed, while* FIREFLY *stands beside her talking into the phone.*)
FIREFLY: Get me headquarters; not hindquarters – headquarters.
　　　(*Seen in close-up,* CHICOLINI *sticks his head out from under the bed.*)
　　　(*Off*) Hello.
　　　(*Resume on him and* MRS TEASDALE.)
Rush the guards right over to Mrs Teasdale's and have 'em surround the house.

(Down in the drawing room, PINKY *turns away from the window and sees . . .*

FIREFLY *coming down the stairs.*

PINKY *looks panic-stricken and runs off.*

He rushes across the drawing room and crashes straight into large mirror seen previously. It shatters on the floor.

FIREFLY, *at the bottom of the stairs, hears the noise and lopes off towards the drawing room.*

Camera pans with him as he runs across to the gap left by the smashed mirror (the alcove beyond is furnished in a mirror image of the drawing room). As he searches to and fro, PINKY *peeps round the corner. They start simultaneously across the gap, but halfway across* FIREFLY *notices* PINKY, *and they stop.*

Shot of the two of them as they stare at one another. FIREFLY *leans forward suspiciously;* PINKY *mirrors his actions.*

Shot of the scene. FIREFLY *walks away from the 'mirror' pondering;* PINKY *does likewise.* FIREFLY *turns suddenly, trying to catch him out; bends down and wiggles his behind; comes up to the mirror again.* PINKY *mirrors his every move.*

Camera pans as they walk to the edge of the alcove. FIREFLY *nods: 'You can't fool me.'* PINKY *does likewise, and disappears round the corner.* FIREFLY *has an idea; he peers forward round the edge of the alcove, and meets* PINKY *doing the same.*

Close-up of FIREFLY. *He has another idea.*

He gets down on all fours and peers round the corner again – and meets PINKY *doing the same. He gets up again.*

FIREFLY *ponders. He has a better idea.*

He trots across the gap, high-stepping; so does PINKY. *He hops back sideways facing the 'mirror'; so does* PINKY. *They skip across, jigging one leg up and down.*

In a longer shot, FIREFLY *walks slowly to the centre and does a wild charleston, facing the mirror;* PINKY *does likewise, grinning.* FIREFLY *spins round;* PINKY *doesn't, but strikes the right pose when* FIREFLY *ends up facing him again.* FIREFLY *moves to the edge of the alcove, fluttering his hands like part of a Negro hallelujah chorus;* PINKY *disappears round the corner doing the same.* FIREFLY *has another idea and goes off. Back to the previous shot as* FIREFLY *enters slowly with a panama hat*

behind his back; PINKY *does likewise, but we see that he has his
black top hat. Convinced that he's caught him out this time,*
FIREFLY *laughs and steps up to the 'mirror'; so does* PINKY.
They circle round through the 'mirror', reversing their positions.
FIREFLY *spots the black hat and heaves with silent laughter –
now he's got him – and* PINKY *does the same. They circle back
through the 'mirror', and suddenly* FIREFLY *puts on his hat.
Seen in a closer shot,* PINKY *does likewise – producing a panama
hat he has been hiding.* FIREFLY *points – 'Haha, I caught you';*
PINKY *mirrors him – 'Haha I caught you'.*
PINKY *is so pleased with himself that he points out of turn, then
pulls a face as he realizes.*
Back to the scene as they both take off their hats and bow.
PINKY *drops his and* FIREFLY *hands it back to him.* PINKY
grins thank you. FIREFLY *slowly puts his hat on and takes it off
again;* PINKY *does likewise, but getting more and more out of
phase.*
A closer shot as FIREFLY, *mirrored by* PINKY, *turns away and
ponders. At that moment,* CHICOLINI *enters on* PINKY's *side of
the 'mirror'.* PINKY *gazes in horror at his nightshirted figure and
hurriedly pushes him out of sight. He just recovers his pose as*
FIREFLY *turns towards him again.* CHICOLINI *wanders on
again and* PINKY *runs off, while* FIREFLY *grabs* CHICOLINI *by
the tail of his nightshirt and holds him fast.)*

The scene dissolves to a newspaper headline: 'CHICOLINI
UNDER ARREST; FACES COURT-MARTIAL FOR
TREASON: SPY TRAPPED ATTEMPTING TO STEAL WAR PLANS
AT GLORIA TEASDALE HOME. Firefly to prosecute: quick
conviction is promised.'
*Dissolve again to the Freedonian Council Chamber, seen from a very
high angle, filled with ministries, generals, trumpeters and guards, and
the Freedonian people in rustic dress. A* LACKEY *steps forward and
announces:*

LACKEY: His Excellency, Rufus T. Firefly.
    (*Music; the people sing.*)
PEOPLE: (*Singing*) Hail, hail Freedonia,

Land of . . .

(*A closer shot looking down on the scene as* FIREFLY *enters.*)

(*Singing*) . . . the brave and free.

(*Camera pans with* FIREFLY *as he steps up to his desk at the end of the council table.* BOB *and the ministers are waiting for him. We now see* BOB *in the foreground. The ministers sit down, while* FIREFLY *opens his brief-case and takes out his lunch.*)

FIREFLY: Lieutenant . . .

(BOB *springs to his feet.*)

. . . why weren't the original indictment papers placed in my portfolio?

(*He pours himself a glass of milk.*)

BOB: Why . . . er . . . I didn't think those papers were important at this time, Your Excellency.

(*Shot of the two of them, with a* GENERAL *sitting beside them.*)

FIREFLY: You didn't think they were important? You realize I had my dessert wrapped in those papers? (*He hands the empty milk bottle to the* GENERAL.) Here, take this bottle back and get two cents for it.

(*Cut to show* CHICOLINI *in the dock. He gets up with a cheery wave, and shouts across to* FIREFLY.)

CHICOLINI: Hello, boss!

(*We see* FIREFLY *seated at the bench, flanked by the* JUDGE, *the* GENERAL *and the ministers.* CHICOLINI *is in the dock in the foreground.*)

FIREFLY: Chicolini, I'll bet you eight to one we find you guilty.

CHICOLINI: 'At's-a no good. I can get ten to one at the barber shop.

(*The* PROSECUTOR *enters from the left.*)

PROSECUTOR: Chicolini, you are charged with high treason, and if found guilty, you'll be shot.

(*He is seen in back view, standing over* CHICOLINI.)

CHICOLINI: I object.

PROSECUTOR: Huh! You object! On what grounds?

CHICOLINI: I couldn't think of anything else to say.

(FIREFLY *is seen from a low angle with the* GENERAL *beside him. He bangs the gavel on the table.*)

FIREFLY: Objection sustained.

(*Resume on* CHICOLINI *and the* PROSECUTOR.)

PROSECUTOR: (*Turning to* FIREFLY) Your Excellency! You
  sustain the objection?
  (*Back to* FIREFLY *and the* GENERAL.)
FIREFLY: Sure. I couldn't think of anything else to say, either.
  Why don't you object?
  (*Shot of the whole bench, with the* PROSECUTOR *and*
  CHICOLINI *in the foreground*.)
PROSECUTOR: Chicolini, when were you born?
  (*Resume on just the two of them*.)
CHICOLINI: I don't remember. I was just a little baby.
PROSECUTOR: Isn't it true you tried to sell Freedonia's secret
  war code and plans?
CHICOLINI: Sure. I sold a code and two pair of plans. (*He laughs
  and slaps the edge of the desk*.)
  (*Back to the scene*.)
  (*To* FIREFLY) 'At's some joke, eh, boss?
FIREFLY: Now I'll bet you twenty to one we find you guilty!
  (*Shot of the* JUDGE.)
JUDGE: Chicolini, have you anyone here to defend you?
  (*Back to* CHICOLINI *and the* PROSECUTOR.)
CHICOLINI: It's-a no use. I even offered to pay as high as
  eighteen dollars, but I no coulda get somebody to defend me.
  (*Resume on the bench*.)
FIREFLY: My friends, this man's case moves me deeply.
  (*He climbs over the desk and jumps to the floor, then we cut
  back to* CHICOLINI, *head bowed*.)
  (*Off*) Look at Chicolini!
  (*Resume on the scene*.)
  (*Dramatically*) He sits there alone, an abject figure.
CHICOLINI: I abject!
FIREFLY: (*Declaiming*) I say look at Chicolini. He sits there
  alone, a pitiable object . . . (*In an aside to* CHICOLINI) Let's
  see you get out of that one! . . . Surrounded by a . . .
  (*Shot of the crowd of Freedonians watching in the gallery*.)
  (*Off*) . . . sea of unfriendly . . .
  (*Then another part of the crowd*.)
  (*Off*) . . . faces.
  (*We now see* FIREFLY *standing over* CHICOLINI, *with the*

people above him in the background.)
Chicolini, give me a number from one to ten.

CHICOLINI: Eleven.

FIREFLY: Right.

CHICOLINI: Now, I ask you one. What is it has a trunk, but no
key, weighs two thousand pounds and lives in a circus?
(*Cut to include the* PROSECUTOR *in the foreground.*)

PROSECUTOR: That's irrelevant.

CHICOLINI: A relephant! Hey, that's the answer. There's a whole
lotta relephants in a circus.
(*Shot of the* JUDGE.)

JUDGE: That sort of testimony we can eliminate.
(*Resume on* FIREFLY *and* CHICOLINI.)

CHICOLINI: 'At's-a fine. I'll take some.
(*The* JUDGE *again.*)

JUDGE: You'll take what?
(*Back to* FIREFLY *and* CHICOLINI.)

CHICOLINI: Eliminate. A nice cold glass eliminate. (*To* FIREFLY)
Hey, boss, I'm goin' good, eh? (*He laughs.*) Yeah.

FIREFLY: (*Addressing the bench*) Gentlemen, Chicolini here may
talk like an idiot, and look like an idiot, but don't let that fool
you. He really is an idiot. I implore you, send him back to his
father and brothers who are waiting for him with open arms
in the penitentiary. I suggest that we give him ten years in
Leavenworth, or eleven years in Twelveworth.

CHICOLINI: I tell you what I'll do. I'll take five and ten in
Woolworth.

FIREFLY: I wanted to get a writ of habeas corpus, but I should
have gotten a writ of you instead.
(*A longer shot includes the* PROSECUTOR, *the* JUDGE *and the
people in the background.*)

PROSECUTOR: I object!

FIREFLY: Even I object.

CHICOLINI: Then I object too.
(*Shot of the* JUDGE.)

JUDGE: You're on trial. You can't object.
(*Resume on the scene as a military courier enters in the
background.*)

COURIER: Your Excellency! General Cooper says that the Sylvanian troops are about to land on Freedonia's soil. This means war!

(*He goes out again as the* MINISTER OF FINANCE *leaps up in the foreground.*)

MINISTER OF FINANCE: Something must be done! War would mean a prohibitive increase in our taxes.

(*Shot of* CHICOLINI, FIREFLY *and the* MINISTER OF FINANCE.)

CHICOLINI: Hey, I got an uncle lives in Taxes.

MINISTER OF FINANCE: No. I'm talking about taxes – money – dollars.

CHICOLINI: Dollas! That's where my uncle lives. Dollas, Taxes.

(*He laughs and shakes hands with* FIREFLY.)

MINISTER OF FINANCE: Aww!

(*Back to the scene again as the* PROSECUTOR *sits* CHICOLINI *down in the dock while* FIREFLY *shakes hands with the* MINISTER OF FINANCE. *The trumpeters enter in the background and blow a fanfare.*)

FIREFLY: More bad news!

(*Some guards come in and flank the entrance with crossed swords as* MRS TEASDALE *hurries in after them.*)

Didn't I tell you?

MRS TEASDALE: Your Excellency!

(*Shot of the two of them.*)

FIREFLY: What's on your mind, babe?

MRS TEASDALE: (*Clasping his arm*) On behalf of the women of Freedonia, I have taken it upon myself to make one final effort to prevent war.

(*The guards march out in the background.*)

FIREFLY: No kidding!

MRS TEASDALE: I've talked to Ambassador Trentino and he says Sylvania doesn't want war either.

FIREFLY: Eether.

MRS TEASDALE: Doesn't want war eether.

FIREFLY: Either.

(MRS TEASDALE *sighs.*)

Skip it.

MRS TEASDALE: I've taken the liberty of asking the Ambassador to come over here because we both felt that a friendly conference would settle everything peacefully. He'll be here any moment. (*Music over another shot of the two of them.*)

FIREFLY: (*Patting her hand*) Mrs Teasdale, you did a noble deed! (*Camera pans as he walks across in front of her.*) I'd be unworthy of the high trust that's been placed in me if I didn't do everything within my power to keep our beloved Freedonia at peace with the world. I'll be only too happy to meet Ambassador Trentino and offer him, on behalf of my country, the right hand of good fellowship. (*Jovially*) And I feel sure that he will accept this gesture in the spirit in which it is offered . . . But suppose he doesn't? A fine thing that'll be! I hold out my hand and he refuses to accept it! That'll add a lot to my prestige, won't it? (*Shouting indignantly*) Me, the head of a country, snubbed by a foreign ambassador! Who does he think he is that he can come here and make a sap out of me in front of all my people? Think of it!

(*Shot of the scene. Camera pans as he moves back across her again. The music continues.*)

(*Working himself up*) I hold out my hand and that hyena refuses to accept it! Why, the cheap, four-flushing swine! He'll never get away with it, I tell you!

MRS TEASDALE: Oh!

FIREFLY: He'll never get away with it.

(*At that moment,* TRENTINO *enters with a retinue of Sylvanian officers.*)

MRS TEASDALE: Oh please!

(FIREFLY *rounds on* TRENTINO *before he can get a word out.*)

FIREFLY: So! You refuse to shake hands with me, eh?

(*He slaps* TRENTINO *with his gloves. The music stops.* MRS TEASDALE *wails:*)

MRS TEASDALE: Ohhh!

(*They are all seen from a low angle.* TRENTINO *is furious.*)

TRENTINO: (*Waving his forefinger*) Mrs Teasdale, this is the last straw! There's no turning back now. This means war!

(*He goes out with the Sylvanian officers, followed by* MRS TEASDALE.*)

FIREFLY: Then it's war!
  (*Back to the scene. We follow* FIREFLY *as he strides to the head of the council table. The trumpeters raise their instruments.*)
  Then it's war!
  (*Fanfare.*)
  Gather the forces!
  (*Fanfare.*)
  Harness the horses!
  (*Fanfare.*)
  Then it's war!
  (*Music, as the* JUDGE, *in close-up, rises and salutes.*
  The GENERAL *does the same.*
  Then a minister.
  And ANOTHER MINISTER, *who sings:*)
MINISTER: (*Singing*) Freedonia's going to war!
  (*Back to the* GENERAL.)
GENERAL: (*Singing*) Each native son will grab a gun.
  (*Shot of a* STENOGRAPHER.)
STENOGRAPHER: (*Singing*) And run away to war!
  (*Camera shows a row of generals and ministers with the Freedonian people in the background.*)
ALL: (*Singing*) At last we're going to . . .
  (*Shot of* FIREFLY, BOB *and the ministers at the bench.*)
  (*Singing*) Feet will beat along the street to . . . war!
  (*Resume on the scene as* BOB *exits. The music continues.*)
  (*Singing*) We're going to war!
CHICOLINI and BOB: At last the country's going to war.
ALL: It seems the country's going to war.
MINISTERS: At last the country's going to war.
ALL: We're going to war!
PROSECUTOR: This is a fact we can't ignore.
ALL: We're going to war!
  This is a fact we can't ignore
  We're going to war!
FIREFLY: In case you haven't heard before
  I think they think we're going to war
  I think they think we're going to war
ALL: We're going to war!

BOB: I think they think we're going to war.

ALL: We're going to war!

(CHICOLINI *appears from under the council table*.)

CHICOLINI: (*Singing*) We're going to war!

GUARDS: (*Singing*) We're going to war!

> (FIREFLY *crawls under the table, then we cut to show* CHICOLINI *appearing over the top of the table with* FIREFLY *on all fours beneath*.)

CHICOLINI: We're going to war!

> (*Sound of drums, as we see the entrance to the council chamber. Camera pans as* PINKY *marches in at the head of a group of guards, twirling a drum-major's baton.*
>
> *In a closer shot,* PINKY *halts and marks time, wielding the baton, as the guards form up in a row behind him. He throws the baton high in the air and it brings a large crystal chandelier crashing down on his head. He extricates himself from the chandelier and goes off while* BOB, FIREFLY *and* CHICOLINI *enter behind the row of guards.*
>
> *We hear xylophone music as* CHICOLINI, BOB *and* FIREFLY *play on the guards' helmets with sticks.*
>
> *The guards mark time to the music as a longer shot includes* PINKY, *who has joined in at the end of the row, and the ministers watching in the foreground.*
>
> *Seen in a closer shot again, the guards turn and start marching out.* PINKY *produces his scissors and starts snipping at the plumes on their helmets.*
>
> PINKY *snips off the plumes as the guards march past in front of him.*
>
> *As the guards march out, seen from below,* PINKY *grabs his drum-major's baton and hits the last one over the head with it. We look down on the whole scene. As the guards file out in the centre, everyone gets up and starts surging to and fro.*)

ALL: (*Singing*) To war, to war, to war we're gonna go!

> (FIREFLY, BOB, CHICOLINI *and* PINKY *sing in a row, fluttering their hands like a Negro chorus.*

THE FOUR: (*Singing*) Oh, hi-de, hi-de, hi-de, hi-de, hi-de, hi-de-ho.

> (*Shot of the scene as everyone sings, shaking their fists in emphasis.*)

ALL: (*Singing*) To war, to war, to war we're gonna go.
  (*The four sing again on their knees, fluttering their hands.*)
THE FOUR: (*Singing*) Oh, hi-de, hi-de, hi-de, hi-de, hi-de, hi-de-
  ho.
  (*Back to the scene as they stop and everyone else takes up the
  refrain, fluttering their hands.*)
ALL: (*Singing*) Oh, hi-de, hi-de, hi-de, hi-de, hi-de, hi-de-ho.
  (*The four kick up their legs as they sing.*)
THE FOUR: (*Singing*) Oh, hi-de, hi-de, hi-de, hi-de, hi-de, hi-de-
  ho.
  (*We look down on the scene as they stop and everyone else kicks
  up their legs.*)
ALL: (*Singing*) Oh, hi-de, hi-de, hi-de, hi-de, hi-de, hi-de-ho.
  FIREFLY, BOB, CHICOLINI *and* PINKY sing, *hauling on an
  imaginary rope.*)
THE FOUR: (*Singing*) Oh-ho, oh-ho, oh-ho, oh-ho, oh-ho.
  (*Resume on the scene. They stop and everyone else starts rope-
  hauling.*)
ALL: (*Singing*) Oh-ho, oh-ho, oh-ho, oh-ho, oh-oh,
  hoooooooo . . .
  (*Back to the group, with the people behind.*)
  (*Singing*) Hooooooo.
  (*Camera tracks out as the four advance towards us with
  watermelon, grins, swaying from side to side.*)
THE FOUR: (*Singing*) They got guns,
   We got guns,
   All God's chillun got guns.
  (*They turn away from camera, which pans to show the people
  swinging their arms.*)
ALL: (*Singing*) We gonna walk all o'er the battlefield
   'Cause all God's chillun got guns.
  (*Pan back to the group, sitting up on the judges' bench,
  strumming banjos, then cut to a closer shot of them.*)
THE FOUR: (*Singing*) Oh, Freedonia,
   Oh donya cry for me,
   Cos I'm comin' round the mountain
   With a banjo on my knee.
  (*They jump down from the bench and we cut back to the scene as*

148

they advance towards camera, playing their banjos.)

ALL: (*Singing*) Oh, Freedonia,
    Oh, donya cry for me.

THE FOUR: (*Singing*) Cos I'm comin' round the mountain . . .
    (*They kneel with their banjos, seen in a medium close-up.*)
    (*Singing*) With a banjo on my . . .
    (*Cut to include the people around them as they get up and start a
    country-style dance. Music.*
    *We look down on the scene as everyone gets up and dances round,
    shouting to the music.*
    THE FOUR *are seen dancing amidst the people, then we cut in to
    *FIREFLY, BOB *and* CHICOLINI. *The trumpets sound and
    everyone freezes, listening.*)

ALL: (*Singing, hands to ears*) To war, to war, to war we're gonna
    go.
    (*Seen in a medium shot, everyone advances towards camera, with
    *FIREFLY, BOB *and* CHICOLINI *in the centre.*)
    (*Singing*) To war, to war, to war . . .
    (*A violin is heard off-screen, and we cut to show* PINKY *playing
    it, surrounded by the people.*
    A closer shot of PINKY *with the people dancing behind him.*
    *He plays the violin above his head, behind his back, then finds
    he's lost the bow. He turns round – the bow is sticking out of the
    back of his trousers.*
    Resume on CHICOLINI, BOB *and* FIREFLY *with the people
    behind. There is another fanfare and they all hearken.*)
    (*Singing*) To war, to war,
    We soon will say goodbye.
    (*Cut in on the three of them*)

BOB: (*Singing tearfully*) Oh, how we'd cry for Firefly.
    If Firefly should die.
    (*We look down on the whole scene.*)

ALL: (*Singing*) A mighty man is he.
    (*The people of Freedonia, in a medium shot, start surging down
    from the gallery.*)
    (*Singing*) A man of brawn who'll carry on
    Till dawn of . . .
    (*Cut in on them jumping over the benches.*)

(*Singing*) . . . victory.

   With him to lead the way . . .

(*Seen in reverse angle they surge towards the council table where everyone has gathered, and turn to face camera.*)

(*Singing*) Our spirits will not lag,

   Until the judgment day.

(*We look down on the council table. Everyone throws up their hands and sings.*)

(*Singing*) We'll rally round the flag, the flag, the flag, the flag!

(*Dissolve to the Freedonian flag, which is drawn aside revealing* FIREFLY, CHICOLINI, PINKY *and* BOB, *posing as statues in eighteenth-century soldier's costumes.* PINKY *is mounted on a horse. There is a roll of drums.*

Shot of the group as FIREFLY *looks off, sabre in hand.*)

FIREFLY: The enemy is coming. There'll be two lamps in the steeple if they're coming by land, and one if they're coming by sea.

(*He exits.*)

(*He reappears at a casement window and opens it. It is night. One, two, then three lamps appear at the top of a church tower in the distance.*)

(*Turning*) They've double-crossed me! They're coming by land and sea. (*He starts out.*)

(*Resume on* CHICOLINI, PINKY *and* BOB *in the same pose as before.* FIREFLY *enters and shouts to* PINKY, *waving his sabre.*)

Ride through every village and town,

Wake every citizen up hill and down.

(FIREFLY *is seen from a low angle.*)

Tell 'em the enemy comes from afar,

(*He dances a jig.*)

With a hey nonny-nonny and a ha-cha-cha.

(*Resume on the group as* BOB *and* CHICOLINI *exit to the left.*)

(*Waving his sabre*) Be off, my lad.

(PINKY *rides his horse down from the plinth and off in the foreground. Dramatic music begins.*)

The scene dissolves to the streets of Freedonia at night. Camera tracks with PINKY *in close-up as he gallops along, blowing a bugle. Sound of hoofbeats as the music continues.*

Dissolve to a shot of a darkened street. People run out of the houses as PINKY *gallops towards us, blowing his bugle.*

Resume on the tracking shot; PINKY *blows his bugle.*

He passes down another street and gallops off. People run out in their nightshirts, one carrying a lantern.

Seen from a high angle, PINKY *slows to a halt. He looks off and grins as he sees . . .*

A girl undressing through a window.

PINKY *dismounts and goes off in the foreground, grinning, while the music changes to 'Ain't she sweet?'*

Inside the house, the GIRL *comes into the bathroom in her underclothes and turns on the bath tap.*

While PINKY *strides into the bedroom in his Paul Revere outfit, his bugle slung round his neck. Camera pans with him to the bathroom door.*

Resume on the bathroom. PINKY *opens the door and looks in, sees the* GIRL *bent over the bath and goes out again.*

Outside the house, we follow PINKY *as he comes down the steps to his horse, which is standing in the foreground. He takes a nosebag from the saddle and puts it on the horse.*

Cut to show the horse tossing its head, eating, as PINKY *goes up the steps into the house again in the background.*

We return to the bedroom, where the GIRL *is now in a dressing-gown. She looks up in surprise as* PINKY *leaps in through the door and lands with a crash.*

GIRL: Oh!
     (Camera pans as he advances on her lustfully and she backs away, gasping.
     Outside, the LEMONADE VENDOR *is seen from above, coming up the steps.*
     In the bedroom, PINKY *is lolling on the bed while the* GIRL *looks out of the window. She hurries across to him and he gets up.)*
     My husband! Quick! *(She pushes him towards the bathroom.)* Hide in there!

(In a closer shot, he tries to pull her into the bathroom with him. There is a violent struggle.)

Oh, don't!

(She finally breaks free; PINKY exits into the bathroom and the door slams.

Resume on the scene in the bedroom as the VENDOR strides in through the door. The GIRL goes up to him hurriedly from beside the bed and thrusts a gun into his hands.)

Freedonia's going to war!

(He hands it back, ignoring her.)

VENDOR: I'm goin' to take a bath!

GIRL: Oh!

(She watches desperately, holding the gun, as camera follows the VENDOR to the bathroom door. He goes in.

Dissolve to show the VENDOR in the bathroom, a little later, sitting in the bathtub. He leans back and PINKY's hooter sounds. The VENDOR, in close-up, looks up in surprise. He looks round, then underneath him.

Back to the scene as he sits down in the bath again. The horn sounds from underneath him.

The VENDOR looks round again, bewildered.

He sits back in the bath again. The horn sounds long and loud from underneath.

The VENDOR starts, in close-up, as PINKY's bugle sounds a loud fanfare . . .

And PINKY rises from the tub in front of the VENDOR, sopping wet and blowing his bugle.)

VENDOR: Oh!

(PINKY drops the bugle and runs for the door, while the VENDOR buries his face in his hands.

Dissolve to another street as PINKY appears on his horse and stops beneath a window with a girl looking out. Romantic music. Seen from below, the girl waves invitingly and blows a kiss. Camera tilts down on to PINKY as he rides through the doorway and into the house.

Dissolve to the bedroom in the house: we see PINKY's boots lying under the bed, then camera pans to show the girl's slippers next to them, and finally four horse shoes lying on the floor. A clock

strikes three.
Shot of the bedroom. PINKY *and the horse are sharing a double*
bed in the foreground, while the girl is in a single bed beyond.
They are all asleep. Fade out.)

The scene changes to FIREFLY's *war headquarters. Bombs and shells*
are heard exploding intermittently off-screen. We follow FIREFLY *as*
he paces to and fro, accompanied by his military staff. He consults a
map, then crosses to the wireless set. Camera tracks in as he addresses
the operator.

FIREFLY: Clear all the wires.
  (*The wireless crackles, and* FIREFLY *dictates a message.*)
  The enemy has captured Hills 27 and 28, throwing thirteen
  hillbillies out of work. Last night two snipers crept into our
  machine-gun nest and laid an egg. Send reinforcements
  immediately. Send that off collect.
  (*He paces across the room again and a* GENERAL *enters in the*
  background.
  Cut to the two of them; as they talk, the wireless crackles and the
  shells explode in the distance.)
GENERAL: Your Excellency, our men are being badly beaten in
  open warfare. I suggest we dig trenches.
FIREFLY: Dig trenches? With our men being killed off like
  flies? There isn't time to dig trenches. We'll buy 'em ready-
  made. Here, run out and get some trenches. (*He hands him a*
  note.)
GENERAL: (*Saluting*) Yes sir. (*He starts out.*)
FIREFLY: Wait a minute.
  (*The* GENERAL *pauses.* FIREFLY *holds a hand up at chin-level.*)
  Get 'em this high and our soldiers won't need any pants.
GENERAL: (*Saluting*) Yes, sir. (*He starts out again.*)
FIREFLY: Wait a minute.
  (*The* GENERAL *pauses.* FIREFLY *holds a hand above his head.*)
  Get 'em this high and we won't need any soldiers.
GENERAL: Yes, sir. (*He goes out.*)
  (*In the Sylvanian headquarters,* TRENTINO *is seated at a table*
  with CHICOLINI *and an officer standing on either side.*

CHICOLINI *is wearing Freedonian uniform. The sound of shells continues.*)

TRENTINO: Chicolini, your partner's deserted us, but I'm still counting on you. There's a machine-gun nest near Hill 28. I want it cleaned out.

CHICOLINI: All right, I'll tell the janitor.

(*Back in the Freedonian headquarters,* FIREFLY *is pacing up and down – now wearing a Unionist uniform.* BOB *hurries in in the background.*)

BOB: A message from the front, sir. (*He hands him an envelope.*)

(*There are distant explosions as we cut to a shot of the two of them.*)

FIREFLY: I'm sick of messages from the front. Don't we ever get a message from the side? (*He takes the envelope and opens it, holding it so that* BOB *can't see.*) What is it?

BOB: General Smith reports a gas attack. He wants to know what to do.

FIREFLY: Tell him to take a teaspoonful of bicarbonate in a half a glass of water.

BOB: (*Saluting*) Yes, sir.

(*He exits.* FIREFLY *hears a crackle from the wireless and looks off. Shot of* FIREFLY *and his officers. Camera follows him to the wireless post.*)

FIREFLY: Any answer to that message?

OPERATOR: No, sir.

FIREFLY: Well, in that case don't send it.

(*He moves away and looks out of the window in the background, followed by the officers. There is the whine of a shell.*

Seen in a long shot, FIREFLY *and the officers duck as a shell flies through the window . . .*

Crashes through a wall on the other side of the room and explodes outside.

FIREFLY *and his staff rush across the room.*

They appear in the foreground and go up to the large gap in the wall made by the shell, FIREFLY *bends down among the rubble. Medium shot of* FIREFLY *and the officers. He picks up a straw boater with its crown flapping.*)

Gentlemen, this is the last straw. Where's my Stradivarius?

A GENERAL: Here, sir. (*He hands him a violin case.*)

(*Camera pans with* FIREFLY *as he puts the case on a table and takes out a machine-gun.*)

FIREFLY: I'll show 'em they can't fiddle around with old Firefly.
(*We now see him through the gap in the wall. The officers scatter in the background as* FIREFLY *looses off a burst with the machine-gun.*)
Look at 'em run. Now they know they've been in a war.
(BOB *comes up behind him.*)

BOB: (*Saluting*) Your Excellency!
(*The two of them are seen facing camera.* FIREFLY *swings the gun to and fro, imitating the noise of it firing and laughing gleefully.*)

FIREFLY: They're fleeing like rats.

BOB: But sir, I've got to tell you . . .
(*We see them from the side.*)

FIREFLY: Remind me to give myself the Firefly medal for this.
(*He fires another burst.*)

BOB: But Your Excellency, you're shooting your own men.
(FIREFLY *stops firing and turns to him.*)

FIREFLY: What?

BOB: You're shooting your own men.
(FIREFLY *puts down the gun and produces some notes from his pocket.*)

FIREFLY: Here's five dollars. Keep it under your hat. Never mind. I'll keep it under my hat.
(*He holds out his hat.* BOB *puts in the money and exits. Two officers stand talking as the explosions continue in the distance.*)

FIRST OFFICER: Now we've got to have more men or we're lost.

SECOND OFFICER: Don't be alarmed. I've got a man combing the countryside for volunteers.
(*Shot of a battlefield. There are loud explosions; tanks rumble past amid smoke. In the foreground,* PINKY *stands with his back to us, wearing a cocked hat and a sandwich board, which reads:* 'JOIN THE ARMY AND SEE THE NAVY'. *A shell bursts in front of him and smoke fills the screen. Resume on the headquarters, where we follow* FIREFLY *as he crosses the room, now wearing a Confederate uniform. The*

155

GENERAL *seen earlier enters in the background and camera*
tracks in on him and FIREFLY.)

GENERAL: Your Excellency, the army's morale is crumbling. The
men are breaking ranks.

FIREFLY: Where's the Secretary of War?

GENERAL: That's it! Where *is* the Secretary of War? The soldiers
are waiting for his orders.

(*A* SENTRY *appears in the background and announces:*)

SENTRY: His Excellency, the Secretary of War!

(CHICOLINI *enters and clocks in at the time clock by the door.*
He comes up to FIREFLY *and the* GENERAL *and salutes.*
Shot of the three of them. The explosions continue off.
FIREFLY *takes off his hat and bows sarcastically.*)

FIREFLY: Awfully decent of you to drop in today. Do you realize
our army's facing disastrous defeat? What do you intend to
do about it?

CHICOLINI: I've done it already.

FIREFLY: You've done what?

CHICOLINI: I've changed to the other side.

(*Cut and pan with* FIREFLY *and* CHICOLINI *as they walk*
across the room.)

FIREFLY: So you're on the other side, eh? Well, what are you
doing over here?

CHICOLINI: Well, the food is better over there.

(*They hear the whine of a shell and we cut to a long shot.*
FIREFLY, CHICOLINI *and the* GENERAL *all duck as shell flies*
in through the window and across the room.
Seen in a closer shot, they turn to look as the shell crashes through
the wall off-screen and explodes.
FIREFLY *appears at the window the shell entered by and pulls*
down the blind. Then he goes off again . . .
And comes back to CHICOLINI *and the* GENERAL.)

FIREFLY: Chicolini, I need you badly right now. What'll you take
to come back and work for me again?

CHICOLINI: I'll take a vacation.

FIREFLY: Good! You're hired. Now, go out in that battlefield and
lead those men to victory. Go on, they're waiting for you.

(*As he speaks, he takes a canvas bag down from the wall and*

hangs it round CHICOLINI's *neck. Camera pans as he pushes*
CHICOLINI *to the door.* CHICOLINI *looks out and sees . . .*
A murky battlefield with tanks rumbling past amid loud
explosions.
Resume on FIREFLY, CHICOLINI *and the* GENERAL.
CHICOLINI *turns away from the door.*)

CHICOLINI: I wouldn't go out there unless I was in one of those
   big iron things go up and down like this. What do you call
   those things?

FIREFLY: Tanks.

CHICOLINI: You're welcome. (*He goes out of the door.*)
   (*The headquarters is seen from a distance as a shell hits it.*
   There is a flash and a loud explosion.
   We see MRS TEASDALE *at the telephone.*)

MRS TEASDALE: Your Excellency, you must come over here at
   once. There is danger here.
   (*In the headquarters,* FIREFLY *is now wearing a scout uniform.*
   He replies on the telephone:)

FIREFLY: Why not come over here? There's no danger here.
   (*Outside the headquarters, a line of Sylvanian soldiers appears*
   over a bank of sandbags, firing.
   At a wooden barricade in front of the headquarters, PINKY *is*
   reloading his gun.
   A soldier fires a shot from the line of sandbags . . .
   And PINKY's *cocked hat spins round once.*
   A soldier fires a burst with a machine-gun . . .
   And PINKY's *hat whirls round like a windmill. He clutches at it*
   nervously.
   We see MRS TEASDALE *again, sitting at a table in what appears*
   to be a farmhouse kitchen. FIREFLY, CHICOLINI *and* BOB *enter*
   in the background. FIREFLY *is now wearing a bearskin on his*
   head.
   In a medium shot of the group, MRS TEASDALE *turns to face*
   them; they put their fingers to their lips.)
Sssh!
   (MRS TEASDALE *springs joyfully to her feet.*)

MRS TEASDALE: Rufus!
   (*Cut to a longer shot as she tries to throw herself into his arms, but*

FIREFLY *dodges. He and the other two make for the table and descend on a bowl of fruit like starving men.*
Another shot of Sylvanian soldiers firing over a line of sandbags.
Resume on MRS TEASDALE, FIREFLY *and* CHICOLINI *crouching by the window.* FIREFLY *restrains* CHICOLINI, *who is about to look out.)*

FIREFLY: Wait a minute. I want to find out something.
(*He takes a plate from a dresser and holds it up above the window sill. Nothing happens.*)
Just as I thought. The coast is clear.
(*He stands up and his bearskin is immediately shot off his head. He falls to the floor.*)

MRS TEASDALE: Rufus!

FIREFLY: Chicolini, to your post!
(CHICOLINI *climbs on a box with his gun and takes aim through the window.*)
Remember you're fighting for this woman's honour – which is probably more than she ever did.
(*He gets up and takes aim also; at that moment* BOB *runs in.*)

BOB: (*Loudly*) Your Excellency!
(FIREFLY *starts at the sound and drops his gun out of the window.*)

FIREFLY: There goes my gun. (*To* MRS TEASDALE) Run out and get that like a good girl.

MRS TEASDALE: Oh, I'm afraid.

BOB: We can't last much longer. Our ammunition supplies are very low.

FIREFLY: Man the boats, lieutenant. I'll get help.
(*We see the house from a distance as a shell hits it. There is a flash and a loud explosion.*
Inside the house, the ceiling starts to fall in, and a great beam nearly kills FIREFLY *in the foreground. Camera pans as he runs to the wireless set by the wall.*
Shot of him holding the microphone.)
Calling all nations! Calling all nations! This is Rufus T. . . .
(*A shower of plaster and rubble falls on his head; he puts on a tin helmet and then continues.*)
This is Rufus T. Firefly, coming to you through the courtesy of the enemy.

(*Cut to show* PINKY *coming in through the door.*)
(*Off*) We're in a mess, folks, we're in a mess!
(*Resume on* FIREFLY *at the microphone.*)
Rush to Freedonia. Three men and one woman are trapped in a building. Send help at once. If you can't send help, send two more women.
(*At the door,* PINKY *holds up three fingers.*)
Make it three more women.
(*We see the house from a distance as another shell hits it and there is a loud explosion.*
Resume on the four men in the ruined kitchen. FIREFLY *is now wearing a raccoon hat.*)

BOB: Your Excellency, we can't hold out much longer. We must have help.
(PINKY *grins and slaps himself on the chest, then exits.*
Seen from outside, PINKY *opens the door, hangs up a sign which says* 'HELP WANTED', *and goes back into the house.*
Inside, FIREFLY, BOB *and* CHICOLINI *walk towards camera,* FIREFLY *first.*)

FIREFLY: One of us has to break through the lines and get word to General Cooper and his men.
(*We hear the whine of a shell off-screen.*)
Which one . . .
(*There is a loud explosion as* PINKY *enters. They all look round.*)
Quiet back there! Which one of us . . .
(*Cut to a closer shot.*)
. . . is going to have the rare privilege of sacrificing his life for his country?

BOB: We'll draw lots . . .

CHICOLINI: Wait, I got it! (*He starts counting round the four of them.*) Rrrrrrinspot, vonza, twoza, zig-zag-zav. Popti, vinaga, tin-li-tav. Harem, scarem, merchan tarem. Tier, tore . . .
(CHICOLINI *is counted out.* PINKY *grins and points at him.*)
I did it wrong. Wait, wait! (*He points at* BOB.) I start here. Rrrrrrinspot, vonza, twoza, zig-zag-zav. Popti, vinaga, tin-li-tav. Harem, scarem, merchan tarem. Tier, tore . . .
(*He counts himself out again.* PINKY *grins and points at him.*)

At's-a no good, too. Oh, I got it! I got it! Rrrrrrinspot, buck!

(*He counts out* PINKY, *who looks bewildered as everyone shakes him vigorously by the hand.*)

FIREFLY: You're a brave man. Go and break through the lines . . .

(*He lays a hand on his shoulder.*) . . . and remember, while you're out there risking life and limb, through shot and shell, we'll be in here thinking what a sucker you are!

(*Cut to a medium shot.*)

Goodbye, Mont Blanc, goodbye.

(*He makes the motion of kissing* PINKY *on both cheeks, while* CHICOLINI *opens the door behind him.* FIREFLY *turns to* BOB, *and* PINKY *snips off his raccoon tail with his scissors.*)

CHICOLINI: (*Saluting*) For Freedonia!

BOB: (*Saluting*) For Freedonia!

FIREFLY: (*Saluting*) For Freedonia!

(PINKY *flourishes the scissors and falls backwards through the door . . .*

And finds himself in the ammunition store. A shell whines over and explodes off-screen.

Out in the kitchen, the explosion brings a cartwheel chandelier crashing down on MRS TEASDALE. FIREFLY *runs up as she sinks to the ground.*)

Gloria! Gloria!

(*She moans, and we cut in on the two of them as* FIREFLY *kneels beside her.*)

Where did they get you?

(*She groans; we hear shots off-screen, while* FIREFLY *takes a jug of water from the table.*

BOB *and* CHICOLINI *are firing out of the window.*)

CHICOLINI: Hey, careful with the water. It's the only water we got.

(*Resume on* FIREFLY *and* MRS TEASDALE. *She groans.*)

FIREFLY: Well, it's the only woman we got. (*He splashes water on her face.*)

(*In the ammunition store,* PINKY *has been having a quiet smoke. He tosses his cigarette end away . . .*

And it lands on some kegs of gunpowder. They explode.
Resume on PINKY, *who struggles wildly, trying to open the door,*
as the ammunition starts exploding like fireworks all around him.
Long shot of the kitchen. BOB *and* CHICOLINI *are at the window*
in the background. FIREFLY *gets up from beside* MRS TEASDALE
and CHICOLINI *follows him across to the door through which*
PINKY *went out. We hear the ammunition exploding off-screen.*)
We're surrounded! They're attacking from the rear.

CHICOLINI: They're comin' this way.

FIREFLY: We'll barricade the door.

CHICOLINI: Come on, let's go.

(They start to barricade the door with a large cupboard.
Inside, PINKY *is pounding at the door with the ammunition*
exploding all around him.
The pounding continues as we resume on the outside, where
FIREFLY *and* CHICOLINI *are piling things on top of the*
cupboard. A chair falls on FIREFLY'S *head from the top of the*
barricade.
Inside, PINKY *struggles wildly amid more and more explosions.*
More pounding and explosions, heard from outside as CHICOLINI
replaces the chair, while FIREFLY *runs across to the wireless.*
Shot of FIREFLY *at the wireless.*)

FIREFLY: This is Firefly talking. Send help at once.

(A voice answers from the wireless.)

VOICE: Help is on the way!

(Resume on CHICOLINI, *holding up the barricade, as* FIREFLY
shouts, waving his arms.)

FIREFLY: Carry on, men, help is on the way!

(We see two fire engines driving out of a fire station with their sirens
going, in a speeded-up shot.
Then a troop of motorcycle police speeding along a road, also in
fast motion. The engines roar; camera tracks ahead of them.
Marathon runners come towards us along a road, flanked by
cheering spectators.
More cheering as camera pans with rowing eights on a river.
A line of swimmers leaps into the water. More cheering.
Shot of some monkeys crossing a rope bridge over a jungle stream,
howling.

*A mother elephant and her baby thunder towards camera, seen in
fast motion . . .
Then a whole herd of elephants, also speeded up, trumpeting as
they go.
Resume on the howling monkeys . . .
The trumpeting elephants . . .
Then we see a whole school of porpoises leaping through the water
in fast motion.
We see the Sylvanian soldiers again, firing from behind the row of
sandbags.
Seen through a gap in the farmhouse wall,* FIREFLY *rises into view
behind a palisade and looks to and fro. He has a large white
bandage tied round his head with the ends sticking up like rabbit's
ears.
Shot of the scene inside the house.* CHICOLINI, FIREFLY *and* BOB
are firing through part of the ruined wall, while MRS TEASDALE
*loads a gun in the foreground. A soldier rises from behind a
palisade in the background and shoots* FIREFLY *in the backside.
Then he ducks down again.)*
(*Clutching his backside*) They got me! They got me! Water!
(*We return to* PINKY *inside the ammunition store. As he tries to
break down the door, there is a loud explosion . . .
And* PINKY *is blown out into the room.
Resume on the others.* FIREFLY *is leaning back against the
palisade while* CHICOLINI *pours water down his throat from the
jug.)*
(*Faintly*) Water!
(*Outside the house, a Sylvanian soldier is seen from below as he
climbs over the palisade.
We see him again from the inside – he has put his foot on the jug,
which is now stuck over* FIREFLY'S *head.* BOB *watches while*
CHICOLINI *hits the soldier over the head with a brick and he falls
back out of sight.* FIREFLY *gets up and calls in a muffled voice:)*
Get me out of this! Get me out of this!
(*Resume on the Sylvanian soldiers behind the sandbags. They fire
a volley.
While inside the house,* FIREFLY *and* PINKY *try to remove the jug
from* FIREFLY'S *head.)*

(In a muffled voice) The last time this happened to me, I was crawling under a bed.

(Shot of BOB *and* MRS TEASDALE *aiming their guns over the palisade.)*

MRS TEASDALE: Oh, if help would only come!

(Resume on FIREFLY *and* PINKY – *who has painted a picture of* FIREFLY's *face on the jug. He lays down the barrel lid he has been using as a palette and admires his handiwork as* BOB *comes up and salutes.)*

BOB: Your Excellency!

(Outside the house, the Sylvanian soldiers start jumping over the sandbag barricade.

Shot of FIREFLY, CHICOLINI *and* PINKY. PINKY *strikes a match.*

We see PINKY's *hands lighting a firecracker.*

PINKY *puts the lighted firecracker inside the jug on* FIREFLY's *head. He and* CHICOLINI *take cover.*

Cut to a closer shot; there is a loud explosion. The smoke clears away to reveal FIREFLY *with the remains of the jug hanging round his neck.)*

FIREFLY: Any mail for me while I was gone?

(Outside the house, the Sylvanian soldiers are now pounding on the door with a battering ram . . .

While inside CHICOLINI, BOB *and* MRS TEASDALE *push furniture up against the door.* PINKY *pushes at* MRS TEASDALE's *backside.)*

MRS TEASDALE: *(Indignantly)* Get away! Get away from me!

(Resume on the soldiers pounding on the door.

Inside everyone stands back as the barricade falls down. MRS TEASDALE *screams.*

The soldiers start going in through the hole in the door.

On the other side, CHICOLINI, PINKY *and* BOB *are waiting to receive them.* CHICOLINI *and* BOB *stand on either side of the door and* CHICOLINI *lifts the first soldier's tin helmet while* PINKY *hits him on the head with a brick. He staggers out of shot.*

On the other side of the room, FIREFLY *starts counting the heads – moving curtain rings along a pole slung from the ceiling with the bayonet on his rifle.)*

CHICOLINI *and* PINKY *deal with the next soldier in the same
way. He staggers off . . .*
And FIREFLY *moves another ring along the pole.*
Resume on the scene at the door. CHICOLINI *lifts the helmet of
the next soldier and shouts:)*
CHICOLINI: Hey! Trentino!
 (They grab him, and we cut back to FIREFLY.)
FIREFLY: Trentino, eh? That's game.
 (He shoves all the rings along the pole.
 At the door, CHICOLINI *and* PINKY *wedge* TRENTINO's *head
 in the broken door and exit.*
 Seen in a medium shot, FIREFLY, CHICOLINI, PINKY *and* BOB
 run up to the table. MRS TEASDALE *is in the background.)*
CHICOLINI: Trentino!
FIREFLY: Trentino, eh?
 (They start throwing fruit.)
 Ahh! Call me an upstart, eh?
 (We see TRENTINO *as the fruit hits him with a thud, then cut to a
 closer shot as the bombardment continues.)*
TRENTINO: *(Shouting)* I surrender! I surrender!
 (Back to FIREFLY *and the others.)*
FIREFLY: I'm sorry, you'll have to wait till the fruit runs out.
 (They carry on throwing.
 In the corner, MRS TEASDALE *shouts joyfully:)*
MRS TEASDALE: Victory is ours!
 (We see the others again as MRS TEASDALE, *in the background,
 breaks into triumphant song:)*
 (Piercingly, with arms upraised) Hail, hail Freedonia,
   Land of the brave . . .
 *(They all turn and start throwing fruit at her. Then the orchestra
 takes up the tune as the picture fades, and the words THE END
 appear.)*

A Day at the Races

CAST

DR HUGO Z. HACKENBUSH	Groucho
TONY	Chico
STUFFY	Harpo
GIL STEWART	Allan Jones
JUDY STANDISH	Maureen O'Sullivan
EMILY UPJOHN	Margaret Dumont
WHITMORE	Leonard Ceeley
MORGAN	Douglass Dumbrille
FLO MARLOWE	Esther Muir
DR LEOPOLD X. STEINBERG	Sig Rumann
SHERIFF	Robert Middlemass
SOLO DANCER	Vivien Fay
DR WILMERDING	Charles Trowbridge

Directed by	Sam Wood
Screenplay by	Robert Pirosh, George Seaton and George Oppenheimer
Additional dialogue by	Al Boasberg
Director of photography	Joseph Ruttenberg
Art direction	Cedric Gibbons
Edited by	Frank E. Hull
Music by	Bronislau Kaper and Walter Jurmann
Musical Director	Franz Waxman
Running time	111 minutes
Released by	Metro-Goldwyn-Mayer, 11 June 1937

Fade in to the railroad depot, Sparkling Springs Lake. A porter steps off the train; passengers follow and move towards a row of snappy-looking buses that belong to Morgan Enterprises, and one beat-up station wagon that belongs to the Standish Sanitarium.
Cut to TONY (CHICO). *He calls to people as they pass by the Standish Sanitarium station wagon, ignoring him.*

TONY: Free bus to the sanitarium. This way to the Standish
    Sanitarium. Standish San – Standish San – This – this way to
    the Standish – Standish – free bus! Free bus! Standish
    Sanitarium!
    (*The passengers board the buses to the Morgan Hotel.*)
    Free bus to the sanitarium. (*He gestures towards his empty
    station wagon.*) Just got room for a few more!
    (*He stops a well-dressed* MAN *in a panama hat.*)
    Sanitarium?
MAN: No. Racetrack.
TONY: Hey, you don't want to go to the races. You're too sick.
MAN: I'm going to the races!
TONY: All right. You want something hot in the fifth race?
    (*The* MAN *gives him a dirty look which* TONY *ignores as he turns
    to the other people.*)
    Sanitarium? Bus to the sanitarium! Standish Sanitarium!
    (*Cut to close up of* JUDY; *she is a beautiful young girl, standing
    by the Standish Sanitarium station wagon.* TONY *joins her.*)
    Free bus to the sanitarium.
JUDY: It's no use, Tony. If business keeps up like this, I'm afraid
    I'll have to drive the station wagon myself.
TONY: Oh, no, Miss Judy. You can't fire me.
JUDY: But what if I can't pay your salary?
TONY: That's different. You don't have to pay me, but you can't
    fire me.
    (JUDY *is now in the station wagon.*)

JUDY: Oh, Tony, you're sweet.
  (TONY *closes her door.*)
TONY: Yeah. And don't worry, Miss Judy. I'm gonna get some customers if I have to make them sick myself. (*He gets in the driver's seat.*)
JUDY: Oh, Tony, I'm afraid we need more than customers. You don't understand – I owe a great deal of money – far more than I can ever pay.
TONY: Let me see – who do I know that's rich? Hey, how about that big, strong sick woman at the sanitarium?
JUDY: You mean Mrs Upjohn?
TONY: Yeah, that's the one! She'd be glad to lend you the money.
JUDY: Oh, no.
TONY: Oh, she's rich! Why, last week she gave me a dollar tip!
JUDY: She did once offer to help, but it doesn't seem right to borrow from the patients.
TONY: All right, we make her a partner.
JUDY: Oh, Tony!
TONY: Hey, we gotta hurry before she changes her mind. (*He closes the station-wagon door.*)

Dissolve to Standish Sanitarium, exterior.
The station wagon pulls up in front of a Victorian mansion.
Dissolve to interior, Sanitarium, main floor. JUDY *and* TONY *enter.*)
TONY: Go ahead, Miss Judy. (*Whispering*) There's Mrs Upjohn now.
  (MRS UPJOHN *is a stout dowager; she is with* DR WILMERDING, *whose back is partially to camera.*)
DR WILMERDING: But, Mrs Upjohn –
MRS UPJOHN: Now, there's no use talking any more, Doctor! I'm leaving! (*She turns to go, speaks to* MR WHITMORE, *the business manager of the Sanitarium, at the front desk.*) Mr Whitmore, I want my bill made out at once!
  (JUDY *turns and walks towards* MRS UPJOHN.)
WHITMORE: Just as you say, Mrs Upjohn.
JUDY: What's the matter, Mrs Upjohn?
MRS UPJOHN: It's no fault of yours, my dear. It's the doctor! The idea of telling me I'm perfectly well when I know I'm on the

verge of a nervous collapse. Goodbye, Judy dear. (*She clasps*
JUDY's *hands, then hurries up the stairs.*) Have the boy come
up and get my bags, please.
  (JUDY *is heartbroken;* WILMERDING *is frustrated, but resigned.*
  JUDY *walks across the room.*
  Close-up on TONY: *he looks sadly at* JUDY.
  JUDY *hurries out of the room and into her office.*)

Interior, Office.
Medium long shot of GIL, *Judy's boyfriend, who is standing in a set of*
french doors as JUDY *enters.*)
JUDY: Gil! Oh, Gil!
  (*She runs to him and they embrace. She is on the edge of tears.*)
  I'm glad you're here?
GIL: What is it, honey?
JUDY: Hold me tight. I'll be all right. (*She cries.*)
GIL: Come on, honey, tell me.
JUDY: It's Mrs Upjohn – she's leaving.
GIL: Oh, let her leave! Say, I have something here worth a
  hundred Upjohns! (*He pulls a paper out of his jacket.*)
JUDY: You don't understand – I'm going to lose this place!
GIL: No, you're not. That's what I'm trying to tell you. Honey,
  from me to you, with love!
  (GIL *hands* JUDY *an official-looking paper.*)
JUDY: Your radio contract! You've got it! (*She reads:*) 'Gelding –
  out of Honey Lamb by Blue Bolt – two year – Hi-Hat' – (*To*
  GIL) Why, Gil, this doesn't make sense!
GIL: It's a horse, a racehorse.
JUDY: Perhaps I'm awfully stupid, but what do we want with a
  horse?
GIL: Now wait till I tell you. Horse wins race – owner wins money
  – owner gives money to girl he loves – girl saves sanitarium.
  Why, it's very simple!
JUDY: Very simple. But what happens if horse loses race?
GIL: Oh, but he can't lose. He's a wonder! I picked him up for a
  song. Only . . . fifteen hundred dollars.
JUDY: Fifteen hundred dollars?
GIL: Um-hmm.

JUDY: Why, Gil, that's all the money you had in the world!

GIL: Well, I still have my job singing at the casino.

JUDY: Now, Gil, you return that horse at once, and get your money back. You've got to go on with your music – your career!

GIL: Judy, you need money fast – more money than I could make in ten years of singing.

JUDY: I don't care! I want you to be a great singer, not a racetrack tout!

GIL: Oh, wait a minute! That isn't fair!

JUDY: Are you going to return that horse?

GIL: I can't do that. I just bought him!

JUDY: You mean you don't want to. You'd rather bet on a horse than on yourself!

GIL: Of all the ungrateful people! (*He turns away from her and walks towards the french doors.*)

JUDY: Well, what have I got to be grateful for? You've thrown your career away on a long shot, and gambled away our happiness! Here, take your horse! (*She hands him the contract.*)

GIL: All right! (*He leaves through the french doors.*)

JUDY: And I hope you're very happy with it!

Interior, main floor, lobby.

TONY *looks through a door into the lobby.*

Medium shot of MRS UPJOHN *and* DR WILMERDING *on the stairway.* MRS UPJOHN *and a series of bellboys come down the stairs.* WHITMORE *joins them.*

MRS UPJOHN: I'm going to someone who understands me. I'm going to Dr Hackenbush.

DR WILMERDING: Dr Hackenbush? Why, I've never heard of him. Has he a sanitarium?

MRS UPJOHN: The biggest in Florida . . .

(*Close-up on* TONY. *He hears her mention* DR HACKENBUSH *and snaps his fingers: an idea.*)

(*Offscreen*) That's what he told me. Of course, I was never there.

(*Camera on* DR WILMERDING, MRS UPJOHN *and* WHITMORE.)

Hugo – Oh, I mean Dr Hackenbush – always insisted on
treating me in my home. Why, I didn't know there was a
thing the matter with me until I met him.

Exterior, Sanitarium.
TONY *watches the bellboys carry* MRS UPJOHN's *luggage. He runs
after the first boy and takes* MRS UPJOHN's *bags.*
TONY *leads the series of bellboys back into the sanitarium, past* DR
WILMERDING *and on upstairs.*
TONY: Excuse, please. We're sure getting a lot of new customers
since they heard Dr Hackinapuss is coming.
MRS UPJOHN: Did you say Hackenbush?
TONY: Yes, ma'am.
MRS UPJOHN: I wonder if that could be the same one? Where
does he . . . come from?
TONY: Where's your Hackinapuss come from?
MRS UPJOHN: Palmville, Florida.
TONY: That's the one! (*He goes upstairs after the bellboys.*)
(*Medium shot of* MRS UPJOHN, WHITMORE *and* DR
WILMERDING.)
MRS UPJOHN: (*Very excited*) Why – ! Why – Judy! (*She hurries to*
JUDY.) Judy, why didn't you tell me Dr Hackenbush was
coming here?
JUDY: Dr Hackenbush – ? (*She turns to look for* TONY.)
(TONY *comes downstairs, looking innocent.*)
MRS UPJOHN: (*Off-screen*) Oh, I'm so excited!
(TONY *hurries to the door – he is on his way to try and find* DR
HACKENBUSH.)
Judy, why don't you make him chief of staff? He'd do
wonders for the sanitarium. With Dr Hackenbush in charge,
I might help you financially. I don't say I will, but I might.
(*She turns to leave;* JUDY *watches her, hopeful.*)
Oh, Mr Whitmore, have my bags sent right up. I'm staying!
(JUDY *runs to her office.*)

Interior, Office.
TONY *is sitting at the desk, writing.* JUDY *enters.*
JUDY: Who's Dr Hackenbush?

TONY: I don't know. But if she wants a Hackinapuss – she gonna get a Hackinapuss!
(*Close-up on telegram blank.* TONY *writes:* Dr Hackenbush's Sanitarium, Palmville, Florida. Come up and . . .)

Dissolve to close-up on sign:

DR
HACKENBUSH'S
SANITARIUM
FOR
SMALL ANIMALS
AND HORSES

Dissolve to interior, Hackenbush's Sanitarium. It's a barn. Camera pans dogs, chickens, ducks, and their friends. We hear animal sounds in the background.)

HACKENBUSH (GROUCHO): (*Off-screen*) Inhale – exhale – inhale –
(*The camera stops on* DR HACKENBUSH. *He's leaning over a horse, examining it.*)
Inhale – (*He comes up from under the horse, smoking his cigar.*)

HANDY MAN: (*Off-screen*) Here's a telegram . . .
(HANDY MAN *hurries in with a telegram.*)
. . . for you, doc.
(*He hands it to* HACKENBUSH, *whose stethoscope is still in his ears.*)

HACKENBUSH: What does it say?

HANDY MAN: Well it goes on to say that – How should I know?

HACKENBUSH: (*Reading*) 'Come up and take care of Mrs Upjohn. Stop . . . You can write your own ticket. Stop. Come at once Standish Sanitarium.' (*Remembering*) Mrs Upjohn! Ah, Emily – she never forgot that hayride! (*He raises his eyebrows and slouches off past the* HANDY MAN.)

HANDY MAN: Don't Mrs Upjohn know you're a vet?

HACKENBUSH: No. She's so in love with me she doesn't know anything. That's why she's in love with me.
(*The* HANDY MAN *comes over and helps him on with his coat.*)

HANDY MAN: Well, they can throw a horse doctor in gaol for treatin' people.

HACKENBUSH: Yes – they can throw a horse doctor in gaol for not paying his rent, too. (*His arm won't go into his sleeve – he tries to force it.*)

HANDY MAN: Something there –

HACKENBUSH: So what have I got to –

(*The* HANDY MAN *takes a puppy out of the sleeve.*)

(HACKENBUSH *grabs his cane and medical bag and heads for the door, his stethoscope still in his ears. He reacts to a horse whinny off-screen, goes back to the horse, opens his bag, takes out a huge pill and feeds it to the horse.*)

Take one of those every half mile. And call me if there's any change.

Dissolve to interior, Conference Room of Sanitarium.

MORGAN, WHITMORE, *and* JUDY, *with the sanitarium's medical staff is in the background.* JUDY *is looking over a contract.*

JUDY: But, Mr Morgan, if I sign this, it means I turn the sanitarium over to you today!

MORGAN: That's right, Miss Standish. And I'll give you five thousand dollars.

JUDY: But the notes aren't due. I've got almost a month.

MORGAN: Miss Standish, this place has been losing money steadily. You'll never be able to pay. If you wait, I'll take it over and you won't get a cent.

WHITMORE: As your business manager, Judy, I strongly advise you to take Mr Morgan's offer. (*He offers her his pen.*)

JUDY: Oh, but you're forgetting about that doctor Mrs Upjohn recommended. Surely with him in charge, we'll be able to pay Mr Morgan.

WHITMORE: Oh, Judy, are you going to take the advice of a hysterical patient?

MORGAN: Now look here, Miss Standish –

MRS UPJOHN: (*Off-screen*) Judy!

(*She burst into the room. Camera pans her to* JUDY *and* WHITMORE.)

Judy, he's here! He's here!

JUDY: Why, who's here?

MRS UPJOHN: Dr Hackenbush!

MORGAN: Are you going to sign that or not?

JUDY: Uh – no.

MRS UPJOHN: Of course, she's not going to sign it!

JUDY: Why, I have a month – I can at least try this new doctor.

MORGAN: (*Grabbing the contract from her*) You're going to wish you'd taken that check!

(*He leaves and* WHITMORE *follows.*)

MRS UPJOHN: Well!

WHITMORE: Mr Morgan, Mr Morgan!

(*They stand in the doorway.*)

MORGAN: You fixed that all right!

WHITMORE: How did I know that old battle-axe was going to butt in? But don't worry, I'll get to work on this new doctor.

MORGAN: Work fast!

(*Medium shot on* MRS UPJOHN *and* JUDY, *with the medical staff still standing at attention in the background.*)

MRS UPJOHN: Don't let them bully you, my dear. With Dr Hackenbush in charge, I'm sure my trustees will let me help you.

(WHITMORE *comes back.*)

WHITMORE: Mrs Upjohn, I think I am better able to advise Miss –

MRS UPJOHN: I don't want to hear any more about it! Oh, I – I can't stand this excitement! I know this will cause a relapse! Oh, my metabolism! Doctor! (*She throws her hands in the air and moves away from* JUDY *towards the door.*)

(*Hallway: camera shoots at a low angle, revealing first* HACKENBUSH's *shadow and then his legs and two satchels as he slouches into the corridor.*)

(*Off-screen*) Oh, Doctor!

(*The camera pans him into the room as he passes* MRS UPJOHN, *not noticing her.*)

HACKENBUSH: (*To* WHITMORE) Here, boy. Here, boy . . . (*To* WHITMORE) Take these bags and run up to my room. And here's a dime for yourself.

MRS UPJOHN: Oh, no, no, no, no, no! This is Mr Whitmore, our business manager.

HACKENBUSH: Oh, I'm terribly sorry. Here's a quarter.

MRS UPJOHN: Oh! You mustn't take the doctor too seriously. He probably feels tired after his long trip.

HACKENBUSH: Why shouldn't I be tired? Did you ever ride four on a motorcycle? And me – top man!

(*A long shot of the entire room: the four of them and the medical staff.*)

MRS UPJOHN: Oh, this is Dr Hugo Z. Hackenbush, your new chief of staff.

(HACKENBUSH *bows to the doctors; they bow to him.*)

And now, doctor, I'd like you to meet Miss Standish.

(*He bows again and the medical staff return his bow.*)

Oh, doctor –

(HACKENBUSH *bows a third time; the doctors do likewise.*)

Uh, doctor . . .

(HACKENBUSH *bows yet another time; the doctors bow back.*)

HACKENBUSH: Just a moment, till I calm these paralytics.

(*He bows again; they bow with him.*)

MRS UPJOHN: Oh, dear. Oh, doctor . . . Oh, doctor, this is Miss Standish.

(*Medium close-up on* JUDY.)

(*Off-screen*) Owner of the sanitarium.

(HACKENBUSH *oozes over to* JUDY *and shakes her hand.*)

HACKENBUSH: Oh, how do you do, Miss Standish.

JUDY: How do you do.

(*They shake hands.*)

HACKENBUSH: You're the prettiest owner of a sanitarium I've ever seen.

JUDY: Thank you.

HACKENBUSH: You have a charming place here.

(*He looks at a portrait of a distinguished-looking patriarch that is over the fireplace.*)

Ah, I knew your mother very well. I'll let you in on a little secret. Many, many years ago in the dear dim past, I proposed to your mother.

JUDY: Oh, but that's my father.

HACKENBUSH: No wonder he turned me down.

MRS UPJOHN: Now, doctor, I'd like you to meet your new associates.

(*Long shot of everyone. The* FIRST DOCTOR *steps forward*.)

FIRST DOCTOR: Johnson, Bellevue Hospital, Nineteen eighteen. (*He steps back*.)

SECOND DOCTOR: (*Steps forward*) Franko, Johns Hopkins, twenty-two. (*He steps back*.)

THIRD DOCTOR: (*Steps forward*) Wilderming, Mayo Brothers, twenty-four. (*He steps back*.)

(HACKENBUSH *steps forward, clicks his heels*.)

HACKENBUSH: Dodge Brothers, late twenty-nine. (*He steps back*.)

(JUDY *walks over to them*.)

JUDY: Doctor, I'm happy to welcome you as chief of staff. I hope you'll be able to pull the sanitarium out of its difficulties.

MRS UPJOHN: Oh, the sanitarium is having a little financial trouble.

HACKENBUSH: I get it. I'm not going to get paid, huh?

(*He picks up his bag and starts to leave.* MRS UPJOHN *grabs him by the coat-tails and pulls him back*.)

MRS UPJOHN: Oh, no – no – no, doctor – please don't go. I'll take care of your salary.

HACKENBUSH: Oh, yeah? The last job I had, I had to take it out in trade and this is no butcher shop – not yet, anyhow.

(*Close-up on* WHITMORE.)

WHITMORE: Judy, it seems to me, if I may say so, we are making rather a hasty decision.

(*Medium long shot of* JUDY, MRS UPJOHN, HACKENBUSH, *and* WHITMORE.)

MRS UPJOHN: Surely, you don't question the doctor's ability?

WHITMORE: No, not exactly. But running a sanitarium calls for a man with peculiar talents.

HACKENBUSH: You don't have to look any further. I've got the most peculiar talents of any doctor you ever met.

JUDY: I'm satisfied with Mrs Upjohn's recommendations. And, if you'll excuse me, I'll go and bring in the rest of the staff. (*She turns to leave*.)

HACKENBUSH: (*To* WHITMORE) Why don't you go out and bring in something? Preferably your resignation?

WHITMORE: Tell me, Dr Hackenbush, just what was your medical background?

HACKENBUSH: Medically?

WHITMORE: Yes.

HACKENBUSH: Well, uh, at the age of fifteen I got a job in a drugstore, filling prescriptions.

WHITMORE: Don't you have to be twenty-one to fill prescriptions?

HACKENBUSH: Well, ah, that's for grown-ups. I just filled them for children.

WHITMORE: No, no, doctor. I mean, where did you get your training as a physician?

HACKENBUSH: Oh, well, to begin with, I took four years at Vassar.

(*Camera pans left to include* MRS UPJOHN.)

MRS UPJOHN: Vassar! But that's a girls' college.

HACKENBUSH: I found that out the third year. I'd've been there yet but I went out for the swimming team.

(*Close-up on* WHITMORE.)

WHITMORE: The doctor seems reluctant to discuss his medical experiences.

HACKENBUSH: Well, medically, my experiences have been most unexciting, except during the flu epidemic.

WHITMORE: Ah, and what happened?

HACKENBUSH: I got the flu.

MRS UPJOHN: Oh, doctor, I think it's time for my pill.

HACKENBUSH: (*Privately, to* MRS UPJOHN) Ixnay on the opeday.

MRS UPJOHN: Now you told me to take them regularly.

(HACKENBUSH *rummages through his bag, pulls out some pills and hands them secretively to* MRS UPJOHN, *making sure* WHITMORE *can't see.*)

WHITMORE: Just a minute, Mrs Upjohn, that looks like a horse pill to me.

HACKENBUSH: Oh, you've taken them before?

MRS UPJOHN: Are you sure, doctor, you haven't made a mistake?

HACKENBUSH: You have nothing to worry about. The last patient I gave one of those to won the Kentucky Derby.

WHITMORE: (*Takes a pill from* MRS UPJOHN) Uh, may I examine this, please? (*Holding up the pill.*) Do you actually give those to your patients? Isn't that awfully large for a pill?

HACKENBUSH: No. It was too small for a basketball and I didn't
know what to do with it. Say, you're awfully large for a pill
yourself.

WHITMORE: (*Walks over to the line of doctors*) Dr Wilmerding, just
what is your opinion?

WILMERDING: It must take a lot of water to swallow that.

HACKENBUSH: Nonsense, you can swallow that with five gallons.

WHITMORE: Isn't that a lot of water for a patient to take?

HACKENBUSH: Not if the patient has a bridge in her mouth. You
see, the water flows under the bridge and the patient walks
over the bridge and meets the pill on the other side.
(*The* THREE DOCTORS *are appalled at* HACKENBUSH's
*remarks. In the distance, a bugle sounds the beginning of a horse
race.*)
(*Hearing the bugle*) So it's war! I'm off to the battlefield! (*He
starts to leave.*)
(MRS UPJOHN *grabs him by the coat-tails again.*)

MRS UPJOHN: No – no, doctor, that's from the racetrack.

HACKENBUSH: Racetrack? Well, what am I doing here?

MRS UPJOHN: Oh, doctor – don't leave me!
(HACKENBUSH *runs out between the doctors.*)

*Dissolve to exterior, racetrack, seen from the stands. The horses are off
and running.*
WHITMORE *and* MORGAN *are seated in the best seats in the
grandstand, watching the race.*
STUFFY (HARPO) *is riding neck and neck with another* JOCKEY.
JOCKEY: Well, you won it, Stuffy.
(STUFFY *puts his riding crop in his mouth.*
WHITMORE *and* MORGAN *get up to leave.*)

Dissolve to interior, stable with STUFFY *and the grooms.*
STUFFY *walks through a stable door, carrying a racing saddle which
he hangs on a peg.*
GROOM: Nice work Stuffy.
(MORGAN *enters and kicks* STUFFY *in the behind.* STUFFY *flies
up into the air.*
He flies face first into the wall.

MORGAN *pulls* STUFFY *down from the wall and punches him in the face.* STUFFY *falls to the ground.*)

MORGAN: I told you to lose that race!

(MORGAN *takes another swing at* STUFFY, *misses and drives his fist into the wall.*)

(*In pain*) Ohhh!!

(STUFFY *crawls out from underneath and runs out of the stable door.*

He closes the dutch stable doors. MORGAN *lunges at him, through the top half, but* STUFFY *gets away.* MORGAN *opens the bottom half and runs after him.*

A row of horses are in their stalls. STUFFY *runs in past the horses and dives into a stall.*

STUFFY *burrows into a haystack and hides near* GIL *who is taping Hi-Hat's foot.*)

(*Off-screen*) Stuffy, where are you? Where's Stuffy?

(MORGAN *comes to the stable door and startles Hi-Hat.*)

(*Off-screen*) Have you seen my jockey?

(GIL *tries to soothe Hi-Hat.*)

GIL: Whoa, boy! Please, Mr Morgan, don't stay here!

MORGAN: (*At the entrance to the stall*) You ought to beat the head off that ornery devil!

(GIL *tries to calm Hi-Hat as he rears.*)

GIL: He only acts this way when he sees or hears you!

(MORGAN's *afraid of Hi-Hat.*)

MORGAN: Aw!

(STUFFY *sticks his leg out of the hay and kicks* MORGAN. MORGAN *thinks it's Hi-Hat.*)

I should have plugged that nag when I owned him!

(*Hi-Hat's tail swats* MORGAN *in the face.* GIL *struggles with Hi-Hat.*)

GIL: Please, Mr Morgan, don't stay here!

(MORGAN *leaves.*

STUFFY *gets out of the haystack.*)

(*Off-screen*) Calm down now – he's gone now – that's the boy.

(STUFFY *comes over to* GIL *and Hi-Hat, pats* GIL *on the back, and embraces Hi-Hat.*)

You better stay out of Morgan's way for a while.

TONY: (*Off-screen*) Get your ice-cream. Get your tootsie-frootsie ice-cream.

(STUFFY *runs off in the direction of the tootsie-frootsie ice-cream. Outside the stable,* STUFFY *whistles to* TONY. TONY *is pulling his ice-cream cart.*)

Stuffy!

(STUFFY *runs to embrace* TONY, *but at the last minute goes around him and heads for the ice-cream.* TONY *slams the ice-cream-wagon lid down.*)

Hey, hey, get out of there! Yeah, that was some ride you put up. I had five bucks right on the nose. I won sixty cents. Who you ridin' tomorrow? What's the matter?

(STUFFY *strikes a match.*)

What happened? You fired?

(STUFFY *blows out the match and nods his head, 'yes'.*)

Oh, Morgan fired you, eh?

(STUFFY *nods, 'yes'.*)

He wanted you to throw the race?

(*He nods 'yes' again.*

GIL *comes out of the stable behind them.*)

GIL: He wanted Stuffy to be crooked, eh?

TONY: Yeah. You know he's honest.

(STUFFY *reaches into the ice-cream wagon and* TONY *slams the lid on his hand.*)

He's honest but you gotta watch him a little. Hey, Gil, why don't you give Stuffy a job? Let him ride Hi-Hat.

GIL: Why Tony, you know we can't afford a jockey. We haven't enough money to eat on ourselves.

TONY: Eat – eat – eat, all the time eat! We don't have to eat. I'll eat!

SHERIFF: (*Off-screen*) Hey, you!

GIL: Why, hello, sheriff.

SHERIFF: (*Enters*) Well, have you got the money for the feed bill?

GIL: You see, sheriff, it's this way –

SHERIFF: Say, listen . . .

(*Standing behind the* SHERIFF, STUFFY *mimics his anger.*)

. . . you guys have been stallin' me for weeks. Either I get some money on account right now or I'm taking Hi-Hat.

TONY: Hey wait – wait, I give you some money. (*He reaches into his pocket and hands the* SHERIFF *a bill.*) There you are.

SHERIFF: Five dollars! (*He pockets it.*) That's not enough.

(STUFFY *picks the* SHERIFF'*s pocket and hands the five-dollar bill back to* TONY, *behind the* SHERIFF'*s back.*)

Come on, well!

TONY: All right, all right, I gotta some more. There you are.

(*He hands him the same five-dollar bill.*)

SHERIFF: That makes ten.

(*He pockets it, but this time keeps his hand in his pocket.* STUFFY *tickles his neck with a piece of straw.*)

Chicken feed. Come on, you got some more!

TONY: (*Stalling*) yeah, I got some more but it's hard to get at, you know.

(*The* SHERIFF *scratches his neck.*)

SHERIFF: Come on, come on!

TONY: All right, don't hurry. I got it some place. I know it's some place.

(*While the* SHERIFF *is scratching,* STUFFY *takes the five-dollar bill from the* SHERIFF'*s pants pocket and hands it back to* TONY.)

There, I knew it was some place. (*He hands the five back to the* SHERIFF.)

SHERIFF: Well, that's fifteen. (*He puts the bill in his vest pocket.*) Have you got any more?

(STUFFY *reaches into the* SHERIFF'*s pants pocket, but the bill is not there. He digs deeper and deeper, surprised there's no money.*)

TONY: Ah – I let you know in a minute.

SHERIFF: Quit stallin' – come on, hurry!

TONY: All right, I got some more but I can't hurry.

SHERIFF: (*To* STUFFY) Hey, what're you doing there!

(STUFFY *goes limp, his hand is in the* SHERIFF'*s pants pocket to deeply that he pulls out a sock. The* SHERIFF *lifts his pants leg, looks at his bare ankle, and chases* STUFFY.)

Hey, come back here!

TONY: Well, that's-a fine. Now we owe the sheriff a hundred and twenty dollars and a sock.

GIL: Well, it's a good thing Judy doesn't have to depend on me. I can't even hold on to the horse.

TONY: No? Well, we hold on to the horse. (*He closes the stable door.*)

GIL: Say, if we only had some dough. I got a tip on Sun-Up!

TONY: Sun-Up?

GIL: Yeah.

TONY: He's in the next race. We no gotta much time!

GIL: Hey, wait a minute! What're we going to use for money? (TONY *hurriedly pushes his ice-cream wagon underneath the horse.* GIL *runs after him.*)

Dissolve to exterior, betting windows.

TONY *and* GIL *look at the odds board for the next race.* TONY *is still pushing the ice-cream wagon.*

TONY: Hey, boy, look – look! Sun-Up, he's ten to one! (*Among the other names, it reads:* 'SUN-UP 10–1.')
Boy, are we going to clean up! Ten to one.

GIL: We haven't any money to bet.

TONY: Don't worry, I getta some money. I find a sucker some place. Scram, I think I see a sucker coming now. Get out of here.
(HACKENBUSH *enters, wearing a white linen jacket and a panama hat. He looks at the betting windows and steps up to the two-dollar window.*)
(*Off-screen*) Get your ice-cream!

HACKENBUSH: (*At the two-dollar window*) Two dollars on Sun-Up.

TONY: Hey! Hey, boss! Boss! (*Yanking* HACKENBUSH *by the coat-tails*) Come here, You wanna something hot?

HACKENBUSH: Not now, I just had lunch. Anyhow, I don't like hot ice-cream.

TONY: Hey!
(HACKENBUSH *goes back to the betting window.* TONY *pulls him by the coat-tails again*)
Come here! I no sella ice-cream. That's a fake to foola the police. I sella tips on the horses. I gotta something today can't lose. One dollar.

HACKENBUSH: No, some other time. I'm sorry, I'm betting on Sun-Up. Some other time, eh? (*He goes to the window.*) Two dollars on Sun-Up.

(TONY *pulls him back by the coat.*)

TONY: Hey, come here. Sun-Up is the worst horse on the track.

HACKENBUSH: I notice he wins all the time.

TONY: Aw, that's-a just because he comes in first.

HACKENBUSH: Well, I don't want him any better than first. (*He goes back to the window.*) Two dollars on Sun-Up.

(TONY *pulls him back by his coat-tails.*)

TONY: Hey, boss, come here. Come here. Suppose you bet on Sun-Up. What are you gonna get for your money? Two to one. One dollar and you remember me all your life.

HACKENBUSH: That's the most nauseating proposition I ever had.

TONY: Come on, come on, you look like a sport. Come on, boss – don't be a crunger for one buck.

(HACKENBUSH *thinks about it, hands him the dollar, and takes the envelope.*)

Thank you.

HACKENBUSH: What's this?

TONY: That's-a the horse.

HACKENBUSH: How'd he get in here?

TONY: Get your ice-cream. Tootsie-frootsie ice-cream. (*He walks away from* HACKENBUSH.)

HACKENBUSH: (*Reading from the paper that* TONY *gave him*) Z . . .

(*Close-up on the paper:* ZVBXRPL.)

(*Off-screen*) V–B–X–R–P–L–

(*Close-up on* HACKENBUSH.)

I had that same horse when I had my eyes examined. Hey, Ice-Cream. What about this optical illusion you just slipped me? I don't understand it.

TONY: Oh, that's not the real name of the horse, that's the name of the horse in code. Look in your code book.

HACKENBUSH: What do you mean, code?

TONY: Yeah, look in the code book. That'll tell you what horse you got.

HACKENBUSH: Well, I haven't got any code book.

TONY: You no gotta code book?

HACKENBUSH: You know where I can get one?

TONY: (*Opens ice-cream wagon*) Well, just by accident, I think I got one here. Here you are. (*He holds up the book.*)

HACKENBUSH: How much is it?

TONY: That's free.

HACKENBUSH: Oh, thanks. (*He takes the book from* TONY.)

TONY: Justa one-dollar printing charge.

HACKENBUSH: Well give me one without printing. I'm sick of printing. (*He tosses the book back to* TONY.)

TONY: Aw come on, you want to win.

HACKENBUSH: Yeah, sure, of course I want to win.

TONY: Well then, you gotta have this. (*He gives the book back.*)

HACKENBUSH: I want to win but I don't want the savings of a lifetime wiped out in the twinkling of an eye. (*He takes his money out secretively and gives it to* TONY.) Here.

TONY: Thank you very much. (TONY *goes back to his ice-cream wagon.*) Ice-cream! (*He exits, singing 'Tootsie-Frootsie Ice-Cream'.*)

(HACKENBUSH *begins leafing through the book.*)

HACKENBUSH: (*Reading*) Z–V–B–X–R–P–L. Page thirty-four. (*Calling off-screen*) Hey, Ice-Cream, I can't make head or tail out of this.

(TONY *is rolling his ice-cream wagon along.*)

TONY: Oh, that's all right, look in the master code book . . . that'll tell you where to look.

HACKENBUSH: Master code? I haven't got any master code book.

TONY: You no gotta master code book?

HACKENBUSH: No, do you . . . do you know where I can get one?

TONY: Well, just by accident, I think I got one right here. (*He takes another book from the ice-cream wagon.*) Huh – here you are.

HACKENBUSH: Lots of quick accidents around here for a quiet neighbourhood. Just a minute, ah, is there a printing charge on this?

TONY: No.

HACKENBUSH: Oh, thanks. (*He takes the book.*)

TONY: Just a two-dollar delivery charge.

HACKENBUSH: What do you mean, delivery charge? I'm standing right next to you.

TONY: Well, for such a short distance, I make it a dollar.

HACKENBUSH: Couldn't I move over here . . . (*He steps closer to* TONY.) . . . and make it – uh – fifty cents?

TONY: (*Stepping away*) Yes, but I'd move over here and make it a dollar just the same.

HACKENBUSH: Say, maybe I better open a charge account, huh?

TONY: You gotta some references?

HACKENBUSH: Well, the only one I know around here is you.

TONY: That's-a no good. You'll have to pay cash.

HACKENBUSH: (*Turning to the side to hide his money*) You know, a little while ago I could have put two dollars on – on Sun-Up and avoided all this.

TONY: Yeah, I know – throw your money away. (*He takes the money.*) Thank you very much.

HACKENBUSH: Now I'm all set, huh?

TONY: Yes, sir.

(*As* TONY *turns to his ice-cream wagon,* HACKENBUSH *looks over his books.*)

Get your tootsie-frootsie ice-cream.

(*Medium close-up on* HACKENBUSH.)

(*Off-screen*) Get your ice-cream . . . tootsie-frootsie . . .

HACKENBUSH: (*Reading*) Master code . . . plain code . . . X–V–B–X–R–P–L. 'The letter Z stands for J unless the horse is a filly.'

TONY: (*Off-screen*) Get your tootsie-frootsie ice-cream.

HACKENBUSH: Hey, Tootsie-Frootsie . . .

(*Medium close-up on* TONY.)

(*Off-screen*) Is the horse a filly?

TONY: I don't know. Look in your breeder's guide.

(*Medium close-up on* HACKENBUSH.)

(*Off-screen*) Get your ice-cream. Tootsie . . .

HACKENBUSH: What do you mean, breeder's guide? I haven't got a breeder's guide.

TONY: You haven't got a breeder's guide?

HACKENBUSH: (*Embarrassed*) Shh. Not so loud. I don't want it to get around that I haven't got a breeder's guide. Even my best friends don't know I haven't got a breeder's guide.

TONY: Well, boss, I feel pretty sorry for you walking around without a breeder's guide. Why you're just throwing your money away buying those other books without a breeder's guide.

(*A long wait while* HACKENBUSH *thinks about it. Medium close-up:* HACKENBUSH *is still thinking about it.*)

HACKENBUSH: (*Finally*) Where can I get one, as though I didn't know.

(*Medium close-up on* TONY.)

TONY: One is no good. You got to have the whole set.

(*Close-up on* HACKENBUSH.)

(*Off-screen*) Get your tootsie-frootsie . . .

HACKENBUSH: Hey, you know, all I wanted was a horse, not a public library. What d'you mean? How much is the set?

TONY: One dollar.

HACKENBUSH: One dollar?

TONY: Yeah, four for five. (*He goes back into his wagon and pulls out a stack of books.*)

HACKENBUSH: Well, all right, I'll . . . I'll . . . Give me the four of them. There's no use throwing away money, eh?

TONY: Oh, yeah, here you are.

HACKENBUSH: This is all I'm buying, too. I didn't want so many.

(TONY *hands the stack to* HACKENBUSH.)

I thought you could do this quickly.

TONY: Here you are. (*He crosses to the betting window behind* HACKENBUSH.) Six dollars on Sun-Up.

(HACKENBUSH *is in the foreground leafing through his guides;* TONY *leaves the betting window and heads for his ice-cream wagon.*)

Hurry up – tootsie-frootsie ice-cream!

(*Medium close-up on* HACKENBUSH. *His arms are filled with guidebooks and codes.*)

HACKENBUSH: Z–V–B–X–R–P–L is Burns.

TONY: (*Off-screen*) Yeah, that's-a right.

HACKENBUSH: Heh, Burns?

(TONY *joins him.*)

TONY: Yeah, yeah. Someday the code gives you the name of the jockey instead of the horse. Now you find out who jockey Burns is riding and that's the horse you bet on. It's easy. Get your ice-cream, tootsie-frootsie . . .

HACKENBUSH: Oh, I'm . . . I'm gettin' the idea of it . . .
(HACKENBUSH *looks through his load of books, two of which are between his legs.*) I didn't get it for a long time, you know. It's pretty tricky when you don't know it, isn't it, huh? (*He leafs through one of the books.*)

TONY: It's not that book.

HACKENBUSH: Huh?

TONY: It's not that book.

HACKENBUSH: It's not – it's not that book . . . ?

TONY: No.

HACKENBUSH: Oh, I see. (*He leafs through another.*)

TONY: No, it's not that book.

HACKENBUSH: Huh? (*He checks the books that are between his legs.*)

TONY: No, you haven't got that book.
(HACKENBUSH *is leafing through all his books.*)

HACKENBUSH: You've got it, huh?
(TONY *nods 'yes'.* HACKENBUSH *nods 'yes' with him.*)
I'll get it in a minute, though, won't I?

TONY: Get your tootsie-frootsie . . .

HACKENBUSH: I'm getting a fine tootsie-frootsie right here.

TONY: Get your ice-cream . . .

HACKENBUSH: How much is it?

TONY: One dollar. (*He reaches back into the wagon.*)

HACKENBUSH: And it's the last book I'm buying.

TONY: Sure, you don't need no more. Here . . . (*He hands* HACKENBUSH *the book.*)
(*We hear the bugle calling the horses to post.*)

HACKENBUSH: Here's . . . ah . . . here's ah . . . ten-dollar bill (*He hands him the money*) and shoot the change, will you. They're going to the post.

TONY: I gotta no change. I'll have to give you nine more books. You don't mind, huh, boss? You take nine more books. (*He pulls lots of books out.*)

HACKENBUSH: Nine more . . .

TONY: Yeah.

HACKENBUSH: Say, you don't handle any bookcases there, do you?

TONY: Well, you come tomorrow, anyhow.

(*He piles the additional books on to* HACKENBUSH's *arms.*)

HACKENBUSH: I didn't know that you needed so many.

TONY: That's all right, you're going to win on the horses today.

HACKENBUSH: (*Mumbling to himself*) Just walk up and bet on a horse.

TONY: Yeah. Open . . .

HACKENBUSH: Huh?

TONY: Open . . . open . . .

(HACKENBUSH *opens his legs;* TONY *stuffs the books between his knees.*)

HACKENBUSH: Say, am I shedding books down there?

TONY: Close.

HACKENBUSH: Huh?

TONY: Close . . .

(HACKENBUSH *closes his legs, locks the books in place.*)
. . . that's-a it. Now . . .

HACKENBUSH: Good thing I brought my legs with me, huh?

TONY: Yeah, yeah.

HACKENBUSH: Tell me what horse have I got? Hurry up, will you.

TONY: I'll find it . . . (*He looks through one of the books.*) . . . here it is, here it is . . . right here . . .

HACKENBUSH: I just heard the fellow blowing his horn.

TONY: Here it is, here . . . Jockey Burns – hundred and fifty two . . . that's-a Rosie . . .

HACKENBUSH: Rosie, huh?

TONY: Sure . . . oh, boy, look – forty to one.

HACKENBUSH: Forty to one.

TONY: Oh, what a horse, Rosie. Look. (*He points to the odds board.*)

HACKENBUSH: Am I going to give that bookie a whipping.

TONY: Oh, boy . . .

HACKENBUSH: I was going to bet on Sun-Up at ten to one. (*He hobbles over to the betting window.*)

TONY: Look – forty to one. Thatsa it.

HACKENBUSH: I'll show them a thing or two. Say, there . . .
   (HACKENBUSH *and* TONY *at the betting window.*)
   Hey there! Big boy, two dollars on Rosie, huh?
BOOKIE: Sorry, that race is over.
HACKENBUSH: Huh?
BOOKIE: I say, the race is over.
HACKENBUSH: Over? Who won?
BOOKIE: Sun-Up.
TONY: Sun-Up! That's-a my horse. (*He runs off.*)
   (TONY *runs to the window to collect.* HACKENBUSH, *stunned, watches him.*)
   Sun-Up! Sun-Up! Hurry . . . Good-ah-by, boss. (*Counting his money.*) Ten . . . twenty . . . thirty . . . (*He walks off.*)
   (HACKENBUSH *dumps all his books back into the ice-cream wagon and pushes it off, trailing books as he goes.*)
HACKENBUSH: Get your tootsie-frootsie nice ice-cream . . . nice tootsie-frootsie ice-cream . . .
   (*Fade out.*)

Fade in interior, Sanitarium. The telephone switchboard. We see part of the OPERATOR.
OPERATOR: (*Off-screen*) Oh, Miss Standish.
JUDY: (*Off-screen*) Yes.
OPERATOR: (*Off-screen*) These calls came for you while you were out.
JUDY: (*Off-screen*) Oh, thank you.
   (*The* OPERATOR *hands a stack of phone messages to* JUDY. *We see the messages and the* OPERATOR's *and* JUDY's *hands.* JUDY *leafs through the stack of messages. Camera pans up to* JUDY's *face as she tears the messages in half and dumps them in the* OPERATOR's *wastebasket.*)
OPERATOR: (*Into telephone mouthpiece*) Hello . . . Mr Stewart?
JUDY: (*To the* OPERATOR) I'm still out.
OPERATOR: I'm sorry but Miss Standish is still out. . . . (*She plugs in another call.*) Yes, Mr Whitmore.
   (WHITMORE *and* MORGAN *in* WHITMORE's *office.* WHITMORE *is on the phone.* MORGAN *listens.*)
WHITMORE: (*Into phone*) What about that call to the Florida

Medical Board? What? Well, keep on trying. Call me the
moment you get it. (*He hangs up and sits on the desk.*)

MORGAN: That's great. You can't even get any action out of your
own telephone operator.

WHITMORE: Don't worry, I'll get the dope on that Florida quack.

MORGAN: Now listen, Whitmore. I want to turn this place into a
gambling casino before the season ends. With my race track,
my night club and this, I'll have every sucker in America
flocking here. But every day counts.

WHITMORE: I'll let you know the moment I get the call.

MORGAN: I'll be waiting. (*He turns to leave.*)

Interior, lobby. JUDY *and* HACKENBUSH. *He is wearing a white
doctor's coat. Patients lounge about in the background.*

JUDY: Doctor, may I have one of your photographs?

HACKENBUSH: Why, I haven't one. I can let you have my
footprints, but they're upstairs in my socks.

JUDY: No. I want to announce your association with the
sanitarium. We'll send your picture to all the papers.
(*They move across the room;* JUDY *sits down.*)

HACKENBUSH: The Florida papers?

JUDY: Yes, it'll be wonderful publicity.

HACKENBUSH: Publicity? Oh, we mustn't have any of that, Miss
Standish. You know, the ethics of my profession. (*He sits
next to her.*)

JUDY: But – we have to get new patients.

HACKENBUSH: Well, after all, the old patients were good enough
for your father. Besides, who wants to see my picture – I'm
not a famous man. I'm just a simple country doctor with
horse sense.

JUDY: Oh, you're too modest. Never mind, we'll forget about the
pictures. And doctor, remember – I'm counting on you. The
success of the sanitarium is in your hands.

HACKENBUSH: Ummm . . . Look, Miss Standish . . . Suppose,
suppose that I were to tell you that . . . that I'm not the
doctor you think I am.

JUDY: Well, you're the only one that can help me. (*She stands.*)
And do be nice to Mrs Upjohn, won't you?

HACKENBUSH: Well, she's not exactly my type, but for you, I'd make love to a crocodile.

JUDY: Silly. (*She giggles and leaves.*)

(HACKENBUSH *moves quickly over to the telephone* OPERATOR.)

HACKENBUSH: Have the florist send some roses to Mrs Upjohn, and write 'Emily, I love you' on the back of the bill.

OPERATOR: Oh, just a moment, Dr Hackenbush. Yes, Mr Whitmore. No, I haven't been able to get that call through to the Florida Medical Board.

(HACKENBUSH *reacts to her saying 'call through to the Florida Medical Board'.*)

Well, I'm doing the best I can! It ought to be here any minute.

HACKENBUSH: If that call's what I think it is, she can cancel those roses and make it lilies for me!

(*Camera pans* HACKENBUSH *as he hurries away from the* OPERATOR.)

Interior, office. HACKENBUSH *hurries in, sits at the desk and grabs the telephone.*

HACKENBUSH: (*Into the phone*) Get me Mr Whitmore.

(*The screen splits diagonally:* HACKENBUSH *on the phone in his office on the left, and* WHITMORE *in his office picking up the ringing phone on the right.* HACKENBUSH *holds his nose and talks like an operator.*)

WHITMORE: Hello.

HACKENBUSH: (*Operator's voice*) Here's your Florida call, Mr Whitmore.

WHITMORE: All right. Hello.

HACKENBUSH: (*In a Southern woman's voice*) Florida Medical Board. Good morning.

WHITMORE: I'd like to talk to the man in charge of the records, please.

HACKENBUSH: (*Southern woman's voice*) Record department? Just a moment, sugar. (*Putting on his Southern-colonel voice*) Record department. Colonel Hawkins talking.

WHITMORE: (*Into phone*) Colonel Hawkins, did you get a wire from me regarding Dr Hackenbush?

(HACKENBUSH *turns on a small table fan next to the telephone.*)

HACKENBUSH: I'm sorry, sir, but there's a hurricane blowing down here . . . (*He puts paper into it to make more noise*) . . . and you'll have to talk a little louder. Whew – it certainly is the windiest day we ever did have!
(WHITMORE *looks at his phone receiver, trying to figure out what's going on.*)
(*Off-screen*) Whew! It certainly is windy!
WHITMORE: I want to know about Doctor . . .
(HACKENBUSH *leans back in his chair and lifts his leg.*)
(*Off-screen*) . . . Hackenbush.
(*Close-up on* HACKENBUSH's *foot. He buzzes* WHITMORE's *intercom, pushing the button with his foot.*
WHITMORE *hears the intercom, gets up, walks over to it.*)
WHITMORE: (*Into the intercom*) Yes.
HACKENBUSH: (*In his own voice*) Whitmore, you'll have to cut out that squawkin'. The patients are all complaining.
(WHITMORE *turns off the intercom and hurries back to the telephone.*)
(*Off-screen, back to his Colonel Hawkins voice*) And I hope sir, that is the information that you require.
WHITMORE: (*Seated*) I'm sorry, colonel, I didn't hear it. I was called to the dictograph.
HACKENBUSH: (*As* COLONEL HAWKINS) What was that you said, sir?
WHITMORE: I was called to the dictograph.
(HACKENBUSH *moves his foot to the intercom and buzzes.*
WHITMORE *moves to the intercom and clicks it on.*)
HACKENBUSH: (*Into the intercom in his own voice*) Whitmore, one more yelp out of you and I'll have you bounced out of here.
(WHITMORE *goes back to his desk and the phone.*)
(*Off-screen, Colonel Hawkins voice*) And I trust, suh, that that answers your question.
WHITMORE: I'm terribly sorry, colonel, I didn't hear you.
HACKENBUSH: (*Colonel Hawkins voice*) I can't hear you. You'll have to talk a little louder.
WHITMORE: I want to find out something about Hackenbush!
(*The intercom buzzes.*)
Well, what is it now? (*Furious, he rushes to the intercom.*)

HACKENBUSH: (*Leaning back in his chair with his foot on the intercom button; in his own voice*) Whitmore, that's the last time I'm going to warn you about that yowling!
(WHITMORE *goes back to his desk.*)
(*Off-screen, Colonel Hawkins voice*) And in conclusion, let me say –

WHITMORE: I'm sorry, colonel. What was that you said about Hackenbush?

HACKENBUSH: (*Into the phone, Colonel Hawkins voice*) Hacken– You mean Dr Hackenbush? Oh, no . . . (*Off-screen*) . . . he's not here.

WHITMORE: (*Into phone*) I know he's not there. He's here.

HACKENBUSH: (*Colonel Hawkins voice*) Then what are you bothering me for, yankee?

WHITMORE: But I want to know something about his Florida record!

HACKENBUSH: (*Holds his nose; the operator's voice again*) Here's your Florida call, Mr Whitmore.

WHITMORE: Operator, will you get off the line! Hello. Hello, colonel.

HACKENBUSH: (*Off-screen, Colonel Hawkins voice*) Yes?

WHITMORE: Are you sure you're speaking of Doctor . . . (*Off-screen*) Hugo Z. Hackenbush?

HACKENBUSH: (*Colonel Hawkins voice*) Who?

WHITMORE: Hugo Z. Hackenbush.

HACKENBUSH: (*Colonel Hawkins voice*) Who's calling him?

WHITMORE: The Standish Sanitarium.

HACKENBUSH: (*Colonel Hawkins voice*) Yes, that's where he works. Say, I understand he's doing a mighty fine job up there.

WHITMORE: I . . . I want to get some information regarding his qualifications for the job.

HACKENBUSH: (*Colonel Hawkins voice*) What job?

WHITMORE: As head of the sanitarium.

HACKENBUSH: (*Colonel Hawkins voice*) Who?

WHITMORE: Hackenbush.
(HACKENBUSH *buzzes the intercom.*
WHITMORE *turns to the buzzing intercom.*)

HACKENBUSH: (*In his own voice*) Whitmore, you calling me?

WHITMORE: (*Into intercom*) No, you sap! (*Into phone*) Hello . . .

HACKENBUSH: (*Colonel Hawkins voice*) Yes, now . . . now what was that name?

WHITMORE: Hackenbush! Hackenbush!

HACKENBUSH: (*Colonel Hawkins voice*) Uh, huh, well as soon as he comes in I'll have him get in touch with you.

WHITMORE: Bah! (*He slams the receiver down.*)

(*The windows behind him open slightly and someone peers in as* WHITMORE *storms out of the room.*

STUFFY *and* TONY *are seen through the open window.*)

TONY: You see that sourpuss? That's-a Whitmore, the man you gotta watch. He's-a no good. He's ina with Morgan and I think they're trying to get the sanitarium away from Miss Judy.

(*That angers* STUFFY *and he jumps into the room head first.* TONY *follows him.* STUFFY *moves towards the door as though he's going to find* WHITMORE *and kill him.*)

(*Stopping him*) Hey, hey, hey! No! No! You no gonna fight him. You're gonna watch 'im. You gotta watch him like a hawk.

(STUFFY *nods 'yes' and tries to run to the door anyway.* TONY *stops him.*)

Not so fast. No! Not so fast. Now look, first I gotta get you in here as a patient or elsa Whitmore is gonna get wise to you. Come on, I take you to the doctor.

(STUFFY *doesn't like that and makes a dash for the window.* STUFFY *goes out the window head first.* TONY *grabs him and pulls him back into the room.*)

Hey, Stuffy, Stuffy, hey, come here! Hey, he won't hurt you.

(STUFFY *mimes his arm being cut off.*)

No, no, come here. This fellow's a nice doc. You're hungry, eh?

(STUFFY *nods his head, 'yes'.*)

You wanna some ice-cream?

(STUFFY *again nods 'yes'.*)

You wanna a nice big steak?

(STUFFY *nods 'yes'*.)

With spinach?

(STUFFY *turns to dive out of the window;* TONY *pulls him back*.)

All righta, all right, no spinach, no spinach. Apple pie? Anda beautiful nurses?

(TONY *shows how curvy the nurses are and* STUFFY *begins to grin*.)

Oh, baby, come on, you're gonna get a nurse.

(TONY *leads* STUFFY *to the door*.)

Come on, you're gonna get plenty eat.

Interior, Sanitarium examination room.

Long shot of WILMERDING *and* INTERN.

WILMERDING: Have you seen Doctor Hackenbush?

INTERN: No, I haven't, doctor.

WILMERDING: Well, go and find him right away. Mrs Upjohn wants him.

(*The door opens and a* SECRETARY *followed by a nurse enters. Another nurse moves quickly across the room in the background*.)

INTERN: What's the matter with Mrs Upjohn?

WILMERDING: Nothing. In its most violent form.

(*The door opens and* DR HACKENBUSH, *in a wheelchair pushed by an* ORDERLY, *is rolled to the centre of the room. He rises, puffs on his cigar*.)

HACKENBUSH: (*To the* ORDERLY) Ah, pick me up at five.

ORDERLY: Yes, sir.

(HACKENBUSH *goes to his desk, hangs his head reflector on a clothes tree and sits.*

The SECRETARY *hands* HACKENBUSH *a note.*)

SECRETARY: Doctor, may I have an OK on this, please?

HACKENBUSH: Ummm, I'm too busy right now. I'll tell you what. I'll put the 'O' on now and come back later for the 'K'.

(WILMERDING *steps forward*.)

WILMERDING: Doctor Hackenbush . . .

HACKENBUSH: Ummm – a little later. Get me the Turkish bath.

(*A* NURSE *picks up the phone*.)

WILMERDING: Doctor Hackenbush . . . Mrs Upjohn is

complaining again – and these X-rays show absolutely nothing wrong with her.

(*The* NURSE *is on the phone, trying to reach the Turkish bath.*)

HACKENBUSH: Is that so? Who are you going to believe – me or those crooked X-rays?

NURSE: Doctor – the Turkish bath. (*She hands him the phone.*)

HACKENBUSH: (*Into phone*) Oh, hello. Gus, will you look in the steam room and see if my frankfurters are done?

(HACKENBUSH *hangs up the phone and stands.*)

That will be all. I have some important research.

(*Everyone leaves.*)

HACKENBUSH *opens the drawer and pulls out the racing chart. Camera pulls back as he puts his feet up on the desk and reads.* TONY *enters.*

HACKENBUSH *is behind the racing chart, reading.*

TONY *walks to* HACKENBUSH *and leans over the racing chart.*)

TONY: Excuse me.

(HACKENBUSH *puts the racing chart away and sits up.* TONY *recognizes him from the race track and backs away.*)

Oh, so you're the doctor?

HACKENBUSH: Yeah, remember me? I used to be in the book business.

(TONY *backs away as* HACKENBUSH *follows him around the room.*)

TONY: Hey, forgetta about that, doc. I gotta some good news for you.

HACKENBUSH: Yeah, what are the odds?

TONY: No, no, it's no horse. I gotta patient for you.

HACKENBUSH: Oh, a patient. Oh, fine. (*Wiggling his foot in the air*) What size?

(STUFFY *comes through the door dancing and playing his flute. Camera pans him into the room with* TONY *and* HACKENBUSH.*)

Well, you didn't get him here any too soon.

TONY: Hey, Stuffy!

(HACKENBUSH *grabs* STUFFY *as he goes by and puts him in a chair.*)

HACKENBUSH: Sit down here till I snatch you from the jaws of death. Just sit quiet there. Now, that's it.

TONY: That's-a doctor.

> (HACKENBUSH *is taking* STUFFY's *pulse.* STUFFY *looks very nervous as* HACKENBUSH *stares at his watch.*)

HACKENBUSH: Either he's dead or my watch has stopped. (*He goes to a cabinet and takes a thermometer.*)

TONY: He's a good doctor. He knows his business.

> (HACKENBUSH *shakes the thermometer down and sings.* STUFFY *watches him and plays his flute.*)

HACKENBUSH: Goodbye for ever, goodbye for ever. Here you are.

> (STUFFY *shuts his mouth tight; he doesn't want any part of the thermometer.*)

Oh, come on, this isn't going to hurt.

TONY: Oh, come on – everybody gets this.

HACKENBUSH: Come on, open up those pearly gates. Just flip this under your flapper. (*He slips the thermometer into* STUFFY's *mouth.*) Atta boy. It didn't hurt, did it, huh?

> (STUFFY *shakes his head – 'yes', it did.*)

TONY: He's pretty sick, eh, Doc?

> (STUFFY *starts to chew up the thermometer.*
> STUFFY *chews.* HACKENBUSH *looks at his watch.*)

HACKENBUSH: (*When the thermometer is gone*) Well, that temperature certainly went down fast.

> (STUFFY *gets up and goes to the cabinet.*
> *Close-up on a bottle in the cabinet.*
> STUFFY's *hand takes the bottle with a skull and crossbones, marked: POISON.*
> STUFFY *starts to drink the poison.* HACKENBUSH *grabs the bottle away from him.*)

Hey, don't drink that poison. That's four dollars an ounce.

> (HACKENBUSH *kneels in front of* STUFFY. *He looks through the mirror at* STUFFY *who jumps up, frightened.* TONY *grabs him.* HACKENBUSH *pushes up* STUFFY's *pants leg and begins tapping on his knee and then his foot and then his other foot.*)

TONY: I think we better put him to bed, doc. He looks awfully sick today. Better get him a nurse too.

HACKENBUSH: (*Muttering*) If he knows that, he'll go to bed.

TONY: Come on.

(HACKENBUSH *puts on his head mirror and goes back to* STUFFY
to continue the examination.)

HACKENBUSH: There now, take it easy, will ya, take it easy.

TONY: He's been a doctor for years, this fella.

HACKENBUSH: I've been a doctor longer than you've been a
patient, I'll tell you that.

(STUFFY *climbs on* HACKENBUSH's *back as if he were a horse.*
HACKENBUSH *immediately dumps him back in the chair.*)

TONY: Come here! What makes you do like that? What do you
think he's gonna play with you?

(HACKENBUSH *tries to look through his head mirror at* STUFFY's
eyes. STUFFY *peers back at* HACKENBUSH *through the head
mirror; they stare into each other's eyes.*)

HACKENBUSH: No, don't look at me – let me look at you, huh?
No, don't look at me – what do you think I am – a peep
show?

(STUFFY *pulls his head away, shakes it, and looks back into the
head mirror.*)

Get away there, will you? Hmmm. Rather a strange-looking
sight.

TONY: It's serious, eh, Doc?

HACKENBUSH: I haven't seen anything like this in years. The last
time I saw a head like that was in a bottle of formaldehyde.

TONY: I told you he was sick.

HACKENBUSH: (*Touches* STUFFY's *neck*) That's all pure
desiccation along there.

(HACKENBUSH's *hands inspect the side of* STUFFY's *neck.*)

He's got about a 15 per cent metabolism with an overactive
thyroid and a glandular affectation of about 3 per cent.

TONY: That's bad, huh?

HACKENBUSH: With a one per cent mentality.

(STUFFY *grins and leans back.*)

He's what we designate as the Crummy Moronic type.
Mmmm.

(HACKENBUSH *continues his examination.*)

All in all, this is the most gruesome-looking piece of blubber
I've ever peered at . . .

TONY: Hey, doc! Hey, doc!

HACKENBUSH: Huh?

TONY: You gotta da looking glass turned around – you're looking at yourself!

HACKENBUSH: I knew it all the time. (*He skips and dances across the room, laughing and singing.*) That was a good joke on all of us, wasn't it? Let's do it again sometime, huh?

(HACKENBUSH *leans over next to* STUFFY. STUFFY *opens his mouth but of course nothing comes out.*)

Say 'Ah'. Louder!

(*Still nothing.*)

Louder!

(*He opens* STUFFY's *mouth wider still – nothing.*

HACKENBUSH *runs across the room to the door.*)

TONY: (*Off-screen*) Hey, doc, where you going?

HACKENBUSH: I'm going to the ear doctor. I'm deaf.

TONY: (*Off-screen*) Aw, come on back. It's notta you – it's him.

HACKENBUSH: Well, sometimes I'm not sure who's getting the examination here.

(*He crosses back to* STUFFY. HACKENBUSH *puts his hand on* STUFFY's *heart.*)

Now take it easy, huh?

(*He then pushes on his chest; as he does* STUFFY *begins to blow a bubble. When* HACKENBUSH *lets up the pressure the bubble disappears.*)

Say, am I stewed or did a grapefruit just fly past? (*He means the bubble.*)

TONY: I don't see nothing.

(HACKENBUSH *pushes lightly on* STUFFY's *chest, then on the mid-chest, then on his stomach and the bubble comes out again. He lets up his pressure and looks up at* STUFFY's *face but the bubble disappears before he can see it.*)

HACKENBUSH: If that's his Adam's apple – he's got yellow fever.

TONY: He's got ingrown balloons.

HACKENBUSH: He has, huh? Well, we'll soon find out.

(*He presses on* STUFFY's *chest, mid-chest and stomach. On the third press the bubble comes out again. This time* HACKENBUSH *sees it, grabs* STUFFY *by the throat so the bubble will last.*)

Hold it till I get a rock, will you?

TONY: Look – look – he's got a blister on his tongue.

HACKENBUSH: Is that what it is?

TONY: Yeah – I think it's a Ubangi.

HACKENBUSH: Well, I'll get a hammer and Ubangi that right off.
(*He leans over and picks up a mallet.*) I had a case like that
once in Dusseldorf, many years ago. And a – (STUFFY *is
leaning over and* HACKENBUSH *sees the top of his head and
thinks it's the bubble.*) – Say, it's grown considerably, hasn't
it, huh? What's that hairy fungus all over it?

TONY: Some fungus, hey, doc?

HACKENBUSH: Not a great deal, no. I don't know . . .

TONY: Hey, you're making a mistake – that's his head.

HACKENBUSH: Well, if that's his head, he's making a mistake,
not me.
(HACKENBUSH *puts the hammer down.*)
I can't do anything for him. That's a case for Frank Buck.
(STUFFY *has a stethoscope stuck to his forehead.*)

TONY: All right, put him in the room until Frank Buck gets here.

HACKENBUSH: Oh, fine, shall we say a fifty-buck room – or would
you prefer something better?

TONY: We'll take something better.

HACKENBUSH: Oh, that will be nice.

TONY: Yeah, but we'll talk about the money tomorrow.

HACKENBUSH: Oh, no, money on the line or out you go.
(STUFFY'*s playing with the stethoscope.*
TONY *picks up* HACKENBUSH'*s watch from the desk and reads
the inscription.*)

TONY: 'To Dr Hugo Z. Hackenbush for saving my horse'.

HACKENBUSH: Here, gimme that. Come here with that watch.

TONY: You – a horse doctor!

HACKENBUSH: Shhh! A little easy with that talk.

TONY: A horse doctor.

HACKENBUSH: Don't mention that word around here.

TONY: Hey, that's terrible. I'm gonna tell Miss Judy, quick.
(*He walks to the door, followed by* HACKENBUSH.)
No, that's no good.
(*He turns and follows* HACKENBUSH *back into the centre of the
room.*)

Miss Judy, she's-a depending on you. A horse doctor.

HACKENBUSH: Now listen, boys, I admit it. You've caught me with my coat down. Well, it's been nice knowing you.

(*He starts running away;* TONY *stops him.*)

TONY: Oh, no you don't. Oh, no.

HACKENBUSH: Now let's get together on this. I'm open to any kind of a proposition.

TONY: All right. You stick on to this job, You make Mrs Upjohn happy or we're gonna have you thrown in gaol.

HACKENBUSH: Well, that – that doesn't leave me much choice, does it.

(STUFFY *picks up a hypodermic syringe and starts to fill it from a pan under the cabinet.*)

TONY: (*Off-screen*) Listen, Hackenapuss, nobody must know you're a horse doctor.

(*Close-up of the hypodermic syringe and bottle. The label on the bottle reads: 'Novocaine – for hypodermic use only'.*)

(*Off-screen*) You understand, you make one false move and we fix you . . .

(STUFFY *jabs the needle into* HACKENBUSH's *leg.*)

(*Off-screen*) . . . good.

HACKENBUSH: I hate to admit it, but – I haven't got a leg to stand on. Now let's (*He stands on his Novocained leg and collapses*) . . . hey, wait a minute. Hey, bring that over here, will ya.

TONY: Hey, Stuff– . . .

(HACKENBUSH's *numb leg spins and turns freely.*)

There it goes.

HACKENBUSH: Now . . .

(TONY *and* STUFFY *try to help him to his feet.*)

TONY: Get it around, Stuffy.

(STUFFY *grabs the numb leg.*)

HACKENBUSH: No, whip it around the other way.

TONY: You keep quiet – we know . . .

HACKENBUSH: You're goin' the wrong way.

TONY: We know what we're doin'.

HACKENBUSH: OK. (*He walks around the room with his legs crossed.*) There. For a while I thought I wasn't going to be able to walk again.

TONY: Hey, look, I got it too. (*He walks with his legs crossed.*)

HACKENBUSH: It worked out fine. It's fine now. Yes, it's . . .

TONY: Hey, Stuffy, I got it. Come on.

HACKENBUSH: . . . better than it ever was . . .

> (TONY *and* STUFFY *follow* HACKENBUSH *out, walking with their legs crossed, imitating him.*
> *Fade out.*)

Fade in exterior, race track.

GIL *is timing Hi-Hat with* STUFFY *riding him. As Hi-Hat whizzes by,* TONY *comes over to* GIL.

GIL: One forty-four. That's bad.

TONY: You thinka that's bad. I know something worse than that. Did Stuffy tell you?

GIL: Tell me what?

TONY: Hackenapuss – he's a horse doctor.

GIL: What!

TONY: Sure. Here, ask Stuffy.

> (STUFFY *comes in leading Hi-Hat.*)

GIL: A horse doctor! Does anyone else know about this?

TONY: Only Hackenapuss and he won't talk.

GIL: Ah, it's bound to get out sooner or later. There must be something we can do to help Judy.

TONY: Yes! Hi-Hat. (*He strokes Hi-Hat's nose and talks to him.*) You gotta wina race and maka us plenty a money.
> (STUFFY *rubs his stomach and points to his mouth.*)
Stuffy's right. Hi-Hat's too hungry to run.

GIL: Oh, I can take care of that. I'm going to get paid extra for singing at the water carnival tonight.

TONY: Ah, that's-a fine. You sing – I sella some more books and Stuffy, he's goin' to put Hi-Hat to bed.

GIL: OK, boys, I've got to go to rehearsal. See you later.

TONY: All right, good luck.

> (GIL *leaves.*)

SHERIFF: (*Off-screen*) Hey, you!

TONY: Hello, Sheriff.

SHERIFF: (*Walking to them*) I thought I told you guys not to take this horse out of the stable until I got the rest of my dough.

TONY: Hey, we didn't take him out. He walked out and we
   followed him.

SHERIFF: Well, I warned you. Now I'm taking the nag.

TONY: Hey, Sheriff, you can't take that horse. We're just getting
   him into condition. How we gonna win the money to pay the
   feed bill?

SHERIFF: That don't mean a thing to me. I'm gonna put him
   where nobody'll take him out. (*He leads Hi-Hat off.*)
   (*The* SHERIFF *doesn't see* TONY *and* STUFFY *next to Hi-Hat.*
   They untie his bridle.
   As he walks across the field, we see that the bridle is now attached
   to STUFFY, *who lopes along behind him.* STUFFY *stops for a*
   moment and the SHERIFF *turns and sees that Hi-Hat is gone.*
   STUFFY *runs away and the* SHERIFF *chases him.*
   TONY *climbs on Hi-Hat, and starts to ride away.* STUFFY *runs*
   up to them and jumps on the back of the horse. They ride off
   across the track, the SHERIFF *shaking his fist after them.*
   Fade out.)

Fade in – Insert of Programme:

TONIGHT
GALA
WATER CARNIVAL
SPARKLING SPRINGS LAKE
DINING   DANCING   ENTERTAINMENT

A hand turns the page to:

Picture	*Picture*
of	*of*
VIVIEN FAY	GIL

Captioned:	*Captioned:*
VIVIEN FAY	GIL STEWART
and her ballet	*tenor*

Dissolve to exterior, lake and fountain.
Elegant people walk in front of the spray.
A waiter comes up to people at a table in a boat.
People sit at tables in front of the fountain.
As the fountain stops and the spray dies, it reveals GIL *in a white*

dinner-jacket standing in a boat surrounded by beautiful girls strumming mandolines.

GIL: (*Singing*) Tonight, we will be gay

Turning away from all regret.

Tonight, saying goodbye to every sigh, we will . . .

(HACKENBUSH *and* JUDY *are in* MRS UPJOHN'*s boat.*)

HACKENBUSH: He couldn't get you, so he took six other girls.

GIL: (*Off-screen, singing*)

. . . forget. And in fancy 'neath a distant moon.

(JUDY *pouts.*)

(*Off-screen, singing*) You and I will drift upon a blue lagoon.

On blue Venetian waters, together we'll dream.

(*The fountain cascades behind him.*)

(*Singing*) On blue Venetian waters, how lovely 'twill seem.

Starlight tumbling down.

(*Singing to* JUDY *across the water*) You shall wear, as a silver crown for your hair.

(*She looks at him but pretends not to notice.*)

(*Off-screen, singing*) The blue Venetian moonlight will soon light our way.

Your eyes will tell me secrets your lips dare not say.

(GIL'*s boat turns and moves across the lake.*)

(*Singing*) While I'm singing a love song of love dreams come true, of blue Venetian waters and you.

(*His boat disappears at the bottom of the screen and only the water curtain is left. As the water curtain falls away it reveals the corps de ballet: beautiful girls in diaphanous gowns dance out on to the platform and begin their Busby-Berkeley-style ballet.*

They are reflected in the water as they dance.

As they twirl, a lot of attractive legs are shown.

Shooting past people seated at tables.

The lighting changes: dark, and shadowy.

The lighting changes back to bright.

The music becomes Spanish.

Shooting past the Spanish orchestra playing in the foreground.

The girls bow and dip as they cross the stage.

Their skirts fly as they twirl.

Leaves from the trees fall on VIVIEN FAY. *She starts across bridge.*

VIVIEN FAY *starts to toe-dance down the bridge. Girls pose on either side of her.*
She dances her heart out in front of the girls.
STUFFY *and* TONY *are sitting on a diving board, watching the ballet.*
The dancers break their pose and join VIVIEN FAY.
We can see the ballet in the background through the marimba-players in the Spanish orchestra.
The corps de ballet is arranged as a bouquet of flowers, and is reflected in the water.)

GIRLS: (*Singing*) When you're singing a love song, your love dreams come true.
(*A ripple across the lake washes away the reflection.*
VIVIEN FAY *dances away.*
VIVIEN FAY *and the girls dance past the musicians.*
VIVIEN FAY *dances and the girls pose behind her.*
She begins to toe-dance again.
She twirls across the stage.
She twirls around the platform.
She crosses past the camera, still twirling.
Still more twirling.
VIVIEN *dances towards the camera, still twirling.*
She twirls into the foreground and poses victoriously at the height of the crescendo.
Shooting past the people at tables, VIVIEN *takes bows and they applaud.*

HACKENBUSH *and* MRS UPJOHN *are in* MRS UPJOHN'S *canopied boat applauding.* JUDY *is between them.*
FLO *is an attractive blonde. She flirts with* HACKENBUSH *as she walks by him.*
MRS UPJOHN *is applauding enthusiastically while* HACKENBUSH *is flirting with* FLO.)

MRS UPJOHN: Isn't it beautiful?

HACKENBUSH: (*Meaning* FLO) The prettiest number I've ever seen. (*He climbs out of the boat.*)
(HACKENBUSH *is climbing on all fours off to the left.* MRS UPJOHN *is still applauding.*)

MRS UPJOHN: Oh, Hugo, it's so impressive . . . (*She sees*

HACKENBUSH *is gone; she rises.*) Now what? (*She stalks off the boat.*) The idea!
(*As she leaves,* GIL *climbs into the boat.* JUDY *rises.* GIL *pushes* JUDY *back into her seat.*)

GIL: Oh now Judy, wait a minute, wait a minute. Look, I want to talk to you. It's about Hackenbush. You can't depend on him.

JUDY: (*Formally*) Mrs Upjohn is perfectly satisfied with Doctor Hackenbush and that's all that matters. As a matter of fact, she may take over the notes tomorrow.

GIL: (*Discouraged*) Well, I guess everything's all right.

JUDY: (*Avoiding him*) Yes.

GIL: Well, there's nothing to worry about, is there?

JUDY: (*Still cool, but obviously wanting something else*) No, not a thing.
(GIL *rises.*)
Except that horse of yours.

GIL: Now wait a minute. That horse is all right. He's in the pink. Why today he ran the mile in one thirty-six.
(JUDY *is cynical but impressed.*)
(*Off-screen*) The horse is going places.

JUDY: Oh, that's wonderful. I wish you luck.

GIL: Thanks. I'm sorry I bothered you.

JUDY: That's all right.

GIL: Aw, now, Judy . . . (*He sits down beside her*) . . . I'm the biggest liar in seven states. He isn't all right – and he isn't in the pink. It was one forty-four instead of one thirty-six. And the only place he'll ever go is where the Sheriff takes him.

JUDY: Oh, you can't possibly mean Hi-Hat.

GIL: Well, there's only one horse in my stable. Come on, let me have the rest of it.

JUDY: The only thing I'm going to say is this, Gil. Don't ever let a horse come between us again!
(STUFFY *and* TONY *are still on the diving board, they're watching* GIL *and* JUDY.)

TONY: She loves him. Everything is going to be all right now.
(*On the dance floor, as* HACKENBUSH *dances with* MRS

UPJOHN, *he ogles* FLO, *off-screen.*
FLO *is on the stairs. She smiles at* HACKENBUSH.
He glances at FLO *as he dances with* MRS UPJOHN.
FLO *smiles back and starts down the steps.*
HACKENBUSH *dances* MRS UPJOHN *around the floor with one eye on* FLO.)

HACKENBUSH: (*Like a square-dance caller*) Change your partners!
(*He twirls* MRS UPJOHN *around and away from him and while she's spinning, he dances away towards* FLO.
HACKENBUSH *spins up towards* FLO, *doing an elaborate improvised dance step. He and* FLO *begin to tango.*
FLO *is tangoing sexily around* HACKENBUSH. *He takes a silk handkerchief and rolls it around his rear end which he thinks is sexy.* FLO *continues to dance.*
MRS UPJOHN *looks through her lorgnette, shocked.*
HACKENBUSH *leaves* FLO *and dances with* MRS UPJOHN.)

MRS UPJOHN: Hugo, I'm surprised at you!
(*He begins to rumba with her.*)

HACKENBUSH: Oh, you didn't know I could rumba?
(FLO's *back is towards them. She turns and smiles at* HACKENBUSH.
HACKENBUSH *and* MRS UPJOHN *are dancing. He glances at* FLO *over* MRS UPJOHN's *shoulder.*
FLO *smiles at* HACKENBUSH *as he dances.*
(*Like a square-dance caller*) Change your partners!
(HACKENBUSH *twirls* MRS UPJOHN *away.*
HACKENBUSH *slouches through the crowd towards* FLO, *takes her in his arms and they begin to dance.*
HACKENBUSH *twirls* FLO *towards the camera and slides along the floor next to her.*
MRS UPJOHN *watches them disapprovingly.*
HACKENBUSH *and* FLO *are tangoing wildly. The music changes.*
HACKENBUSH *dances away from* FLO.
HACKENBUSH *dances back into* MRS UPJOHN's *arms.*)

MRS UPJOHN: How would you like me to dance away from you?

HACKENBUSH: I'd be satisfied if you danced off my feet.
(FLO *watches* HACKENBUSH *and* MRS UPJOHN *dance. She winks at him.*

HACKENBUSH *has his eye on* FLO. *He grins at her through* MRS UPJOHN's *feathered hat.*
FLO *sees* HACKENBUSH *looking at her and moves towards him.*
HACKENBUSH *stoops down, dances in a circle around* MRS UPJOHN *and then dances away from her into the crowded dance floor.*
The music changes again and HACKENBUSH *dances over to* FLO *and they begin to Charleston wildly.* HACKENBUSH *spins away from* FLO *and back to* MRS UPJOHN.

MRS UPJOHN: Hugo, I'm disappointed in you. To think of your dancing with that strange woman.

HACKENBUSH: Well, don't think of it. Think of me dancing with you!

(*He glances over* MRS UPJOHN *to* FLO.
She smiles back at HACKENBUSH.)

HACKENBUSH: I'm crazy about you.

(HACKENBUSH *dances with* MRS UPJOHN *but speaks to* FLO.
MRS UPJOHN *hears him and she's in heaven.*)
Nothing will ever come between us again. You don't know how lonely I get, night after night, in my little room at the sanitarium. Room four-twelve.

MRS UPJOHN: Perhaps I could come in and say good night to you.

(HACKENBUSH *continues to speak to* FLO. MRS UPJOHN *hasn't a clue to what's going on.*)

HACKENBUSH: Yes! We could have a midnight snack.

(FLO *is listening to* HACKENBUSH.)
(*Off-screen*) A nice little steak between us.

MRS UPJOHN: Why Hugo!

HACKENBUSH: (*To* MRS UPJOHN) Oh, you would stay up until midnight! That's the way you follow doctor's orders!

(HACKENBUSH *hustles* MRS UPJOHN *off the floor, past* FLO.)
You're supposed to be in bed by ten o'clock! (*To* FLO)
Twelve o'clock. (*To* MRS UPJOHN) Ten o'clock!

(STUFFY *and* TONY *are still on the diving board.*
STUFFY *looks up, frightened.*
The SHERIFF *is creeping up on the diving board towards* STUFFY *and* TONY.
The SHERIFF *walks on the diving board towards* TONY *and*

STUFFY. *They swing down to a lower diving board to avoid him and the* SHERIFF *lunges at them and tumbles off the diving board.*
The SHERIFF *splashes into the water.*
He thrashes about in the water.
TONY *and* STUFFY *run away towards the orchestra.*
The MANAGER *has joined the* SHERIFF, *who is dripping wet.*)
MANAGER: Sheriff, listen! We mustn't have any disturbance here tonight.
   (TONY *is at the piano and* STUFFY *has the conductor's baton. The* SHERIFF *is wringing out his coat.*)
SHERIFF: All right – I can wait!
   (*The orchestra is tuning up.* STUFFY *begins to conduct.* TONY *begins to play a Rakhmaninov prelude.*
   TONY *continues to play the piano but changes the music to 'On the Beach at Bali Bali'.*
   STUFFY *continues to conduct as* TONY *finishes playing.*
   The SHERIFF *watches, mayhem in his eyes.*
   TONY *sees the* SHERIFF *and runs off.*
   TONY *jumps over a low wall, and over the* SHERIFF, *and runs away. The* SHERIFF *chases him.*
   STUFFY *watches* TONY *run away and runs after him.*
   The SHERIFF, *with the* MANAGER, *and two assistants, sees* STUFFY *and runs towards him.*
   He sees the SHERIFF *coming after him and quickly sits down at the piano.*
   The SHERIFF *is stymied. He can't arrest* STUFFY *while he's playing.*
   STUFFY's *at the piano and begins to play the Rakhmaninov prelude.*
   STUFFY *is baffled by the music he's playing.*
   He begins to attack the piano and plays wildly.
   He pounds on the keys.
   The piano begins to fall apart. STUFFY *continues to play.*
   STUFFY *grins and cleans his ear out with his finger. The keys begin to fly off the piano.*
   He tries to keep playing. More of the piano falls apart.
   He plays as the piano disintegrates around him.

STUFFY *dives into what's left of the piano and he pulls the string*
block out of the mess and decides it's a harp. He pulls the harp out
of the rubble.
The SHERIFF, *the* MANAGER, *and an assistant are all furious.*
STUFFY *sits down at the harp and begins to play.*
He continues to play and finishes. The orchestra applauds him and
he raises his clasped hands above his head like a boxer who has just
won his fight.
The SHERIFF, *the* MANAGER, *and an assistant are watching*
STUFFY, *waiting for their opportunity.*
STUFFY *is standing by the harp. He sees the* SHERIFF *and twirls*
the seat of the piano stool up as high as it will go, sits down on it,
and it catapults him up above the harp and into the air.
The SHERIFF, *the* MANAGER, *and an assistant watch* STUFFY *fly*
over their heads.
STUFFY *splashes into the lake.*
STUFFY *splashes about.*
STUFFY *swims away. The* SHERIFF *runs to the edge of the water*
and then runs along the side of the lake.
WHITMORE *is pacing next to a tall hedge near the lake.* FLO *joins*
him.)

WHITMORE: And . . . ?

FLO: Well, it's in the bag. I have a date with him in his room at
twelve.

WHITMORE: Nice going. And see that you stay there till I break in
with Mrs Upjohn. I want Hackenbush fired out of the
sanitarium tonight!

FLO: Don't worry, toots. When you knock on the door, I'll have
that moth-eaten Romeo playing the balcony scene.
(STUFFY, *carrying his wet clothes, bursts through the bottom of the*
hedge. He's heard WHITMORE *and* FLO *plotting. He shakes his*
fist after them.
He tosses his wet clothes over the hedge and runs off.
STUFFY *runs down a small stairway. Camera pans to a group of*
girls in frilly dresses playing blindman's buff. The 'blind man' in
the centre is TONY. *The girls run off.* STUFFY *runs to* TONY.
TONY, *still blindfolded, thinks* STUFFY *is one of the girls and*
embraces him.)

TONY: I gotcha! I gotcha!

(*He pulls his blindfold off, sees it's* STUFFY *he's holding in his arms.*)

Oh, you spoila my game. What's-a matter? What's-a matter?

(STUFFY *whistles through his teeth, holds his fingers under his nose like a moustache.*)

Buffalo Bill?

(STUFFY *slouches in a circle.*)

Buffalo Bill goes ice-skating.

(STUFFY *begins hacking at a bush.*)

Oh, Hackenabush?

(STUFFY *turns and shakes* TONY's *hand wildly, congratulating him for getting it.*)

Oh – what's-a matter with him? Dr Hackenabush –

(STUFFY *makes the outlines of a curvy girl with his hand.*)

He's gotta snake?

(STUFFY *makes the curve again and adds a wolf whistle.*)

No? He's got apple dumpling?

(STUFFY *shakes his head, 'no', makes the moustache sign.*)

Dr Hackenabush – he's got apple dumplings –

(STUFFY *makes an even curvier girl and adds a longer wolf whistle.*)

No, 'at's-a no apple dumpling, no.

(STUFFY *pulls up his pants leg, turns his ankle and demurely shows his calf to* TONY.)

No, no. Oh, it's a woman! A woman!

(STUFFY *shakes his hand, congratulating him.*)

Oh, I get it. Oh, there's a woman . . . yes, smart, eh?

(STUFFY *makes the moustache sign.*)

Dr Hackenabush – there's a woman –

(STUFFY *stomps his foot.*)

She got a wooden leg –

(STUFFY *shakes his head.*)

No? –

(STUFFY *stomps his foot again.*)

She's got a woodpecker?

(STUFFY *slaps his forehead at* TONY's *obtuseness.*)

She got a headache?

213

(STUFFY *shakes his head, 'no', and makes the moustache sign;*
TONY *makes the moustache sign with* STUFFY *as if that will help
him understand.*)
Dr Hackenabush –
(STUFFY *makes the curvy woman sign too.*)
– there's a woman –
(STUFFY *stomps his foot again.*)
She knock on the door –
(STUFFY *clasps his hand to congratulate him for getting it and
jumps up and down, whistling.*)
Ah, she knock on the door! All right, all right –
(STUFFY *makes the moustache sign.*)
– Dr Hackenabush –
(STUFFY *makes the curvy sign.*)
– there's a woman –
(STUFFY *stomps his foot.*)
– she knocks on the door.
(STUFFY *points over* TONY's *shoulder, does all the gestures at
once rapidly, hopelessly confusing* TONY.)
– Ah, you're crazy, you maka me sick.
(STUFFY *grabs a 'House Rules Card' which is conveniently
tacked to a nearby tree.*)
What's-a matter now?
(STUFFY *hits it with his foot, knocks it out of the frame and holds
the empty frame in front of his face.*)
Oh, she's gonna frame him.
(STUFFY, *overjoyed that* TONY *finally gets it, collapses into his
arms.* TONY *drags him away.*)
Oh, come on – hurry up – hurry up!
(*Fade out.*)

Fade in interior, Hackenbush's room.
The table is set for two. HACKENBUSH *is wearing a silk robe. He
pirouettes and waltzes around the room to the sound of 'The Blue
Danube' as he brushes his hair and fixes his tie. There's a knock at the
door.*
HACKENBUSH: Who is it?
FLO: (*Off-screen, musically*) It's Miss Marlowe.

HACKENBUSH: Just a moment, fruitcake.

(*He sprays perfume into the air: on the table, on the couch, on his shoes.*)

(*At the door*) Yes?

FLO: Oh, doctor.

(HACKENBUSH *opens the door and* FLO, *carrying a fur stole, oozes her way into the room.*)

Thank-kew.

HACKENBUSH: Thank-yo. (*He picks up a box of flowers.*) Do you like gardenias?

FLO: I adore them. How did you know?

HACKENBUSH: I didn't – so I got you a forget-me-not. (*He hands her a sunflower.*) One whiff of this and you'll forget everything. Won't you sit down?

(*They walk to the table. He pulls out the chair. She sits.*)

FLO: Thank-kew.

HACKENBUSH: Thank-yo.

FLO: (*She hands him her fur*) Oh, ah – do you mind?

HACKENBUSH: Not at all. I always take the wrap. (*He tosses the fur on the floor behind him.*)

FLO: You're such a charming host.

HACKENBUSH: The Hackenbushes were all like that. How about a short beer?

FLO: Nothing, thank-kew.

HACKENBUSH: (*Mimicking her*) Thank-yo.

(*He sits across the table from her. Between them, in the centre of the table, is an enormous floral arrangement.*)

Ah, Miss Marlowe, I've dreamed of this moment ever since I met you.

(*They both lean to the left to see each other around the flowers.*)

For days I've been trying to see you. And I still don't seem to be able to make the grade. Ah, a quiet evening alone with you. What more could anyone ask.

(*He leans to the right; she leans to the left. They both look around opposite sides of the flowers trying to see each other. He looks under the table for her.*)

Say, have you sneaked out of here?

FLO: Yoo-hoo! (*She waves.*)

HACKENBUSH: Oh, there you are. (*He climbs on to the chair.*)
Yoo-hoo! Isn't this too, too devastating?
(*He sits on the back of the chair;* FLO *is doing her best to look enraptured.*)
Would you mind carving? I can't reach the steak from here.

FLO: Me?
(*There's heavy knocking at the door.*)

HACKENBUSH: Yes?
(*The door opens and* STUFFY *and* TONY *enter.*)

TONY: Hey, doc! Hey, doc! Can you see us?

HACKENBUSH: If I can't, there's something wrong with my glasses.
(STUFFY *begins making the curvy-girl sign and points to* FLO.)

TONY: You mean her? She's the one?
(STUFFY *nods 'yes'.*)
We fix her. (*To* FLO) Ah, signorina, *gentile e bella.* [Ah, lady, kind and beautiful.] Oh, baby, you looka good to me.
(*He jumps on her lap and* STUFFY *clasps his hands and pats him on the back approvingly.*)

FLO: Oh, oh – oh, stop it!

HACKENBUSH: Hey, wait a minute, wait a minute. I thought you came here to see me?
(TONY *is on* FLO's *lap;* STUFFY *is behind them.*)

TONY: Well, I can see you from here.
(STUFFY *jumps on* TONY's *lap.*)

FLO: Oh, oh, get up you . . . oh – oh . . .
(STUFFY *pulls up his pants leg, whistles to* HACKENBUSH *and signals to him to come sit on his lap.*)

TONY: You know my friend.
(HACKENBUSH *shakes his head, 'no', indignantly.*
STUFFY *continues to urge* HACKENBUSH *to sit on his lap.*)

HACKENBUSH: (*Shaking his head, 'no'*) No, no. Not for me – three men on a horse.

FLO: Oh, what is the meaning of this? (*She pushes* STUFFY *and* TONY *off her lap.*)
Oh!
(STUFFY *flops right back down.*)
Why you little pest! (*She gets up indignantly and turns to* HACKENBUSH.)

Well!

HACKENBUSH: (*Getting down from his chair*) Say, what's the matter with you mugs? Haven't you got any gallantry at all? (*He walks to* TONY *and* STUFFY, *and* FLO *turns her back on them.*)

TONY: (*Privately*) She's in with Whitmore. She's trying to frame you.

HACKENBUSH: I wouldn't mind framing her. A prettier picture I've never seen.

FLO: Thank-kew.
(*She turns;* HACKENBUSH *bows to her quickly.*)

HACKENBUSH: Thank-yo. (*He turns back to* TONY *and* STUFFY.)

TONY: (*Screaming*) Hey, doc! Doc, I'm-a tell you a secret – she's out to get you.

FLO: Why, I've never been so insulted in my life.

HACKENBUSH: Well, it's early yet.

FLO: Well, I'm leaving. I'm certainly not going to stay here with these men.
(TONY *runs to the door. He opens the door to show her the way out.*)

HACKENBUSH: (*Off-screen*) You're not leaving – they're leaving.
(STUFFY *wraps the fur around* FLO *and starts to drag her to the door.*)
Now come on, I want you fellows to get out of here.
(*He grabs the other side of the fur and pulls in the other direction. The fur rips.*)

FLO: Oh, my cape.

HACKENBUSH: Come back here with my woman.
(TONY *helps* STUFFY *pull* FLO. HACKENBUSH *continues to tug on her other arm trying to keep her in the room.*)

FLO: Oh!

HACKENBUSH: You fellows are busting up a beautiful romance. What's the matter with you?

TONY: Doc, get her out – she's gonna make trouble.

HACKENBUSH: You've got her all wrong. This is my aunt and she's come to talk over some old family matters.

TONY: I wish I had an aunt look like that.

HACKENBUSH: Well, take it up with your uncle.

TONY: Hey, doc!
> (FLO *sits down at the table and begins to powder her nose.*)
> Doc, you're playing with fire.
HACKENBUSH: I notice you didn't mind getting scorched.
TONY: Well, I got fire insurance.
HACKENBUSH: Well, you better get accident.
> (STUFFY *gestures towards the door with his thumb, telling* FLO *to leave.*)
FLO: (*Returning the gesture*) Scram! Blow!
> (STUFFY *leans over and blows the powder in her compact into her face. A great cloud of powder obscures both of them.*)
> Oh! Oh! Oh! Oh!
> (STUFFY *runs to the door and follows* TONY *out of the room.*
> HACKENBUSH *slams the door shut and* FLO *jumps up and dusts herself off.*)
HACKENBUSH: How do you like those cheap chisellers horning in on us? (*He walks back to the table and holds the chair for* FLO.)
FLO: Thank-kew.
HACKENBUSH: Thank-yo.
> (*He starts to sit at the table across from her; he misses the chair and crashes to the floor. She laughs off-screen.*
> *He picks himself and the chair up off the floor and sits. They look around the flowers at each other again.*)
FLO: Oh, ah – how about a little Scotch?
HACKENBUSH: Why, I'd love it. (*He starts to hand her his glass.*)
> Oh – ah – I'll ring for some. (*He walks to the phone.*)
FLO: Thank-kew.
HACKENBUSH: (*Runs back to her*) Thank-yo. (*He goes back to the phone. On the phone*) Will you have the bellhop hop up with some hopscotch? (*He crosses back to* FLO.) I'll flip you to see who pays for it.
FLO: Oh, doctor.
> (*There is a knock at the door.*
> TONY, *in a bowler hat, a huge dime-store handlebar moustache, holding a hotel passkey on a large ring, and smoking a cigar, enters.*
> FLO *and* HACKENBUSH *look at him, perplexed.*
> *He stands there.*)

TONY: (*Trying to add an Irish brogue to his Italian accent*) I'm
    O'Reilly, the house detective.
HACKENBUSH: Don't talk so loud – your moustache will drop
    off.
TONY: (*Looking at* FLO) Have you got a woman in here?
HACKENBUSH: If I haven't, I've wasted thirty minutes of
    valuable time!
TONY: Well, you better get her out of here! This is the last time
    I'm going to tell you.
HACKENBUSH: The last time? Can I depend on that?
TONY: Yes. (*He walks to the couch.*) Because this time I'm going
    to stay all night.
    (TONY *sprawls on the couch.*
    FLO *is furious.*)
    This looks like a tough case.
HACKENBUSH: (*Looking at* FLO) So does this!
TONY: I think I'll call me assistant. (*He toots a whistle.*)
    (FLO *and* HACKENBUSH *look towards the door.*
    The door opens and* STUFFY, *dressed like he thinks Sherlock
    Holmes looks, and leading two bulldogs, enters. He crosses to*
    FLO *and looks through his magnifying glass at her bare
    shoulder.*)
FLO: Oh!
HACKENBUSH: If you're looking for my fingerprints, you're a
    little early.
    (STUFFY *continues to study* FLO's *shoulder. He takes his
    Sherlock Holmes pipe out of his mouth; his moustache is
    attached to the pipe.*
    HACKENBUSH *looks down towards the steak on the table.*
    HACKENBUSH *picks the steak up with his hand and dangles it
    in front of the bulldogs.*
    HACKENBUSH *runs by with the steak; the dogs follow him,
    dragging* STUFFY *behind.*
    TONY's *on the couch, asleep.* HACKENBUSH *runs up to him.*
    HACKENBUSH *puts the steak in* TONY's *pocket.*
    HACKENBUSH *jumps back out of the way as the bulldogs jump
    on* TONY, *growling for the steak.*
    TONY *falls off the couch. The bulldogs go after him.*)

When you get through with that steak, chew him!
(*The dogs chase* TONY *and in the process wind the leash around* STUFFY's *feet.*

STUFFY *falls to the floor tangled in the leash. The dogs pull him behind them, knocking over furniture as they go.*

TONY *dives under the table. The dogs follow.*)

(*To the dogs as they go under the table*) Pull in your ears . . .

(STUFFY *is dragged under the table after them, feet first.*)

(*Off-screen*) . . . you're coming to a tunnel.

(TONY *comes out from the other side of the table. One of the bulldogs jumps out after him.*

TONY *gets up; the dogs nip at his coat and drag* STUFFY *behind him.* FLO *stands in the background baffled. As* STUFFY *slides by, he pulls the rug out from under her. She starts to fall.*

TONY *runs out of the door, followed by* STUFFY *who slides behind the dogs as if he were on a sled. As they slide out,* HACKENBUSH *slams the door behind them.*

HACKENBUSH *looks at the door.*)

FLO: (*Off-screen*) It's been a nice, quiet dinner.

HACKENBUSH: How do you know? You haven't had any yet. Shall we?

(*They cross to the table; he pulls out her chair.*)

FLO: Thank-kew. (*She sits.*)

HACKENBUSH: Thank-yo.

(*He sits and they try to look at each other around the flowers again. He stands.*)

Tomato soup? (*He takes the top off a soup tureen and pulls out a can.*) Have you got a can opener? (*He looks around, finds it on the table.*) Oh, here it is. (*He starts to open the can.*)

FLO: Oh, I'm really not hungry. Couldn't we just sit over here?

(*She leads him away from the table. She takes him in her arms. He embraces her.*)

I want to be near you. I want you to hold me. Oh, hold me closer! (*She squeezes him.*) Closer! (*She squeezes some more.*) Closer! (*And some more.*)

HACKENBUSH: If I hold you any closer, I'll be in back of you.

FLO: You're so comforting. (*She runs her fingers through his hair.*)

HACKENBUSH: The Hackenbushes were all like that. Shall we sit down and bat it around?

(*He leads her to the couch. He sits down and gestures for her to sit next to him. He looks down at the couch waiting for her to sit, and begins to search through the rest of the couch for her. He looks under the cushion, then looks up and sees she's in his lap.*)

You're a little near-seated – a little near-sighted, aren't you? (*She laughs.*

There is a knock at the door.)

Oh, no – there's nobody else going to get in. I bolted the door.

(*There is a louder knock at the door and the door falls forward into the room off its hinges. TONY and STUFFY, dressed as paper hangers, carrying ladders and a great deal of equipment, enter.*)

Say, fun is fun!

(*STUFFY carries one pail of paste in his hand and another balances on his head. He slops the paste wherever he goes.*)

TONY: We come to hang the paper.

HACKENBUSH: How about hanging yourself instead?

(*TONY and STUFFY set up their ladders on either side of the couch, climb up, and get ready to go to work.*)

FLO: (*Gets up*) Well, I'm going to stay right here! (*She sits down again.*)

HACKENBUSH: Thank-yo!

FLO: Ahhh!

(*TONY's on the ladder.*)

TONY: That's right, Stuffy. You work on that side . . .

(*STUFFY's on his ladder. He takes a brush out of his pocket and dips it into the pail on his head.*)

(*Off-screen*) I work on this side, and we meet on the ceiling.

HACKENBUSH: (*To TONY and STUFFY*) You'll wind up on the gallows is my prediction.

(*STUFFY and TONY are papering the wall above HACKENBUSH and FLO.*

The wallpaper drops down in front of FLO and HACKENBUSH; each sheet of wallpaper is different.)

(*Sticking his head out around the paper*) I must be a citizen. I just got my second papers!

(*STUFFY and TONY are on the ladders over HACKENBUSH and*

FLO, *who are still on the couch.*)

TONY: Looks like a wet track tomorrow, Stuffy.

(STUFFY *and* TONY *slop paper and paint on everything.*
They have completely covered HACKENBUSH *and* FLO.)
I think, Stuffy, we put up a border.

MRS UPJOHN: (*Off-screen*) If he's got a woman in his room I'll see
that he's dismissed . . .

(*We see* MRS UPJOHN *and* WHITMORE *in the hallway.*)
. . . immediately!

(MRS UPJOHN *and* WHITMORE *enter the room.*)
What's going on? Good gracious!

(FLO *and* HACKENBUSH *are completely hidden from her.*)

(*To* WHITMORE) You're mistaken! There's no woman here!

WHITMORE: No?

(*The couch is completely covered with wallpaper.* WHITMORE
crosses to it and rips away the paper exposing HACKENBUSH *all*
alone, reading a book.)

MRS UPJOHN: (*Off-screen*) Hugo! What are you doing?

HACKENBUSH: I'm having the place done over. It'll make a lovely
honeymoon suite.

MRS UPJOHN: Oh-h-h-h!

(TONY *unravels a roll of wallpaper in front of* MRS UPJOHN.)

HACKENBUSH: (*On the couch*) You better go, dear. We're tearing
up the floor next.

MRS UPJOHN: Oh, my! Come, Mr Whitmore, I've a few words to
say to you!

(WHITMORE *follows* MRS UPJOHN *out.*)

HACKENBUSH: Boys, you were wonderful!

(*He jumps up; the cushion falls off the couch and an infuriated*
FLO *crawls out of the couch.*)
You saved my life!

FLO: (*To* HACKENBUSH) I'll get even! You – you dirty, low-down,
cheap, double-crossing snake!

HACKENBUSH: Thank-yo!

FLO: Oh! Oh!

(*She turns to leave and as she goes* STUFFY *slaps a piece of*
wallpaper on her rear. She goes out and HACKENBUSH, STUFFY
and TONY *shake hands.*

Fade out.)

Fade in exterior, garden.
HACKENBUSH *and* MRS UPJOHN *are seated on a bench; his back is to her.*
MRS UPJOHN: Hugo . . . (*She moves closer*) . . . speak to me.
　　(*He shakes his head, 'no'.*)
　　I said I was sorry about last night. I never should have
　　mistrusted you. Isn't there anything I can do to make you
　　forgive me?
HACKENBUSH: You could take over the notes from Miss
　　Standish.
MRS UPJOHN: Then would you forgive me?
HACKENBUSH: Well, it would help. (*He turns to her, takes her
　　hand.*)
MRS UPJOHN: Ohhh!
HACKENBUSH: Emily, I can't hide it any longer. I love you.
MRS UPJOHN: Oh, Hugo!
HACKENBUSH: It's the old, old story. 'Boy Meets Girl' – 'Romeo
　　and Juliet' – 'Minneapolis and St Paul'.
　　(GIL *enters from behind them.*)
GIL: Mrs Upjohn! Judy has the papers ready for you to sign.
MRS UPJOHN: Later, later! Can't you see we're busy?
HACKENBUSH: It's all right, Emily, I'll remember where I left off.
　　(HACKENBUSH *leads her back into the sanitarium.* GIL *follows.*)
MRS UPJOHN: Must they do that now? What in the world?
　　(WHITMORE *walks quickly across the patio.*)
WHITMORE: Mrs Upjohn, just a moment, please.
　　(HACKENBUSH, MRS UPJOHN, *and* GIL *cross and stop in front
　　of him; a pompous man with a cane and a bowler hat enters
　　behind* WHITMORE.)
　　Mrs Upjohn, may I present Dr Leopold X. Steinberg of
　　Vienna?
　　(DR STEINBERG *bows to* MRS UPJOHN *and* HACKENBUSH *tries
　　to duck out behind her.* WHITMORE *stops him.*)
MRS UPJOHN: Doctor.
WHITMORE: And this is Dr Hackenbush.
STEINBERG: (*Bows to* HACKENBUSH.) Ah, doctor! I have a few

questions I would like to ask you.

HACKENBUSH: (*Looking closer at his beard*) I've got a question I'd
like to ask you. Steinberg, what do you do with your old
razor blades?

STEINBERG: Huh?!

WHITMORE: (*Off-screen*) I've been telling Dr Steinberg about
your unusual case.

STEINBERG: Yes. And I would like to know – what is this ailment
– double blood pressure?

(HACKENBUSH *raises his eyebrows.*)

MRS UPJOHN: Dr Hackenbush tells me I am the only case in
history. I have high blood pressure on . . .

(HACKENBUSH *rolls his eyes.*)

(*Off-screen*) . . . my right side, and low blood pressure on my
left side!

STEINBERG: Ha! There is no such thing!

MRS UPJOHN: Oh!

STEINBERG: She looks as healthy as any woman I've ever met.

HACKENBUSH: You don't look as though you ever met a healthy
woman!

STEINBERG: (*Snarling*) What?

WHITMORE: (*Off-screen*) Gentlemen, gentlemen! There's a very
simple way to settle this. Why not examine Mrs Upjohn?

MRS UPJOHN: Splendid! Splendid!

WHITMORE: Right this way, Mrs Upjohn.

MRS UPJOHN: Dr Hackenbush will show you. Then I insist that
you apologize to him. Come, Hugo. The idea!

(MRS UPJOHN, DR STEINBERG, *and* WHITMORE *go into the
sanitarium.* HACKENBUSH *turns and runs out the other way.* GIL
follows him.)

HACKENBUSH *runs up the stairs, followed by* GIL.)

GIL: Hey, doc! Where are you going?

(GIL *grabs* HACKENBUSH *by the arm.*)

Don't you realize if Steinberg examines that woman, we're
through?

HACKENBUSH: I'm through right now!

GIL: Oh, no you're not! Now you got to get in there! Do
anything! But stop Steinberg! Come on, you've got to hurry!

HACKENBUSH: I'll say I have to hurry. I'm hopping the next banana boat for Central America! (*He pulls away from* GIL *and runs upstairs.*)

GIL: Hey, doc! Where you going?

Dissolve to interior, Hackenbush's room.

HACKENBUSH *runs into his room, followed by* GIL.

GIL: Wait, doc – wait!

(*The camera pans over to* STUFFY *who is attacking the mattress with a knife and taking out the straw.*

TONY *has joined them. He's wearing a smoking jacket and his hat.*)

HACKENBUSH: It's all right with me – go right ahead. I'm not sleeping here tonight.

(STUFFY *opens the closet door. Hi-Hat is in the closet.* STUFFY *feeds him the straw.*)

GIL: (*Off-screen*) It's Hi-Hat!

(GIL *goes into the closet to talk to his horse.*)

HACKENBUSH: Nonsense – that's a horse!

TONY: No, it's Hi-Hat. We hide him in the closet so the sheriff can't find him.

HACKENBUSH: Is that so? Well, he's not going to find me either, because I'm leaving here right away, boys. (*He takes his suitcase from under the bed.*)

GIL: Doc! Doc – wait a minute now –

HACKENBUSH: No – I'll see you again sometime.

GIL: Please, doc –

HACKENBUSH: Just as soon as I get my effects – (*He takes the smoking jacket off* TONY *and stuffs it into the suitcase.*) Old Hackenbush isn't going to be with you very long! (*He runs to* STUFFY, *takes his tie off, stuffs the tie in the suitcase.*)

GIL: Doc, you can't walk out on us like this!

(HACKENBUSH *takes his suitcase and moves quickly across the room.*)

HACKENBUSH: I'll say I can't. I'm going to run out!

(HACKENBUSH *puts his suitcase on the dresser and begins filling it.* GIL *comes over to him.*)

GIL: You can't go, doc! If you walk out, where will Judy be?

HACKENBUSH: Well, she won't be in gaol, and that's where I'll be if I stay here. Besides, what can I do?

GIL: You've got to stop the examination – somehow!

HACKENBUSH: Not today, I don't.

GIL: Are you a man or a mouse?

HACKENBUSH: You put a piece of cheese down there and you'll find out. Well, it's been nice seeing you! (*He puts his suitcase under his arm and moves towards the door.*)

TONY: Oh, no you don't!

(TONY *and* STUFFY *stop him.*)

If you leave, it's over my dead body!

HACKENBUSH: Well, that's a pleasant way to travel. Look out!

TONY: All right, now look, doc! Look, doc! You can't leave Miss Judy in a fix like this.

HACKENBUSH: I know, but the sheriff –

GIL: Doc – doc! If you leave now, Judy loses the sanitarium.

HACKENBUSH: All right, I'll stay.

TONY: You gonna stay?

(STUFFY *takes* HACKENBUSH's *suitcase and* GIL *helps him off with his jacket.*)

I knew you'd do it, doc.

GIL: Thanks, doc!

Dissolve to interior, examination room.

HACKENBUSH *enters.*

DR STEINBERG: (*Off-screen*) So next we will see –

(MRS UPJOHN *is in an examination chair.* WHITMORE *and* DR STEINBERG *are next to her.*)

HACKENBUSH: Just a moment. Take your hands off her! A fine doctor you are. Don't you know you're not supposed to touch a patient without being sterilized? You don't see me running an examination like that!

MRS UPJOHN: No!

WHITMORE: That's true. And I think it would be very interesting to see just how Dr Hackenbush does conduct an examination.

MRS UPJOHN: (*Off-screen*) Splendid, splendid! Show them, doctor.

HACKENBUSH: If you insist, I'll proceed.

(HACKENBUSH *stands in front of three washbasins, dips his hands and lets the water run to his elbows. He washes again.* DR STEINBERG *comes over to look, and he washes a third time, then a fourth.*)

(*To* STEINBERG) In case you've never done it, this is known as washing your hands.

(MRS UPJOHN *looks embarrassed.*

STEINBERG *watches* HACKENBUSH *as he continues to wash his hands in the same manner.* HACKENBUSH *takes off his watch, puts it on a work table.* STEINBERG *stares at the watch.* HACKENBUSH *picks up the watch and puts it in the washbasin.*)

Rather have it rusty than missing. (*He washes his hands three more times, raises his arms in the air, and lets the water run down to his elbows.*) You'll go a long ways to see prettier drippings than those.

STEINBERG: Why sterilization? After all, this is not an operation, you know.

HACKENBUSH: Not yet, but I may get hot and operate on everybody in the joint, including you!

MRS UPJOHN: Come, come, doctor. Aren't you ready?

HACKENBUSH: (*Drying his hands on a towel*) Now, Mrs Upjohn, I guess I know my business. Of course, that's just a guess on my part, but at any rate, I know a thing or two about cleanliness, and that's more than I can say for that mountain goat standing there!

(STEINBERG *is shocked and infuriated at the insult.*)

MRS UPJOHN: Come, doctor, we're waiting.

HACKENBUSH: All right, if you insist, we'll proceed at once. Now, Mrs Upjohn . . . (*He crosses to her*)

. . . I want you to take your arms and let them wave through the air with the greatest of ease.

(*He waves his own arms through the air with the greatest of ease; she imitates him.*)

Not too swiftly.

MRS UPJOHN: Like that, doctor?

HACKENBUSH: Yes, that's splendid.

MRS UPJOHN: How long do you want me to do this, doctor? (*She continues to flap her arms.*)

HACKENBUSH: Just until you fly away.

(MRS UPJOHN *stops*.

TONY *and* STUFFY, *dressed in surgical gowns and masks, enter.*)
(*Privately*) I told you guys to stay down in that room with those pigeons.

(DR STEINBERG, *between* TONY *and* STUFFY, *scowls at* STUFFY, *who cringes and walks to the washbasins. When* STUFFY *turns to wash his hands we see the back of his surgical gown which says:*

JOE'S
SERVICE
STATION

He dips his fingers in each of the three basins.)

WHITMORE: (*Off-screen*) Dr Hackenbush!

(MRS UPJOHN *is still in the examining chair.*)
Tell me, who sent for these men? (*He means* STUFFY *and* TONY.)

HACKENBUSH: You don't have to send for them. You just rub a lamp and they appear.

TONY: (*Shakes hands with* DR STEINBERG) My name is Steinberg.

STEINBERG: Steinberg?

HACKENBUSH: (*Privately to* TONY) Nix, nix, that's Steinberg. (*To the real* STEINBERG) Dr Steinberg, by a strange coincidence, this is another Dr Steinberg.

(TONY *and* STEINBERG *bow to each other.*)
May I take my great friend and introduce my colleague and good friend, another Dr Steinberg. (STEINBERG *turns to* STUFFY *and bows.* STUFFY *bows backwards, hands on his hips. Behind him,* TONY *continues to bow to* DR STEINBERG – *the real one.*)
This is a Dr Steinberg – Dr Steinberg. Dr Steinberg, and – ah (*Gesturing to* MRS UPJOHN) Mrs Steinberg.

(HACKENBUSH *walks over to an anatomy chart.* TONY *turns to follow him. When he does we see that the back of his surgical gown reads:* 'BRAKES RELINED'.)
And, doctor, I'd like you to meet another Dr Steinberg. (*He*

slaps the picture of the skeleton on the anatomy chart and it rolls up and reveals another anatomy chart.) And that's . . . that's Steinberg Junior.

WHITMORE: If Dr Hackenbush is not going to continue the examination, professor, may we have your diagnosis please?

STEINBERG: (*Takes a paper from his pocket and begins to read*) With pleasure. In all my years of medicine, I have never . . .

HACKENBUSH: (*Takes the paper from* STEINBERG *and tears it up*) In all your years of medicine, why you don't know the first thing about medicine.

(*In the background* STUFFY *is fitting himself out with a head reflector.*

STEINBERG *juts his chin out at* HACKENBUSH.)

And don't point that beard at me. It might go off!

WHITMORE: Dr Steinberg. Do you remember your diagnosis?

STEINBERG: Certainly. To begin with, her pulse is absolutely normal.

HACKENBUSH: I challenge that.

STEINBERG: Challenge that? You take her pulse!

HACKENBUSH: Pulse?

STEINBERG: Take her pulse!

HACKENBUSH: I – I don't do any pulse work. I'm an acute diagnostician. (*To* STUFFY) Take her pulse! Take her pulse!

(STUFFY *reaches for* MRS UPJOHN's *pulse, takes her purse instead, puts it in his pocket, and starts to walk away.*)

MRS UPJOHN: Oh, no, no, no. My purse, my purse, my purse, give me my purse. Oh!

(HACKENBUSH *stops him, takes the purse back, returns it to* MRS UPJOHN.)

HACKENBUSH: You must forgive him – he doesn't spell very well, Mrs Upjohn.

MRS UPJOHN: Oh, dear, come gentlemen, let us begin. (*She takes* TONY *and* HACKENBUSH *by the hand.*)

HACKENBUSH: Oh, you shouldn't have done that. (*Looking at his hands.*) Now we're all unsterilized. What's the matter with you?

(HACKENBUSH, TONY, *and* STUFFY *run to the washbasins.*)

HACKENBUSH *and* TONY: (*Singing*) 'Down by the old mill stream, where I first met you.'

(*They wash their hands slowly and carefully.*
As they continue to sing, they walk in a small circle and dry their
hands on the backs of each other's surgical gowns.)

MRS UPJOHN: (*Off-screen*) Well, I must say I've seen quicker
    examinations.

HACKENBUSH: Maybe, but you'll never see a slippier one.

STEINBERG: Gentlemen, are you ready to proceed?

(*The three boys cross to* MRS UPJOHN *and* WHITMORE.)

HACKENBUSH: We'll proceed immediately.

WHITMORE: Doctor, and what do you expect to do next?

TONY: The next thing I think we shall do isa wash our hands.

(*They run back to the washbasin.*)

MRS UPJOHN: Oh!

HACKENBUSH: You're absolutely right.

MRS UPJOHN: (*Off-screen*) I have never seen . . .

HACKENBUSH *and* TONY: (*Singing and washing their hands again*)
    'Down by the old . . .'

(DR STEINBERG *walks to the washbasins.*)

(*Singing*) '. . . mill . . .'

(STEINBERG *watches* HACKENBUSH, TONY, *and* STUFFY *as*
they wash.)

(*Singing*) '. . . stream . . .'

MRS UPJOHN: (*Off-screen*) What is the matter with them?

(*They finish washing and* STEINBERG *turns away from them.*
TONY *dries his hands on* HACKENBUSH's *gown;* HACKENBUSH
on STUFFY's *gown and* STUFFY *dries his hands on* DR
STEINBERG's *tails.*)

STEINBERG: I don't know – what is this – get away from me. (*He*
pushes STUFFY *away.*)

HACKENBUSH: Everything is going to be all right. Nurse! (*Yelling*)
    Sterilization – sterilization!

(THREE NURSES *enter with clean surgical gowns and hold them*
up. HACKENBUSH, TONY, *and* STUFFY *each step into a gown,*
arms first. TONY *and* STUFFY, *however, embrace the* NURSES.
TONY *lets go but* STUFFY *hangs on to his* NURSE.)

MRS UPJOHN: (*Off-screen*) Oh, are they mad, or what is it?

HACKENBUSH: No, we're not mad, we're just terribly hurt, that's all.

MRS UPJOHN: (*Off-screen*) Ohhh – ohhh!

(HACKENBUSH *separates* STUFFY *and the* NURSE *and as*
STUFFY *pulls away he takes the* NURSE'S *uniform with him*.)

HACKENBUSH: Hey, just a – just a moment. Just put the gown on,
not the nurse, eh? Come here.

(*The nurse in her slip runs out screaming.*
HACKENBUSH *is using the water carafe for a telescope*.)

How is it a dame like that never gets sick.

MRS UPJOHN: But I am sick. Doctor, will you pay attention to
me?

(HACKENBUSH *is still looking through his water-carafe telescope.*
TONY *stares through an ultraviolet light, using it as a telescope*.)

HACKENBUSH: You'll have to get in line, Mrs Upjohn. There's
three orders ahead of you.

(*He and* TONY *put their telescopes down on the desk and cross to
the door*.)

Say, that nurse, poor girl, may be out there catching her
death of cold. (*He looks into the doorway and yells down the
hall*.) Say, nurse – sterilization!

(*In the background,* STUFFY *is playing with a large heat lamp*.)

TONY: (*Off-screen*) Hey, doc, get away from there.

STEINBERG: This is absolutely insane.

HACKENBUSH: Yes, that's what they said about Pasteur.

STEINBERG: Ach, this is ridiculous. Put the patient in a
horizontal position.

(STUFFY *and* TONY *flip* MRS UPJOHN'S *examination chair
backwards and turn it into an examination table but they push it
too high and her feet are above her head*.)

Be careful, gentlemen.

MRS UPJOHN: Oh, oh, oh!

(*They push the table even further until her legs are straight up in
the air.* STUFFY *dangles a sign from her feet:* 'MEN AT WORK'.
HACKENBUSH *runs over, takes the sign off and throws it under*
WHITMORE'S *feet.* STUFFY *begins to drag* MRS UPJOHN, *still
turned upside down on the examination table, around the room.
The table and* MRS UPJOHN *have been forced into a right-angle.
She clings to the sides.* STUFFY *drapes a towel over her and
begins to lather her face.* WHITMORE *tries to pull him away*.)

TONY *adds more towels and begins to shave her, using a blunt medical instrument for a razor.* STUFFY *takes a basin of water and begins to wash* MRS UPJOHN's *hands.*)

WHITMORE: Here, give me that. What are you doing? (*He takes the basin from* STUFFY.)

(*The examination table is now back in its sitting position.* HACKENBUSH *is shining* MRS UPJOHN's *shoes.* STUFFY *is drying her hands and* TONY *is massaging her scalp.* DR STEINBERG *passes in the background and* WHITMORE *is tearing his hair.* HACKENBUSH *stops shining* MRS UPJOHN's *shoes and begins drying his own back and legs with the towel he was using to dry her shoes.* STUFFY *is cranking the examination table up and down.* MRS UPJOHN's *legs fly in the air.*)

STEINBERG: But there is one indisputable test.

WHITMORE: What?

STEINBERG: The X-ray!

WHITMORE: The X-ray!

(TONY, STUFFY, *and* HACKENBUSH *run around the room.*)

TONY *and* HACKENBUSH: (*Shouting*) X-ray . . . X-ray . . .

(STUFFY *pretends to shout and hands out newspapers.*)

TONY: (*Off-screen*) X-ray! Extray! Extray!

(STUFFY *slams a newspaper into* DR STEINBERG's *gut;* HACKENBUSH *slides a chair behind* DR STEINBERG *and he collapses in it.* STUFFY *immediately begins cranking* MRS UPJOHN *up and down again.*

STUFFY *goes to the lever on the wall marked:*

OVERHEAD SPRINKLERS
FIRE ONLY

He looks up at the ceiling and pulls the lever.
The water begins to flow.

HACKENBUSH, TONY, *and* STUFFY *run across the room.* STUFFY *hides under the instrument stand. The water pours on it and knocks him down.*

WHITMORE, MRS UPJOHN, *and* STEINBERG *run to the door and start to leave.*

Hi-Hat comes trotting down the corridor with pigeons riding on his back.

HACKENBUSH *is standing on a desk.* DR STEINBERG *turns and*

runs away from the door as Hi-Hat trots into the room.
HACKENBUSH *jumps off the desk and on to Hi-Hat. The pigeons flutter away.*
TONY *climbs upon the examination table and then jumps on to Hi-Hat's back. By now everything in the room is soaked and water begins to collect on the floor.*
STUFFY *runs behind Hi-Hat and jumps aboard joining* HACKENBUSH *and* TONY, *and Hi-Hat trots out of the room. Fade out.*)

Fade in interior, barn.
STUFFY *is sprawled in the hay. He is holding his sock between his toes, drying it over a small bonfire. As the camera pulls back, we see that he is surrounded by* HACKENBUSH, GIL, *and* TONY. *They all look miserable.*
GIL: Well, I certainly messed things up for Judy.
HACKENBUSH: You messed things up? I suppose Old Doc
    Hackenbush didn't throw a nasty monkey wrench.
TONY: You no throw the monkey wrench. I'm the guy that did it.
HACKENBUSH: Now listen, it was nobody's fault but mine.
    (STUFFY *sits up, whistles for attention, and points to himself.*)
    Now I don't want any more arguments. It was all my fault.
TONY: I think he's right. It was his fault.
HACKENBUSH: Oh, it was my fault, eh? That's the thanks I get. I
    get you the first shower you had in years and you turn on me
    like a snake in the grass.
    (STUFFY *whistles;* GIL *looks up.*)
GIL: Someone's coming.
TONY: The sheriff!
    (STUFFY, HACKENBUSH, GIL, *and* TONY *all get up, run, and hide.*
    The barn door opens. JUDY *comes in carrying blankets.*
    GIL *is hiding in a wagon. He peeks over the side, sees* JUDY, *and smiles.*)
GIL: Judy!
    (GIL *jumps out of the wagon. They all run forward to greet* JUDY.)
HACKENBUSH: You're the prettiest sheriff I've ever seen.
JUDY: Oh, you thought I was the sheriff?

HACKENBUSH: We're taking no chances.

JUDY: No, I just brought you these blankets. I thought it might make it a little more comfortable living out here.
(STUFFY *takes all the blankets and jumps on them.*)

TONY: Hey, get up – get up.

GIL: You should worry about our comfort after the way we bungled your affairs.

JUDY: You did your best, Gil.

GIL: Yes, and our best was none too good.

HACKENBUSH: Ah – tell me, Miss Standish, is the water still running in the examination room?

JUDY: Well, after tomorrow, I'm afraid that's Mr Morgan's worry.

TONY: Morgan, he no gotta the sanitarium yet.

GIL: Oh, a lot of things will happen before tomorrow.

JUDY: The sanitarium doesn't matter any more. Gil, you were right. I've been taking things far too seriously. It's much better this way. Now I can be free, I – I won't be tied down, I – I can enjoy myself and – and really laugh. (*She starts to cry.*)

GIL: Oh, Judy, please.

TONY: Don't cry, Miss Judy. I feel sad, but I laugh – I laugh – Stuffy, he's-a laughing too. Look. Go on and laugh, Stuffy.
(TONY *laughs;* STUFFY *opens his mouth to laugh and collapses in silent hysterics on* TONY's *shoulder.*)
HACKENBUSH *looks very sad.*)
Hey, look. Look – looka Hackenapussa – laugh – go ahead – laugh –

HACKENBUSH: (*A feeble attempt*) Hee-haw. Where did that come from? (*He looks around.*)
JUDY *runs to the window.*)
Several black children are jumping rope in the yard. GIL *joins* JUDY *and tries to comfort her.*

GIL: It can't be that bad, Judy.
(HACKENBUSH *leads* TONY *and* STUFFY *out.*
Look at those kids. Laughing – happy. Come on, you're just a kid. Laugh, be happy. (*He sings:*) 'The day is through . . .'
(*He holds her and sings.*)
'The sun descending has brought to you

No happy ending – but you can face the setting sun and say
Tomorrow is another day.'
(*In another part of the barn we find* HACKENBUSH, TONY, *and*
STUFFY.

HACKENBUSH *is reading the racing sheet*. TONY *is attending to
Hi-Hat and* STUFFY *is sitting by himself, looking glum. Hi-Hat
begins to nibble the straw on* STUFFY's *hat*. STUFFY *doesn't
notice*.)
(*Singing off-screen*) 'You've had your share of tears and
trouble.
But every care will be a bubble.'
(*Singing to* JUDY) 'If you can face the setting sun and say.
Tomorrow is another day.'
(STUFFY *looks around the barn door*.)
(*Singing to* JUDY) 'Some days a little rain must fall
The skies can't all be blue.
Sometimes a little tear must fall
To make a smile break through
Today is gone, it's all behind you
A brighter dawn will surely find you
If you can face the setting sun and say
Tomorrow is another day.'
(*They embrace*.

STUFFY *smiles, watching* GIL *and* JUDY. *He plays a few notes
on a flute*.

STUFFY *plays the flute to* GIL *and* JUDY. *They smile at him and
he dances away from them to where the children are playing. The
children follow him, tugging at his coat as he plays the flute and
dances for them.*

*A group of young boys is shooting craps on the ground. With the
line of children behind him,* STUFFY *dances over to the boys*.)
BOY: O dice, don' come twosies –
CHORUS: Di-a-di-a-di-a-di-a-da – twosies.
BOY: Baby needs new shoesies.
CHORUS: Di-ah-di-a-di-a-di – shoesies.
BOY: Come on.
CHORUS: Yeah.
BOY: Seven.

CHORUS: Man.
  (STUFFY *toots his flute.*)
BOY: (*Pointing at* STUFFY): Who dat man?
  (*All the children follow* STUFFY *as he plays the flute.*)
CHORUS: (*Singing*) 'Who dat man? Who dat man?
  It's Gabriel.
  Oh, Gabriel's blowin' 'cause he needs us.
  We gottta follow where he leads us.
  Blow that horn, Gabe, we is comin'.
  Followin' everywhere you go.'
  (STUFFY *and the children stop in front of a window.* STUFFY
  hears the voices singing and looks in.)
WOMAN'S VOICE: (*Off-screen*) Hal-le-lu-Hal-le-lu–
  (*A group of black people doing various domestic chores.*
  The chorus hums.
  STUFFY *approaches the window and the children follow.*
  Two women are playing checkers.
  A MAN *adjusts his collar and puts a derby on.*)
MAN *and* CHORUS: Hal-le-lu–
  (*The chorus hums.*
  STUFFY *looks in the window, toots his flute.*
  The MAN *in the derby sees* STUFFY.)
  Who dat man?
  (STUFFY *comes to the door, followed by the children, and toots*
  his flute.)
CHORUS: Who dat man?
  (STUFFY *plays his flute.*
  The group in the doorway all looks at STUFFY.)
GROUP: It's Gabriel, it's . . .
  (*The* MAN *with the derby looks at* STUFFY.)
MAN *and* CHORUS: . . . Gabriel! Oh-h-h!
  (STUFFY *dances away from the house. The children follow him.*)
CHORUS: 'Gabriel's blowin' cause he needs us.
  We gotta follow where he leads us.'
  (STUFFY *dances through the barnyard, the children following*
  him.)
  'Blow that horn, Gabe, we is comin'
  Followin' every . . .'

(STUFFY *leads the children. He sees something off-screen and stops.*)
(*Another cabin, crowded. The people are singing and dancing and having a party. The building shakes.*
A group of people is dancing; a band is in the background.
STUFFY *and the children are looking at the party. They walk towards it.*
STUFFY *is at the doorway looking in at the party.*
The band is playing away.
(*Camera shoots past the musicians to* IVIE ANDERSON.)

IVIE: (*Singing*) 'Come on and jam-bo
The jam what am-bo'
(STUFFY *is dancing in the doorway. He's enjoying himself immensely.*)
(*Off-screen, singing*) Jam, Mister Sambo.
(STUFFY *toots on his flute.*
There is a piano-player; other musicians are in the background.)

GROUP: Who dat man?
(STUFFY *toots the flute.*
(*A* MAN, *with a piece of straw in his mouth, playing the banjo. He looks at* STUFFY.)

MAN *and* GROUP: Who dat man?
(STUFFY *is in the doorway. The* MAN *opens the door as* STUFFY *toots the flute.*)

GROUP: Who dat man?

MAN: Why it's Gabriel!
(STUFFY *plays the flute.*
STUFFY, *followed by the group, dances away, having a great time.*)

GROUP: (*Singing*) 'Oh, Gabriel's blowin' cause he needs us . . .'
(*They all dance out of the yard, into the barn to where* GIL *and* JUDY *are waiting for them.* TONY *and* HACKENBUSH *join them.*)

CHORUS: (*Singing*) 'We gotta follow where he leads us
Blow that horn, Gabe, we is comin'
Follow everywhere you go
Oh, Gabriel's blowin' cause he needs us
We gotta follow where he leads us

Blow that horn, Gabe, we is comin'
Follow everywhere you go.'
(STUFFY *plays the flute in the middle of the barn and the chorus dances around him.*)
(*Singing*) Blow that horn – Gabriel
Blow that horn – Gabriel
Blow that horn – Gabriel' –
(STUFFY *is surrounded by the children.*)
(*Singing*) 'Blow – that – horn – '
(*A group of adults blow their trumpets.*)
(*Singing*) 'Blow that horn.'
(GIL *and* JUDY *are on a haystack;* TONY *is at their feet, guzzling booze from a corn jug.* HACKENBUSH *is in the background. They're all watching the singing and dancing.*)

GIL: (*Singing*) 'Tomorrow is another day.'
(STUFFY *joins them*
STUFFY *reaches up to a calendar which is conveniently placed on a beam in the barn and begins tearing off the pages, making the days disappear.*
As the children sing, STUFFY *joins them, dances in the centre and conducts.*

CHORUS: (*Singing*) 'Tomorrow – za-zu-za-zu-zay
Tomorrow – za-zu-za-zu-za
Tomorrow is another day.'
(STUFFY *conducts* IVIE's *solo. She comes to the centre.* STUFFY *follows her.*)

IVIE: (*Singing*) 'I gotta frown, you gotta frown –
All God's chilun gotta . . .'
(JUDY *and* GIL *are listening.*)
(*Off-screen, singing*) '. . . frown on their face.'
(IVIE *cuts loose.*)
(*Singing*) 'Take no chance with that frown
A song and a dance turn it upside down
Ho – ho – ho. Za-zu-za-zu.
All God's chillun got rhythm
All God's chillun got swing
Maybe haven't got money
Maybe haven't got shoes

All God's chillun got rhythm
For to push away their blues – Yeah!
All God's chillun got trouble
Trouble don't mean a thing
When they start to go ho-ho-ho de-ho
All your troubles go 'way – say –
All God's chillun got swing
(*The musicians are playing.*
The children come running in.
IVIE *is surrounded by the musicians and children.*)
CHORUS: (*Singing*) 'All God's chillun got rhythm.'
IVIE: (*Singing*) 'Ba-da-la-da-da-da-da
Ba-da-la-ba-da-whoa-yeah!
CHORUS: (*Singing*) 'All God's chillun got rhythm.'
IVIE: (*Singing*) 'Ba-da-la-da-da-da-da-da
Ba-da-la-ba-da-whoa-yeah!
Maybe haven't got money – ho
Maybe haven't much swing
All God's chillun got rhythm for to push
CHORUS: For to push
IVIE: For to push
CHORUS: Push
IVIE: For to push
CHORUS: Push
IVIE: A . . .
CHORUS: A . . .
IVIE: . . . way
CHORUS: . . . way
IVIE: Their . . .
CHORUS: their . . .
IVIE *and* CHORUS: Blues. . . .'
    IVIE *and a* FAT MAN *begin to jitterbug.*
    He spins.
    The musicians are playing.
    STUFFY *is in the centre;* FOUR COUPLES *jitterbug around him.*
    A GIRL *twirls around.*
    A MAN *dances to her.*
    The camera pans with them as, finally, they dance off.

STUFFY *picks up a pitchfork and dances forward; others follow him.*

HACKENBUSH *is dancing in the background; children in front of him.*

TONY *joins him and dances behind him.*

In the barn, MORGAN, WHITMORE, *and others look suspiciously at the dancers.*

HACKENBUSH, TONY, *and* STUFFY, *in the crowd see* WHITMORE *and* MORGAN. *They run off. The children continue to dance.*

TONY, HACKENBUSH, *and* STUFFY *crawl under a wagon and hide.*

We see MORGAN *and his men through the spokes of the wagon. They're still watching the dancing and looking for* HACKENBUSH, TONY, *and* STUFFY.

HACKENBUSH, TONY, *and* STUFFY *are hiding under the wagon.* HACKENBUSH *takes some axle grease and smears it on his face.)*

CHORUS: (*Off-screen, singing*) 'All God's chillun got rhythm.'

(HACKENBUSH *smears more black grease on his face.* WHITMORE, MORGAN, *and the* SHERIFF *watch.)*

(*Off-screen, singing*) 'All God's chillun got rhythm.'

(HACKENBUSH, TONY, *and* STUFFY *look out from under the wagon.*

HACKENBUSH, TONY, *and* STUFFY *crawl out from under the wagon, their faces covered with black grease. Only one side of* STUFFY's *face is covered with grease. They wave their hands in the air and join the chorus dancing. They move to the front of the line for the finale.)*

(*Singing*) 'Hey – hey, ho – ho, hey – hey, ho – ho

Cause all god's chillun got swing

Swing – swing swing.'

(MORGAN *applauds.*

HACKENBUSH, TONY, *and* STUFFY *look up.)*

MAN: It's de sheriff!

(HACKENBUSH, TONY, *and* STUFFY *run into the crowd and try to sneak out.)*

SHERIFF: Hey, you!

(*He reaches for* HACKENBUSH *and the* FAT MAN *gets in the way.*)

FAT MAN: I ain't done nothing'!

HACKENBUSH: (*Running away*) You've got nothing on me, my skirts are clean!

WHITMORE: Yeah? This letter from Florida says you're a horse doctor!

(WHITMORE, MORGAN, *and the* SHERIFF *run after* HACKENBUSH. *Several bales of hay fall in their way.*)

MORGAN: Put 'em all under arrest!

(*Hi-Hat sees* MORGAN *and gets angry.*

MORGAN *stops in front of Hi-Hat and calls to the* SHERIFF, *who is chasing* HACKENBUSH, TONY, *and* STUFFY.)

They won't run, Sheriff, if you break their legs.

(*Hi-Hat chases* MORGAN *who jumps in a hay wagon to get out of Hi-Hat's way.*)

VOICE: (*Off-screen*) Get that horse – get that horse!

(JUDY *and* GIL *are looking into the barn.*

Hi-Hat has MORGAN *cornered in the hay wagon.*)

JUDY: What's wrong with that horse?

GIL: Why, he goes wild every time he sees Morgan or hears his voice.

(GIL *lifts* JUDY *up over the rail and into the barn.*

Hi-Hat rears up, getting angrier. MORGAN *looks scared.*)

MORGAN: Get out!

(*Hi-Hat moves back, trying to kick* WHITMORE *who is hiding under the wagon.*

Hi-Hat continues to paw the ground and frighten MORGAN.

In the barn, the SHERIFF *and his* DEPUTY *chase* HACKENBUSH *and* TONY *around a bale of hay. They pin* TONY *down.*)

DEPUTY: Hey, come here, you! Where do you think you're goin'?

(*Hi-Hat kicks the wagon with his hind legs, splinters it, and* MORGAN *cowers into the corner.*

Through Hi-Hat's legs we see WHITMORE *under the wagon. Hi-Hat moves around the wagon and kicks viciously at* WHITMORE.

WHITMORE *tries to get out from under the wagon, but Hi-Hat
won't let him.*

MORGAN *is in the wagon;* WHITMORE *is underneath. Hi-Hat
keeps them at bay.*

The SHERIFF *lunges at* TONY *but get tangled in hanging ropes.*

STUFFY *is clinging to a hanging rope up in the rafters. He begins
to swing on it.*

The SHERIFF *is caught in the other end of* STUFFY's *rope. As*
STUFFY *swings above him, the* SHERIFF *is pulled into the air
(off-scene).* STUFFY *descends into the scene as the* SHERIFF *is
yanked up into the rafters.*

The SHERIFF *hangs by a rope in the rafters.)*

SHERIFF: You can't get away with this!

(*Hi-Hat kicks the wagon again.*

HACKENBUSH *is running away: the* DEPUTY *stumbles over a
barrel and falls flat on his face.*

Hi-Hat continues to kick the wagon with his hind legs.

WHITMORE *is under the wagon. Hi-Hat's legs crash into the
wheel.*

MORGAN *jumps out of the wagon and heads for a window.)*

MORGAN: (*Off-screen*) Get the horse!

(JUDY *is in the wagon. She picks up a horse collar.
She drops the horse collar over the* DEPUTY.

Hi-Hat kicks at WHITMORE *under the wagon.*

He kicks WHITMORE *and* MORGAN *who has now joined*
WHITMORE *under the wagon.*

STUFFY *jumps up into the wagon.)*

VOICE: (*Off-screen*) Hey, you!

(STUFFY *jumps on to Hi-Hat and turns and starts to ride away.)*

(*Off-screen*) . . . Nice work, Stuffy!

(MORGAN *and* WHITMORE *are still under the wagon.)*

MORGAN: Stop that horse! Don't let him . . .

(STUFFY, *riding Hi-Hat, leaps over the low barn door.* GIL *and*
JUDY *watch him go.)*

(*Off-screen*) . . . get out of here.

GIL: Did you see that horse jump?

(HACKENBUSH *runs into a wire stall, still chased by the*
DEPUTY *waving a club.)*

HACKENBUSH: And I'm doing some pretty fancy jumping, myself!

(TONY *is in the rafters. He drops a chandelier.*

(*As the* DEPUTY *runs after* HACKENBUSH, *the chandelier drops on his head knocking him down.*)

SHERIFF: (*Off-screen*) Let me off this rope!

(MORGAN *starts to come out, bangs his head on the wagon and knocks himself out.*)

(*Off-screen*) I'll throw you all in gaol! Get me down!

(*The* SHERIFF *is dangling in the ropes and still hanging.*)

Take me out of here!

(HACKENBUSH *and* TONY *run for the gate.* JUDY *and* GIL *join them and they run out.*)

This is no way to treat the law! You'll never get away with this. I'll get you!

(*The* DEPUTY *is sprawled in a corner, gagged, and with the horse collar binding him.*

GIL *and* JUDY, HACKENBUSH *and* TONY *stand at the foot of a haystack, looking for Hi-Hat.*)

GIL: There he goes!

(STUFFY *is riding Hi-Hat. They gallop across a field. Hi-Hat hurdles a fallen tree and then a low stone wall.*)

HACKENBUSH: If he's headed south I'd like to make a reservation.

(*Hi-Hat hurdles a snappy-looking roadster.*)

GIL: Look at that horse! He cleared the automobile!

HACKENBUSH: I wish I could clear mine.

JUDY: Darling, perhaps that's why he never won a race! He's a jumper!

GIL: Am I a sap! I have a steeplechase horse and I don't know it!

(*Long shot of a billboard. It says:*

'GRAND STEEPLECHASE
SPARKLING SPRINGS TRACK
COMING SATURDAY'

STUFFY, *on Hi-Hat, rides up to the billboard.* STUFFY *seems to think that Hi-Hat can hurdle the billboard which is at least twenty feet high. Hi-Hat stops suddenly in front.* STUFFY *sails through the billboard. Hi-Hat whinnies.*

Fade out.)

Fade in exterior, racetrack.
Series of dissolves:
- (a) *Horses walking around the paddock*
- (b) *People walking around the grounds*
- (c) *Crowd in grandstand*
- (d) *Horses walking on the track to starting line*

Dissolve to medium shot of a large blackboard. It reads:

'SIXTH RACE
SPARKLING SPRINGS STEEPLECHASE
$50,000 ADDED 2 MILES 3 YRS & UP'

Camera pans down the list of names to:

'ADDED STARTERS
4804 HI-HAT – STUFFY'

MORGAN *and* WHITMORE *are standing in front of the board.*
MORGAN: We're going to find that added starter and see that he doesn't start.
(MORGAN *and* WHITMORE *exit.*)

Dissolve to exterior, stables.
MORGAN *and* WHITMORE *walk past the stables. The* SHERIFF *enters with his men.*
MORGAN: They're not pulling any fast ones on me. Hi-Hat's not running in this race.
WHITMORE: Ah, but Hi-Hat isn't a jumper.
MORGAN: He was doing plenty of jumping in the barn last night.
WHITMORE: Hmmm, but he can't beat your horse.
MORGAN: Well, I'm not taking any chances. My money's riding on Ski-Ball and that's not all. If Hi-Hat wins, Stewart'll give that money to the girl and we can kiss the sanitarium goodbye.
SHERIFF: Well, Morgan, you've got nothing to worry about. Hi-Hat's not on this track.
MORGAN: Well, you see that he doesn't get on. Put a man at every gate. If that nag slips by you it means your job.
(HACKENBUSH *is sitting on awning looking through field glasses.* TONY *and* STUFFY *jump in and join him.*

Through the field glasses we see an ambulance driving through the gate entrance.

HACKENBUSH *holds the field glasses as* TONY *and* STUFFY *try to look through them at the same time.* HACKENBUSH *breaks the glasses in half and gives* TONY *and* STUFFY *each their own part.*)

HACKENBUSH: Here, keep me posted.

(TONY *and* STUFFY *look through their glasses.*

Through one lens of the field glass we see GIL *and* JUDY *riding in the ambulance. As they pass, we see a sign on the ambulance:*

'SPARKLING SPRINGS RACE TRACK AMBULANCE'

TONY: He's made it! (*He means* GIL *and* JUDY.) He's made it!

(STUFFY *applauds wildly*).

Go ahead, Stuffy, go to it. Good luck!

(STUFFY *runs up the awning and out.*)

HACKENBUSH: Ride 'em, cowboy! Or we're heading for the last lock-up.

TONY: Come on, doc, we get a reserved seat.

(*They go up the awning and leave.*

The ambulance stops near a crowd of people.

JUDY's *in a nurse's outfit and* GIL's *in an ambulance driver's suit.*

JUDY *sees* WHITMORE, MORGAN, *and the* SHERIFF *off-scene and pokes* GIL.)

JUDY: Gil.

(GIL *pulls his hat over his eyes so they can't see him.*)

(*The* SHERIFF *is with* WHITMORE, MORGAN, *and the* DEPUTY.)

SHERIFF: I've got a man on every gate. There's no sign of 'em.

MORGAN: Well, see that there's no sign of 'em until after the race.

(GIL *and* JUDY *are in the ambulance, trying not to be noticed.*

There is a great rumbling in the rear of the ambulance.)

GIL: Whoa! Hi-Hat!

(*The* SHERIFF, MORGAN, WHITMORE, *and the* DEPUTY *look over at the ambulance.*

Hi-Hat is shaking the ambulance. His activity causes the sign to fall off the ambulance. Underneath it, a sign says:

'STANDISH SANITARIUM'.)

MORGAN: If you believe in signs, Sherlock, take a look at that
  ambulance.

  (MORGAN, *the* SHERIFF, *and* WHITMORE *and the* DEPUTY *start
  running towards the ambulance.*

  The SHERIFF *and two deputies run up, see* JUDY *in the front and
  they move around towards the back.*

  GIL *tries to stop the* SHERIFF *and the two deputies from opening
  the ambulance.*)

GIL: Now wait a minute, Sheriff!

SHERIFF: Don't you start anything, Stewart!

  (JUDY *has come around to the back of the ambulance.*

  The SHERIFF *opens the ambulance doors and sees Hi-Hat in the
  back. He puts* GIL *in the ambulance with Hi-Hat and shuts the
  doors.*)

  Ha-ha! We'll put this baby under lock and key. (*To a*
  DEPUTY) You keep searching for those other mugs.

  (JUDY *takes off her cape and nurse's cap.*

  From the upper grandstand, TONY *and* HACKENBUSH *look down
  at the track.*

  STUFFY *looks up at* TONY *and whistles.*

  HACKENBUSH *and* TONY *are at the railing.*)

TONY: Stuffy! What's the matter?

  (STUFFY *opens his arms and gestures wildly. He turns, takes a top
  hat from a passerby and throws it away. The man chases*
  STUFFY.)

  (*Off-screen*) What's the matter? Stuffy! Hi-Hat's gone.

  (*The bugle sounds post time.*)

  The race is going to start.

HACKENBUSH: They won't start the race till we find Hi-Hat!

Dissolve to interior, stable.

Close shot of a can of harness soap

TONY *digs out a paddleful of soap.*

TONY *is standing near a wall with the paddleful of soap.*

TONY *flips the soap under a saddle on to one of the horses just as two
grooms are saddling him.*

Dissolve to exterior, track.
MORGAN *and* WHITMORE *are with a* JOCKEY

MORGAN: (*To the* JOCKEY) Now listen, son, you're riding this race to win. I don't care what you do, as long as the judges don't see you doing it.
(MORGAN *and* WHITMORE *watch the* JOCKEY *mount his horse. Crowds of people are in the background.*)
VOICE: (*Off-screen*) All right men, go to your horses.
(*The* JOCKEY *starts to mount but* TONY's *harness soap was there first and the* JOCKEY *and the saddle fall to the ground at* WHITMORE's *and* MORGAN's *feet.*
All the jockeys are falling to the ground as they try to mount their horses.
We see a jockey on the ground. The harness soap falls on his face.)
MORGAN'S JOCKEY: (*Holding a handful of harness soap*) Soap!

Dissolve to side of grandstand.
There is a bugler; STUFFY *is in the background*
The bugler holds his bugle to his mouth. STUFFY *is behind a tree, watching him.*
The bugler blows on the bugle but no sound comes out. Instead a large soap bubble forms at the end of the horn. The bubble bursts. The bugler looks puzzled.
STUFFY *gets another idea and runs off.*

Dissolve to horses moving towards the track.
ANNOUNCER'S VOICE: (*Off-screen*) We are sorry for the delay, but the horses are now coming on the track.
(*There are* THREE JUDGES *on the platform.*)
A JUDGE: Twenty-five minutes late.
ANNOUNCER'S VOICE: (*Off-screen*) The horses are parading past the grandstand. Only eleven are headed postward.
(STUFFY *walks to the background, turns on a conveniently placed wind-machine. Hundreds of hats blow in the air and on to the track.*)
(*Off-screen*) Hi-Hat, the added starter, is missing. This is the third running of the fifty-thousand-dollar . . .
(MORGAN *and* WHITMORE *are in their box. They hold on to their*

247

hats. *People are screaming as their hats fly off.*)
(*Off-screen*) . . . added jumping classic.
(*Hats fly on to the track.*)
(*Off-screen*) What's this? What's this?
(*The* THREE JUDGES *lose their hats.*
More hats fly over. The horses rear up.
STUFFY *sits in the branches of a tree.*
TONY *and* HACKENBUSH *run over to him.*)

TONY: Hey, Stuffy! Stuffy!
(TONY *and* HACKENBUSH *are on the ground;* STUFFY *is still in the tree.*)
Did you find him? Did you find the ambulance?
(STUFFY *shakes his head, 'no'.*)
Well, keep on looking. We know it came in.
(*Attendants are picking up the hats and tossing them back to the crowd.*)

ANNOUNCER'S VOICE: (*Off-screen*) Now that the storm of hats has subsided, the stewards have ordered the track cleared for action.
(*In* MORGAN's *box.*)

MORGAN: Get all your men. Don't stop searching till you find 'em. (*A* GUARD *brings* MORGAN *and* WHITMORE *their hats.*)

GUARD: Here you are, boss.

ANNOUNCER'S VOICE: (*Off-screen*) And the hats are being returned to the customers. And the horses are back . . .
(MORGAN *and* WHITMORE *put on their hats.* WHITMORE's *is much too small for him and he throws it down in disgust.*)
(*Off-screen*) . . . on parade toward the starting point.
(*The* THREE JUDGES *on the platform put on their hats.*)
(*Off-screen*) They are going back now, up to the starting post.
(*A man in the crowd puts on a hat that is much too small for him.*)
(*Off-screen*) And everyone is getting his own hat . . .
(Another man in the crowd puts on a derby that's much too large for him.)
(*Off-screen*) . . . we hope!
(*The horses are lining up at the starting line.*)
(*Off-screen*) The horses are coming back to the starter now.

They are very fractious. They are . . .

(TONY *runs up and picks up a 'No-Parking' sign and smashes it against a tree and turns it into a 'Parking' sign.*)

(*Off-screen*) . . . giving the boys quite a bit of trouble after the excitement. First Legion is acting very badly. Sun Helmet is . . .

(TONY *is holding the 'Parking' sign as he rides on an auto bumper.*)

TONY: Free parking. Here you are. Free parking.

(TONY *jumps off the bumper of the car. A great many other cars are around him.*)

Get your free parking. (*He motions to other cars to follow.*) Come on – come on . . .

(*The* STARTER *is on the platform.*

The horses line up.)

ANNOUNCER'S VOICE: (*Off-screen*) They're coming up this time. Almost in an even line.

(*Looking down at the entrance tunnel we see dozens of cars driving on to the track. The crowd watches confused.*)

(*Off-screen*) The starter has his flag up. And it looks . . .

(*The* JUDGES *look at the cars pulling on to the track.*)

A JUDGE: Look! Look! Look!

ANNOUNCER'S VOICE: (*Off-screen*) Wait a minute.

(*Cars begin driving on to the track.*)

(*Off-screen*) What is this? A horse race or an automobile race?

(*The* STARTER *sees the cars and turns to look up at the* JUDGES' *stand for directions. The horses rear up.*

The cars drive along the track.)

A JUDGE: Hold those horses!

STARTER: Hold it! Hold it!

(*More cars drive up on the track.*

The STARTER *throws his flag down in disgust. Then he throws his hat away.*

More cars drive up on the track.

HACKENBUSH *sits on a fence, watching the cars drive past.*)

HACKENBUSH: Plenty of room! Nice fresh parking today! Right ahead, folks!

(*The cars are jammed. Cops and attendants try futilely to straighten things out.*

The horses move in a snarl, excited and confused.
At the entrance tunnel THREE COPS *try to stop more cars from coming on to the track.*
As TWO COPS *run towards* HACKENBUSH, *he jumps off the fence and on to a passing car.*
HACKENBUSH *rides on the running board of a limousine.*
Cops run to the back of the tunnel.
He is riding on the running board.
HACKENBUSH *opens the back door of the car, crawls on the floor past three women passengers.*)

HACKENBUSH: You girls got anything on for tonight? (*And he crawls out the other side.*)

(HACKENBUSH *ducks in among the cars.*
TONY, *carrying the parking sign, climbs on to the top of a stalled car. The cops chase him.*)

COP: Hey, get out of here!

(HACKENBUSH *jumps from one roof to another roof with the cops chasing him.*
More cars drive on.
HACKENBUSH *continues over the car roofs. People grab at him and knock him down. He jumps off the roof and runs among the cars. Then he jumps back on to a roof of a car.*
HACKENBUSH *rolls off the roof of one car and down toward the ground.*
HACKENBUSH *appears between two cars. He runs out with cops chasing him.*
TONY *runs in and joins* HACKENBUSH, *who is also running.*)

HACKENBUSH: Going my way?

(TONY *and* HACKENBUSH *run out pursued by the cops. There are dozens of jammed cars as the drivers try to straighten things out.*
The JUDGES *are frantic.*)

A JUDGE: Get 'em out of there! Get em out of there!

(*The cars try to back out of the track.*
People stand on the porch of the clubhouse. STUFFY *enters and whistles.*
HACKENBUSH *and* TONY *join him. All three of them run.*)

TONY: (*Running*) Hey Stuffy? Did you find Hi-Hat?

(STUFFY *shakes his head, 'no'*.)

HACKENBUSH: (*Running*) Well, keep looking, he must be around somewheres.

(*The ambulance drives along the road and stops near a car wreck. The* SHERIFF, *who was driving, jumps out.*
We see JUDY *lying on the ground.*
The SHERIFF *runs to the back, opens the door.* GIL *and Hi-Hat are still in the back.*)

SHERIFF: Get that horse out of there! There's been a terrible wreck. Come on, hurry up! Help me!

(*The* SHERIFF *runs down to where* JUDY *is sprawled in the grass.* GIL *runs to her and kneels next to her.*
JUDY *winks at* GIL *and tells him 'shush'. He smiles and picks her up.*
GIL *picks up* JUDY. *The* SHERIFF *is struggling with a stretcher in the background.*)

GIL: Come on, Sheriff, we've got no time to lose.

(GIL *carries* JUDY *towards the ambulance.*)

SHERIFF: Is she alive?

(GIL *gives* JUDY *a quick kiss when the* SHERIFF *isn't looking and carries her into the ambulance. The* SHERIFF *throws the stretcher back in, goes to the front of the ambulance and* GIL *partially closes the ambulance door. When the* SHERIFF *is gone, he opens the doors and he and* JUDY *climb out.*)

GIL: Get going, Sheriff! I'll take care of her.

SHERIFF: All right.

(*The ambulance drives away.* GIL *runs over to Hi-Hat. All the cars are gone now.*)

STARTER: Come on – come on.

ANNOUNCER'S VOICE: (*Off-screen*) Well, here we are again.

(*The* THREE JUDGES *on the platform look through their field glasses.*)
(*Off-screen*) The horses are coming up. They're not in too even a line.

A JUDGE: Come on, before something else happens.

(*The* STARTER *holds up the flag.*)

STARTER: (*To one of the jockeys*) Turn that horse around!

ANNOUNCER'S VOICE: (*Off-screen*) They're very nervous and

251

skittish – but it looks like he's . . .

(*The* THREE JUDGES *look nervous*.)

(*Off-screen*) . . . going to send them away.

STARTER: Now, easy, easy. . . . Go!

ANNOUNCER'S VOICE: (*Off-screen*) Yes. Yes. . . . and there they go!

A JUDGE: At last!

(HACKENBUSH *and* TONY *hide behind a bush just outside a curve in the track*.)

ANNOUNCER'S VOICE: (*Off-screen*) Demon is third. Sun Helmet is fourth and Green Goddess – there's Ski-Ball . . .

(HACKENBUSH *and* TONY *move to the rail*.)

(*Off-screen*) . . . showing the way in the centre of the track – by two lengths – at least . . .

(HACKENBUSH *and* TONY *lift up the rail and rearrange the track*.)

(*Off-screen*) Sun Helmet is second – Green Goddess is third and Flying Demon is fourth.

(HACKENBUSH *and* TONY *rearrange the rail so that the horses ride into the field*.)

(*Off-screen*) Now they're going around the first turn with Ski-Ball in front by two lengths. First Legion is second by a head – wait . . .

(*The* STARTER *watches the horses leave the track. He's confused*.)

(*Off-screen*) . . . a minute! What is this?

(*The* THREE JUDGES *are stunned*.)

JUDGES: What is . . . what's happened now?

(MORGAN *and* WHITMORE *are furious*.)

MORGAN: Get me the riot squad.

(WHITMORE *leaves*.)

MRS UPJOHN: (*Joining* MORGAN *in his box*) Oh, Mr Morgan, don't get excited.

MORGAN: I'm not excited! Shut up!

MRS UPJOHN: Oh!

(*The horses trot back on to the track.*
The STARTER *watches it all, still confused*.)

ANNOUNCER'S VOICE: (*Off-screen*) Quiet please. Your attention . . .

(*The horses move farther on to the track.*)
(*Off-screen*) Quiet please. Your attention.

(*At the stables* GIL *pulls up in a horse-drawn water wagon.*
STUFFY *runs up to him.*)

GIL: Stuffy!

ANNOUNCER'S VOICE: (*Off-screen*) The stewards have ruled this a
false start . . .

(GIL *is at the reins of the water wagon.* STUFFY *starts to climb up
to join him.*

GIL *gets down from the wagon.*)

(*Off-screen*) . . . and have ordered the horses back to the
starting post. Now, ladies and gentlemen . . .

(GIL *starts to unhitch the horses from the wagon. Two cops approach.*)

GIL: Stuffy! Scram!

(GIL *helps* STUFFY *jump on one of the horses and he gallops away
pulling the water wagon. The* COPS *jump on to the back of the
water wagon.*)

ANNOUNCER'S VOICE: (*Off-screen*) . . . If you will all please be
patient . . . who knows, we may yet have a horse race this
afternoon. The horses . . .

(*The horses come back to the starting line to start the race again.*)

(*Off-screen*) . . . are back at the starting point. And now the
boys are turning them about.

(STUFFY *rides the water wagon on to the track. The* COPS *are still
on the back.*)

(*Off-screen*) They are very nervous – very fractious – they're
having . . .

(*In* MORGAN's *box* MORGAN *and* MRS UPJOHN *watch, stunned,
as the water wagon pulls up to the track.*)

(*Off-screen*) . . . quite a bit of trouble.

JUDGES: Get that wagon off of here.

(STUFFY *races the water wagon down the track. The* COPS *still
cling to the back of the wagon.*

STUFFY *is riding the horse.*

The COPS *are riding on the back of the water wagon.*

STUFFY *turns to crawl back over the horse to the wagon.*

STUFFY *pushes the water-pipe lever.*

*The water from the pipe hits both cops in the face and knocks
them off. They fall to the ground.*
STUFFY *laughs and turns to get back on the horse.*
STUFFY *gets back on his horse.*
STUFFY *throws away his battered top hat.*
MORGAN *is looking through his field glasses.*
STUFFY *puts on his racing cap.*)

A JUDGE: Get off of there!

(*As* STUFFY *passes the* JUDGES' *platform he breaks his mount
loose from the water wagon and flashes ahead. He's riding
Hi-Hat!*

The SHERIFF *and his* DEPUTIES *enter* MORGAN's *box.*

SHERIFF: Hi-Hat . . . Hi-Hat, he got him away from me. I don't
know where he is.

MORGAN: Who do you think that is, stupid? Take a look at the
track!

(STUFFY *is now in his jockey racing silks, hurrying Hi-Hat to the
starting line.*)

A JUDGE: Number seven!

ANOTHER JUDGE: Why, that's Hi-Hat!

(HACKENBUSH *and* TONY *hide behind a hedge to watch the start
of the race. The* STARTER *drops his flag. The race begins.*)

ANNOUNCER'S VOICE: (*Off-screen*) They're coming up to the
start this time – and the starter has his flag raised – and there
they go! Ski-Ball is going to the front . . .

(STUFFY *rides in on Hi-Hat, hurdles the rail and joins the race.*)
(*Off-screen*) . . . But here comes Hi-Hat! He's over the fence
– he's on the track . . .

(STUFFY *is riding Hi-Hat, trying to catch up with the race.*)
(*Off-screen*) . . . and he's in the race!

(TONY *and* HACKENBUSH *are cheering him on.*
He's racing his heart out trying to catch up.)
(*Off-screen*) Ski-Ball is going to the front. First Legion is
second. Flying Demon is third.

(MRS UPJOHN, WHITMORE *and* MORGAN *are watching the
race intently;* MORGAN *through his field glasses.*)
(*Off-screen*) Sun Helmet is fourth . . .

STUFFY *riding Hi-Hat is almost up to the other horses.*)

(*Off-screen*) . . . and Green Goddess is fifth. Now there goes
Hi-Hat . . .

(STUFFY *riding Hi-Hat begins to pass the other horses.*)

(*Off-screen*) . . . he's moving up between horses!

(STUFFY *moves to the head of the race.*)

(*Off-screen*) And look at him go! And he's moving up there at
the leaders – and it's Ski-Ball still in front – but now here
comes Hi-Hat between horses – and now he's challenging the
leader!

(MORGAN'*s* JOCKEY *on Ski-Ball sees* STUFFY.)

(*Off-screen*) There's Ski-Ball in front by a length and one
half. Hi-Hat is second by three quarters of a length. First
Legion is third by a length and one half – and Flying Demon
is fourth. Now Ski-Ball is . . .

(*High in the grandstand* JUDY *and* GILL *join* TONY *and*
HACKENBUSH.)

(*Off-screen*) . . . going out on the edge and they're coming to
the . . .

(*The horses move towards a low stone wall. They all jump except
Hi-Hat.*)

(*Off-screen*) . . . first barrier now. And Ski-Ball . . .

(*Hi-Hat refuses to jump.*)

(*Off-screen*) . . . takes it, but . . .

(STUFFY *shows Hi-Hat a picture of* MORGAN.)

(*Off-screen*) . . . Hi-Hat refuses. He's turning back – but wait
a minute! Wait a minute – he's going to try it . . .

(*Hi-Hat turns, rears up, and goes right over the wall.*)

(*Off-screen*) . . . once more. There he goes! He's going after it
this time – and he's over!

(GILL, JUDY, HACKENBUSH *and* TONY *are watching.*)

GIL: Oh! Your idea worked, Judy!

ANNOUNCER'S VOICE: (*Off-screen*) He's over – and Ski-Ball's
still . . .

(STUFFY *kisses the picture of* MORGAN *and the picture blows out
of his hand.*)

(*Off-screen*) . . . in front by two lengths!

(*The picture of* MORGAN *falls to the ground.*)

JUDY: Oh, he's lost Morgan's picture!

(STUFFY *riding Hi-Hat passes most of the other horses.*)

ANNOUNCER'S VOICE: (*Off-screen*) He's picking up his heels –
and he's going up on the outside this time – and here he is at
the leader!

JUDY: Can you shout like Morgan?

HACKENBUSH: No, but Morgan can.

(*He leaves and* TONY *follows him.*)

(STUFFY *and* MORGAN's JOCKEY *are neck and neck.*

MRS UPJOHN, WHITMORE *and* MORGAN *are watching the
race.*)

MRS UPJOHN: Oh! Something's happened to the loudspeaker!

(*Close-up of the microphone. It has been dropped into a piece of
newspaper.*

TONY *is holding the microphone. He starts up the steps into the
grandstand.*

The horses approach another barrier.

STUFFY *on Hi-Hat searches for the picture of* MORGAN *that he'll
need to get Hi-Hat over the next wall.*)

(MORGAN *is looking through the field glasses.* TONY *grabs them
and looks through.*)

TONY: Let me take a look.

MORGAN: Give me those glasses! (*Grabbing them back.*) You've
got your –

(GILL, JUDY *and* HACKENBUSH *are standing by the
loudspeaker.*)

MORGAN'S VOICE: (*Over the loudspeaker*) It's you!

(*Hi-Hat rears when he hears* MORGAN's *voice.*

Hi-Hat pulls away.

The horses go over the barrier.

STUFFY *nods towards the stands in thanks.*

GILL, JUDY *and* HACKENBUSH *are at the loudspeaker.*)

HACKENBUSH: (*To* GIL) You take care of Judy and I'll take care of
Morgan. (*He leaves.*)

(STUFFY *riding Hi-Hat moves to the front of the pack.*

MORGAN's JOCKEY *on Ski-Ball is still in the lead. He sees*
STUFFY *coming.*

In the tunnel beneath the grandstand TONY, *chased by the cops,
tosses* HACKENBUSH *the microphone and runs out.*)

HACKENBUSH *takes it and runs. The cops don't notice him, and continue to chase* TONY.

MORGAN's JOCKEY *and* STUFFY *are neck and neck.*

MORGAN's JOCKEY *hits* STUFFY *with his crop.*)

MORGAN: (*To* MRS UPJOHN *and* WHITMORE) I hope the judges didn't see that.

(STUFFY *looks ahead, sees the next barrier.*

The horses race towards the next wall.

STUFFY *looks over to the grandstand, clutches his ear.*

HACKENBUSH *comes over to* MORGAN.)

HACKENBUSH: Mr Morgan . . . (*He shoves the microphone in his face*) . . . would you mind telling the radio audience what a heel you are?

MORGAN: Oh, come back later. Oh, I've had enough of this!

(*He gets up and starts to chase* HACKENBUSH.

Hi-Hat hears MORGAN's *voice over the loudspeaker and heads for the wall.*

STUFFY *laughs.*

STUFFY *and Hi-Hat go over the barrier.*)

(*To* HACKENBUSH, *who is running away*) If the police can't take care of you, I'll take care of you myself! (*To cop*) Keep that man away from me, do you understand!

(*We see the race, with Hi-Hat and Ski-Ball neck and neck.*)

(*To cop*) Get around there – and stay there! And see that I'm not disturbed again today!

(*A microphone is tied to the neck of a small dog.*

The dog is in HACKENBUSH's *lap. The dog runs off-screen.*

The dog jumps towards the box containing MRS UPJOHN, MORGAN *and* WHITMORE.

The dog falls on MORGAN.)

(*Screaming at the dog and, without knowing it, into the microphone*) Get out of here! Get out of here!

(*Hi-Hat hears* MORGAN's *voice and rears.*

STUFFY *smiles when he hears* MORGAN's *voice.*

The horses go over the barrier.

One horse and rider fall.

MORGAN's JOCKEY *on Ski-Ball looks at* STUFFY.

MORGAN's JOCKEY's *foot reaches over and pulls* STUFFY's *foot out of his stirrup.*

STUFFY *almost falls from Hi-Hat.*

STUFFY *threatens* MORGAN'S JOCKEY *with his crop.*

MORGAN'S JOCKEY *tries to pull* STUFFY *off of Hi-Hat.*

HACKENBUSH *tumbles over several cops and into* MORGAN'S *box.*

Hi-Hat and Ski Ball are neck and neck in the lead.

Hi-Hat and Ski-Ball approach another barrier. Both horses stumble and both MORGAN'S JOCKEY *and* STUFFY *go into the water.*

JUDY *turns her eyes away.*

MORGAN *looks at the race through his glasses. The cops are holding* HACKENBUSH *and* TONY.

STUFFY *and* MORGAN'S JOCKEY *stagger to their feet in the water and the horses run away.*

STUFFY *staggers out of the water. He,* MORGAN'S JOCKEY, *and both horses are covered with mud.*

MORGAN'S JOCKEY *gets on the horse and gets back in the race.*

STUFFY *gets on the horse and rides after* MORGAN'S JOCKEY.

MORGAN *is looking through his glasses. The cops hold* HACKENBUSH.)

Ski-Ball has the lead!

(MORGAN'S JOCKEY *is ahead of* STUFFY.

They are neck and neck.

GIL *and* JUDY *cheer* STUFFY *on.*

MORGAN'S JOCKEY *is in the lead.*

The cops hold HACKENBUSH *but he manages to shove the microphone, now disguised as a flower, into* MORGAN'S *face.*)

HACKENBUSH: Smell this . . .

MORGAN: Ah, get away . . .

(MORGAN'S JOCKEY *is still ahead.*)

(*Off-screen*) I don't want to smell anything. Get him out of here! Get him out of this box. Get him out of here! How many men does it take to do this. Come on, Ski-Ball!

(*The cops hold on to* HACKENBUSH.)

Come on, Ski-Ball!

STUFFY *and* MORGAN'S JOCKEY *are neck and neck.*

The horses streak across the finish line.)

Ski-Ball wins!
GIL *and* JUDY *are crushed.*
The SHERIFF *is holding* HACKENBUSH.)
HACKENBUSH: OK, Sheriff, where do you arrange for a cell with a southern exposure.
SHERIFF: Come on!
(JUDY *comforts* GIL.)
JUDY: Gil, Hi-Hat couldn't have tried harder. We were just unlucky.
(*In the winner's circle* MORGAN's JOCKEY, *still on his horse, preens.*
STUFFY *looks very disappointed.*
MORGAN *and* WHITMORE *hurry on to the track.*)
MORGAN: Great race, Ski-Ball.
(MORGAN *and* WHITMORE *approach* MORGAN's JOCKEY *to congratulate him.*)
Great race, Ski-Ball.
(*But the horse rears up in anger at* MORGAN *and throws the* JOCKEY *off.*
The horse chases MORGAN *and* WHITMORE *to the rail. They jump over.*
STUFFY *watches* MORGAN *and* WHITMORE *being chased and suspects something is wrong.*
MORGAN *and* WHITMORE *are on the ground with what they think is their horse rearing up, threatening to kick them.*)
Get him out of here! Get him out of here!
STUFFY *jumps off his horse, runs over to the winner's circle, scrapes some mud off, throws it at* MORGAN's JOCKEY.
The mud hits MORGAN's JOCKEY *in the face.*
The THREE JUDGES *watch the winner's circle.*
STUFFY *wipes the mud off the saddle exposing the number seven – Hi-Hat's number. He wipes the mud from his sleeve showing his number seven – Hi-Hat's number. Hi-Hat's the winner after all! He gets very excited.*)
A JUDGE: That's number seven.
(WHITMORE *and* MORGAN *are shocked.*)
(*Off-screen*) Hi-Hat's the winner.
(STUFFY *whistles, kisses Hi-Hat, and everybody cheers.*

WHITMORE AND MORGAN *don't cheer.*

HACKENBUSH *is still under arrest.*)

HACKENBUSH: Hi-Hat wins. Sheriff, cancel my reservations.

TONY: It's Hi-Hat. It's Hi-Hat.

JUDY: (*Grabbing* GIL) Gil, come on. Come on, I want to put the wreath on the winner.

(MORGAN *and* WHITMORE *leave as* HACKENBUSH *and* TONY *go to the winner's circle.*)

HACKENBUSH: One more yell out of you and he'd have jumped over the grandstand.

MORGAN: Ah, ah, you!

TONY: Stuffy!

(STUFFY *and* TONY *hug each other.*

Hi-Hat is in the background.)

HACKENBUSH: Stuffy, you were wonderful!

TONY: Some ride! Oh, boy!

HACKENBUSH: I haven't seen so much mudslinging since the last election.

(STUFFY *whistles;* TONY *and* HACKENBUSH *bend over to make steps next to Hi-Hat.* STUFFY *climbs up on their backs on to Hi-Hat.*

In the winner's circle GIL *and* JUDY *place the wreath around Hi-Hat's neck.*

All the black children from the stables run on to the track.

STUFFY *on Hi-Hat, led by* JUDY *and* GIL, TONY,

HACKENBUSH *and* MRS UPJOHN *join with the black people and sing.*)

CROWD: (*Singing*) 'All Gawd's chillun got money . . .'

(STUFFY *is riding on Hi-Hat.*)

(*Off-screen, singing*) 'All Gawd's chillun got dough . . .'

(*The children follow behind* STUFFY.)

(*Singing*) 'Gabriel's blowin' cause he needs us . . .'

(*We see* GIL, HACKENBUSH *and* MRS UPJOHN.)

(*Singing*) 'We gotta follow where he leads us . . .'

(TONY, JUDY, GIL *and the entire group walk triumphantly forward in front of Hi-Hat.*)

(*Singing*) 'Gabriel, blow that horn!'

STUFFY *on Hi-Hat plays his flute and honks his horn.*)

TONY: (*Singing*) 'On blue Venetian waters together, hi-de-hi-de-
hi-hat!
Get your tootsie-frootsie ice-cream!'
HACKENBUSH (*Singing*) I got a message from the man in the
moon for you – just you!'
(*Spoken to* MRS UPJOHN) Emily, I've a little confession to
make. I really am a horse doctor. But marry me, and I'll
never look at any other horse!
(MRS UPJOHN *throws her arms around him joyously.*
JUDY *and* GIL *are in front of Hi-Hat.*
Everybody is still marching forward in victory.)
GIL: (*Singing*) 'If you can face the setting sun and say . . .'
(HACKENBUSH *grins and chews on his cigar.*)
(*Off-screen, singing*) 'Tomorrow . . .'
CROWD: (*Singing*) 'Za zu – za zu za – za zu!'
(TONY *and* JUDY *are happier with every step.*)
GIL: (*Off-screen, singing*) '. . . tomorrow . . .'
CROWD: (*Singing*) 'Za zu – za zu za – za zu!'
(JUDY *and* GIL *lead Hi-Hat and sing.*)
GIL *and* JUDY: (*Singing*) 'Tomorrow is another day!'
(JUDY, GIL *and everybody walk forward in victory.* STUFFY, *on
Hi-Hat, is in the centre.*
Fade out.)